Be Water

Ming-sho Ho

Be Water

Collective Improvisation in Hong Kong's Anti-Extradition Protests

TEMPLE UNIVERSITY PRESS
Philadelphia • Rome • Tokyo

TEMPLE UNIVERSITY PRESS
Philadelphia, Pennsylvania 19122
tupress.temple.edu

Published 2025

Library of Congress Cataloging-in-Publication Data

Names: He, Mingxiu, author.
Title: Be water : collective improvisation in Hong Kong's anti-extradition protests / Ming-sho Ho.
Description: Philadelphia : Temple University Press, 2025. | Includes bibliographical references and index. | Summary: "This book documents the events of Hong Kong's 2019 protests against China's new extradition policy. In particular, the author highlights how protesters paired a diffuse and improvisational leadership structure with a singular goal to enhance the resiliency of their movement"— Provided by publisher.
Identifiers: LCCN 2024053718 (print) | LCCN 2024053719 (ebook) | ISBN 9781439924846 (cloth) | ISBN 9781439924853 (paperback) | ISBN 9781439924860 (pdf)
Subjects: LCSH: Hong Kong Protests, Hong Kong, China, 2019– | Activism—China—Hong Kong—History—21st century. | Demonstrations—China—Hong Kong—History—21st century. | Protest movements—China—Hong Kong—History—21st century. | Hong Kong (China)—Politics and government—21st century. | Hong Kong (China)—Social conditions—21st century.
Classification: LCC HN752.5 H423 2025 (print) | LCC HN752.5 (ebook) | DDC 951.2506/12—dc23/eng/20250214
LC record available at https://lccn.loc.gov/2024053718
LC ebook record available at https://lccn.loc.gov/2024053719

The manufacturer's authorized representative in the EU for product safety is Temple University Rome, Via di San Sebastianello, 16, 00187 Rome RM, Italy (https://rome.temple.edu/).
tempress@temple.edu

9 8 7 6 5 4 3 2 1

Contents

List of Figures

List of Tables

Acknowledgments

The late Harvard professor Ezra Vogel regularly hosted informal gatherings on Chinese sociology at his home, just a stone's throw away from the Fairbank Center for Chinese Studies, where he had mentored numerous East Asianists over the years. It was in this cozy setting that I had the pleasure to present my book on the Sunflower Movement in Taiwan and the Umbrella Movement in Hong Kong, shortly after its publication in early 2019. On a late April evening, following a delightful food takeout from the nearby Mu Lan Taiwanese Restaurant, I shared my observation on how increasing Chinese interference had sparked resistance among the youths in both societies. The ensuing exchanges were stimulating, but the conversation eventually turned to the grim situation in Hong Kong. Recent harsh sentencings, including the infamous "Case of Occupying the Central Nine," had cast a shadow over the city's political future. Kin-man Chan, a respected sociologist and devoted advocate for civil society in both Hong Kong and mainland China, had recently been sentenced to sixteen months in jail. Chan, who had long overseen the University Service Center at the Chinese University of Hong Kong, was highly regarded among Western scholars of China. As our discussions turned to Chan's plight and the uncertain future of Hong Kong, I couldn't shake the feeling that my research on the city's political activism had reached its terminus. Perhaps it was time to explore new avenues of study as I walked home from Cambridge to my apartment in Coolidge Corner, pondering the path forward in the late evening hours.

Unknown to those of us gathered at Vogel's house, a distant storm in Hong Kong was brewing. A legal dispute over extradition erupted, igniting a city-wide uprising that surpassed all expectations—those of participants, the Chinese rulers, and international observers alike—and irreversibly altered the city's political landscape. What drove the people of Hong Kong to mount a full-scale resistance to defend their legacy of rule of law? How did they conceive so many novel and imaginative protest tactics previously unseen? The trajectory of the city's past offered no clear indications of the Be Water Revolution's eruption, posing an intellectual challenge in pinpointing the origins of the mass rebellion. During subsequent years of investigation, W. B. Yeats' refrain "a terrible beauty is born" in his poetic eulogy to the Irish Easter Uprising of 1916 kept surfacing in my mind. With this book, I concluded that due credit must be accorded to the agentic power of the Hongkongers, whose passionate responses and collaborative efforts fueled an escalating tide of protest devoid of singular leadership. Given that existing literature primarily focuses on the objective conditions precipitating movement emergencies, I endeavor to bridge this gap by introducing the concept of "collective improvisation" to elucidate the surge of such decentralized protest movements. Hong Kong serves as a poignant crystallization of this emerging form of contentious politics, and I aspire for my case study to provide a conceptual clue for comprehending contemporary protest movements worldwide.

The owl of Minerva only takes flight in the dusk, and this book is published after the Be Water Revolution had quieted down and the city was shrouded in a coercively imposed national security regime. There is no telling when Hongkongers could finally regain their freedom. Understanding that the city is forcibly dragged along a path of democratic backsliding in the foreseeable future, my collective improvisation perspective underscores that agentic power cannot be reliably inferred from existing objective conditions. As long as Hongkongers remain united, committed, and prepared, it is always possible to restore their homeland city to its former glory, when there is a sudden change of the circumstances.

The book benefits from many colleagues' comments and criticisms. I appreciate Debby Chan, Adam Chen-Dedman, Silvia Frosina, Ho-fung Hung, Yu-Kai Kenny Liao, Ronex Leung, Thung-Hong Lin, Lake Lui, Ngok Ma, and Kang Yi for offering suggestions to my book manuscript. At various stages, I learned a lot from the discussion with Kin-man Chan, Minchi Chang, King Chuen Chung, Tak Wai Hung, Judy Lee, Kai Chi Leung, Kasey Son Hei Lo, Hans Hanpu Tung, Jeffrey Wasserstrom, and Jieh-min Wu. Without the wonderful assistance of Wei An Chen, Chun-hao Huang, Ronex Leung, Ka Wing Li, Yu-Erh Li, Hawazzi Tsang, Jessie Tse, and Ash Wan, I cannot imagine the herculean task of processing the huge amount of quantitative and qualitative data.

My funding sources include Taiwan's National Science and Technology Council, National Taiwan University's Office of Research and Development, Global Asia Research Center, and Taiwan Social Resilience Research Center. Parts of the book were previously presented in Taiwan's Taipei, New Taipei City, and Pingtung as well as in international locations including Boston, Canberra, Frankfurt, Oxford, Philadelphia, Tokyo, Vancouver, Warsaw, and Zurich, both in person and virtually. My heartfelt appreciation for those constructive comments.

I am deeply thankful for the unwavering support of my family. During the eruption of the Be Water Revolution, my daughter Little Plum and my son Little Sun were still in preschool, their tender age allowing them to equate masked and black-clad Hongkongers with demonstrators. Explaining to children why people are willing to sacrifice for political liberty is always a challenge, isn't it? My heartfelt appreciation goes to my partner, Shuling, who has provided a warm foundation for our family and my research endeavors. I am confident that our Little Plum and Little Sun will one day come to appreciate the courage and determination of Hongkongers in their pursuit of freedom.

Abbreviations

ACG	Animation, Comics, and Games (of Japanese)
BLM	Black Lives Matter
BNO	British National (Overseas)
CCP	Chinese Communist Party
CHRF	Civil Human Rights Front
ELAB	Extradition Law Amendment Bill
HK$	Hong Kong Dollars
HKCTU	Hong Kong Confederation of Trade Unions
HKFS	Hong Kong Federation of Students
HKIAD	Hong Kong Higher Institutions International Affairs Delegation
NSL	National Security Law
OCLP	Occupy Central with Love and Peace
OCTS	One Country Two Systems
PRC	People's Republic of China
SAR	Special Administrative Region
SARS	Severe Acute Respiratory Syndrome
U.K.	United Kingdom
U.S.	United States
US$	United States Dollars

A Note on Romanization

The Sinophone world adopts many romanization systems, reflecting the linguistic diversity and cultural preferences. For proper nouns, such as Mong Kok (rather than Wangjiao) and Joshua Wong (rather than Huang Zhifeng), I follow their conventional spellings. For those rich idioms used by Hong Kong activists, I first use the Cantonese system Jyutping developed by the Linguistic Society of Hong Kong (available at https://lshk.org/jyutping-scheme/) followed by the Pinyin system. In cases of idiosyncratic expressions, where there are no Mandarin equivalents, only Cantonese spelling is provided.

Be Water

Introduction

On August 23, 2019, into a sweltering summer evening, a multitude of Hongkongers poured out of metro stations, converging to form a citywide human chain rally. Known as the "Hong Kong Way," this unprecedented demonstration commenced at 7:00 P.M., coinciding with the departure of workers from their offices of this bustling city. From intersections to underpasses, overpasses, and even atop the iconic Victoria Peak and Lion Rock, alongside the picturesque Victoria Harbor, protesters linked hands, brandished placards, and resolutely chanted slogans such as "Five Demands, Not One Less" and "Liberate Hong Kong, Revolution of Our Time."

At 9:00 P.M., in a symbolic act of unity and empathy, they covered their right eyes, expressing solidarity with a young female first-aider who had tragically lost her vision in her right eye after being struck by a police beanbag bullet a few days earlier. Reports suggest that this event garnered an astounding turnout of two hundred and ten thousand participants, with the human chain spanning an impressive sixty kilometers across Hong Kong Island, Kowloon, and New Territories.

On the exact day thirty years ago, Estonians, Latvians, and Lithuanians demonstrated their commitment to self-determination with the famed "Baltic Way" human chain, which emerged as a series of dramatic events that eventually led to the Soviet Union's dissolution. Like their East European predecessors, Hongkongers were also resisting the encroachment from the central government in Beijing, as a legal revision (the Extradition Law Amendment Bill, or ELAB) would have allowed the transfer of city citizens to be tried in the courts of the People's Republic of China (PRC). Knowing that they needed to enlist support from the international community, Hong Kong's protesters ostensibly displayed various national flags and presented their demands in different languages. They deliberately disregarded the provocation from hundreds of PRC flag–carrying taxicabs mobilized by the progovernment camp and took care not to block the traffic. Human chain participants formed a line on the pedestrian crossing only during the green light and politely yielded the road to motorists with the change of the traffic light. Adopting a protest action familiar to a Western audience, the peaceful event succeeded in obtaining positive coverage on international media such as BBC, CNN, and Al Jazeera. Overseas Hongkongers in Canada, Japan, Taiwan, and other countries joined the effort by staging similar actions in their host societies.

When the Hong Kong Way took place, the city's protest had persisted for seventy-five days. The eventful summer of 2019 witnessed the clash between the growing militancy among protesters and the increasingly brutal use of force among police officers—a major departure from the city's tradition of polite protests. Nevertheless, the extraordinary human chain rally imbued a fresh impetus to the ongoing campaign by creating a brand-new action repertoire. Journalistic sources document 3 incidents of the human chain in August and, in the subsequent months, 105 in September, 11 in October, 9 in November, and 8 in December (see the methodological explanations in Appendix). The September surge was largely due to the massive participation of middle school students in the new semester. In addition, an on-site survey of protest participants indicates that around 60% of respondents had joined human chain actions (Chinese University of Hong Kong Centre for Communication and Public Opinion Survey 2020: 47). Apparently, human chains have become a versatile protest activity particularly suitable for Hong Kong's dense urban ecology where such action easily drew the attention of passersby. It also emerged as an easily replicable repertoire for school students or neighborhood residents who intended to demonstrate their prodemocracy commitment. I found 133 types of activity appearing in Hong Kong's protest events from February 2019 to July 2020. In terms of frequency, the newly minted human chains appeared 137 times, making it the fourth most popular activity, trailing only behind blocking the road (287), singing songs (284), and marching (213).

Given its international attention and reverberations, the Hong Kong Way is intriguing because its initiators remained anonymous and probably can never be identified. In July 2019, a Hong Kong informant who had in-depth knowledge of the Baltic Way was simultaneously approached by different activists who shared the same concern over the "radical" turn of the protest movement. A large-scale peaceful action could have averted such a worrying trend, or so they thought. Another interviewed Hongkonger who previously studied in Barcelona and witnessed Catalonian independence protests pitched the idea of a human chain. Initially, he shared his thoughts with a blogger friend, and, after a round of internet discussion involving many enthusiasts, they found it workable. As the novel proposal was quietly circulating around, Hong Kong's respected columnist Li Yi, upon the request of a young friend, reposted his suggestion for a human chain protest six years ago on Facebook, further popularizing the idea. On August 19, merely four days before the thirtieth anniversary of the Baltic Way, a call-to-action announcement was posted on LIHKG, a popular online chat platform in the city, and immediately went viral. However, despite the enthusiastic response from netizens, there was lingering doubt over whether enough citizens would step forward and fill in along the designated routes.

Unlike conventional protest rallies that gathered participants at a specific site, the Hong Kong Way project required linearly distributed participation spread across different areas, and, for this purpose, many ad hoc Telegram channels were set up to recruit regional coordinators to direct the population flow. Another interviewee signed up for the task in his neighborhood and joined hands with activists whom he had not known previously. Their main tasks were to ensure an even dispersal of participants beyond the metro stations and to avoid blocking traffic. Prior to the event, they put up posters throughout the neighborhood, and they were constantly reminded by friendly local residents to avoid some risky spots where there was a concentration of progovernment store owners. The tasks of these coordinators were also made easier because many district-based online chat groups sprang up with the onset of the protest, and they were able to recruit like-minded partners from these anonymous platforms.

Symptomatically, civil society organizations were conspicuously absent in the historical human chain rally. Hong Kong's prodemocracy movement was traditionally led by advocacy groups like the Civil Human Rights Front (CHRF), the organizer of the annual July First demonstration. CHRF was among the first to raise a red flag against the ELAB proposed by the Hong Kong government in February 2019; in June, it successfully launched two large-scale demonstrations with one million participants at one and two million at the other, kicking off the citywide resistance. Aside from CHRF, established organizations, including prodemocracy parties, student organizations, labor unions, and so on, were not involved in the planning and execution of the Hong Kong Way. At most, their social media pages shared the announcement, and some of their staff chose to join the event in a private capacity.

While the leaders of these organizations were undoubtedly supportive of the protest movement, they chose not to be involved for several reasons. Registered organizations tended to be more mindful of the legality of crowd activities. Without police permission, participants could be indicted on the crime of unlawful assembly punishable by up to three years in prison, which became an increasingly serious concern as the Hong Kong government stepped up its lawfare after the protest flared up in June. Formal organizations operated with stipulated decision rules and were ultimately accountable to their constituencies. They found it difficult to respond to an emergency call for mobilization with an unknown origin and uncertain viability, let alone endorse the action with their organizational legitimacy. Finally, as the protest movement proceeded for more than two months, an antileadership worldview gradually took root among participants, commonly expressed with the slogan "no main stage" (*mou daaitoi/wu datai*) in local parlance. The main stage referred to the makeshift podium erected in Admiralty (the city center where the Central Government Complex is located) during the 2014 Umbrella Movement, functioning as the de facto command center of that seventy-nine-day prodemocracy occupy protest. Since the Umbrella Movement was generally perceived as a failure, participants grew disenchanted with centralized leadership. Sensing this prevalent mood, leaders of preexisting prodemocracy organizations cautiously opted to be on the sidelines.

A successful human chain rally required participants to hold hands with strangers to dramatize their unity, but such physical contact was an outlandish idea for Hongkongers and other East Asians, whose cultural upbringing preferred discreetness and distance. While some movement veterans might be used to hand-holding as a symbolic gesture of solidarity, the physical contact became excruciatingly embarrassing for people at their tender age, especially when teenage students launched their school-based human chains later. To avoid mutual awkwardness, many male and female participants decided to grasp two ends of a pen or other substitutes, rather than direct contact. They often bashfully looked the other way in order not to be taken as a gesture of intimacy. Nevertheless, Hongkongers were willing to act against their cultural predilection because of their strong emotional involvement in the ongoing protest. The controversial ELAB triggered several incidents of suicide protest, and the police's apparent collusion with gangsters fanned the public fury. As such, human chain participants chose to act against their cultural inclinations because of their deep sense of righteous indignation.

The Hong Kong Way episode encapsulates several intellectual puzzles this book seeks to address. Why does a seemingly leaderless protest turn out to be tenaciously durable? How is an innovative repertoire devised and implemented without prior organizing? What are the reasons that motivate many people to voluntarily collaborate with strangers at their personal risk? Without organizational coordination, how is the complex division of labor executed? And, finally, under what circumstances can people invent a new form of action that is not within their cultural stock of knowledge? What makes such impromptu adaptation to become a common language for protesters? This book is an attempt to reframe these questions more reflectively and contextually and offers a new concept of "collective improvisation" to make sense of such a decentralized yet creative way of making protests. Before moving into the theoretical discussion, let us take a closer look at what has unfolded in Hong Kong under the Chinese Communist Party (CCP) rule.

Stalled Democratization

When Hongkongers bid farewell to more than 150 years of British rule in 1997, Beijing's leadership promised a high degree of autonomy and a gradual path toward democracy in the form of the direct election of the chief executive and all Legislative Council members. With the designation as a special administrative region (SAR) of the PRC, the arrangement known as "One Country Two Systems" (OCTS) pledged to preserve the previous institutions and way of living (opaquely defined as "capitalistic" in the law) for fifty years. In the first few years, Beijing largely avoided obtrusive interventions, and some minor regressions, such as the reintroduction of police permission for demonstrations and rallies, did not elicit strong opposition (Pepper 2008: 299). The honeymoon period ended in 2003 when the Hong Kong government attempted to enact a vaguely worded national security bill. The timing could not have been worse. The city had just experienced an epidemic of severe acute respiratory syndrome (SARS), and the inept official responses led to a death toll of 299. A huge demonstration of half a million citizens ensued, leading to a split among the pro-Beijing camp and thus effectively ended the legislative proposal (J. Cheng 2005).

The national security bill fiasco prompted more assertive interventions from Beijing to consolidate its control over this "unruly" city. While many of these efforts proceeded successfully as planned, such as co-opting elite Hongkongers with political titles and privileged access (Fong 2014), improving the electoral competitiveness of pro-Beijing parties (Ma 2012), cultivating an ecology of pro-Beijing media outlets (F. Lee 2018), and fostering a plethora of native-place associations with mainland connections (E. Cheng 2020; Yuen 2021), there were also noticeable blowbacks. The attempt to cleanse the city's colonial past led to a wave of heritage preservation campaigns to safeguard Hongkongers' collective memory (Ku 2012). Gigantic infrastructure projects to bring a closer link between the city and the mainland triggered massive protest actions (Y. Chen and Szeto 2015). The influx of mainland tourists and parallel traders brought about inconveniences and grievances among residents, inviting an angry backlash (Ip 2020). A curriculum reform to implement patriotic education, for example, led to widespread middle school students' mobilization, catapulting Joshua Wong (then sixteen years old) to be one of the world's most recognizable freedom fighters.

At the time when Joshua Wong and his teenager partners successfully forestalled the adaptation of patriotic curriculum, Hong Kong's prodemocracy movement appeared to have lost its steam. Opposition parties were ideologically divided and rife with internecine conflicts; more alarmingly, pro-Beijing parties were gaining electoral ascendency. Beijing has twice postponed the schedule of universal suffrage for the city's chief executive and legislature, and a depleted movement made the goal of democratization even more elusive. Taking cues from occupy movements around the world, Benny Tai, a legal scholar, proposed to paralyze the city's financial center with massive acts of civil disobedience to pressure Beijing to accept a genuine democratic election of the top leadership. In March 2013, an Occupy Central with Love and Peace (OCLP) campaign emerged, with Tai and his associates busy conducting public deliberations, training volunteers, collecting resources, and facilitating other preparatory activities (Yang 2019). While OCLP leaders envisioned an orderly sit-in as the last resort bargaining chip, Beijing reacted harshly by organizing countermovements and publishing two legal documents that imposed exacting conditions for the prospective executive suffrage, which basically denied the opposition the chance of nominating a candidate.

As OCLP campaigners faced a humiliating rejection, the Hong Kong Federation of Students (HKFS), then a formal organization representing student unions of the major eight universities, and Joshua Wong's Scholarism seized the moment by staging a class boycott campaign. On September 26, 2014, students suddenly launched an effort to enter the forecourt of the Central Government Offices. As student leaders were quickly arrested, more and more citizens gathered outside to show their support, leading to an escalating confrontation with the authorities. On the evening of September 28, the police sought to evict protesters by shooting eighty-seven canisters of tear gas. The crowd kept coming back after the tear gas vanished, and the counterproductive use of force galvanized more participation. Knowing that their eviction operation turned out to be futile, the police stopped using force around 10:00 P.M., and, by that time, three occupation zones, in Admiralty, Causeway Bay, and Mong Kok, spontaneously came into being, giving rise to the so-called Umbrella Movement (M. Ho 2019; F. Lee and Chan 2018; C. Lee and Sing 2019).

While a massive sit-in protest for democratic reforms was first broached by OCLP leaders, the scale and length of the Umbrella Movement far exceeded their original planning. An on-site survey reveals that more than half the participants identified HKFS as the legitimate leader (56.5%), rather than the OCLP (17.7%) (E. Cheng and Chan 2017: 226). HKFS delegates held a live broadcast negotiation with the government officials without reaching a consensus. Protesters occupied downtown areas continuously for seventy-nine days, sustaining a community of mutual support and solidarity and braving the constant menace from progovernment gangsters. Encampment zones witnessed the lively experimentation of artistic and cultural production, creatively blending the mundane and the political (Gan 2017; Veg 2016; K. Wang, St. John, and Wong 2017). The authorities applied the tactic of attrition by not actively deploying the police force (Yuen and Cheng 2017); as weeks passed by, popular support declined, participants dwindled, and the remaining protesters grew more impatient with the indecisive student leadership. Finally, the police forcibly evicted depopulated occupation zones one by one, and the exhausted Umbrella Movement ended in frustration and mutual recrimination.

Post-Umbrella Doldrums

In hindsight, the 2014 Umbrella Movement amounted to the last chance of realizing democratic reforms within the OCTS framework, as student leaders explicitly pledged their allegiance to the Basic Law and rejected the internationally prevalent appellation "Umbrella Revolution" to tone down its radicalism. Such well-intended gestures were not reciprocated, and, instead, the central government and the SAR government ratcheted up its control, as CCP leaders instinctively viewed any prodemocracy demands as a Western-instigated Trojan horse to destabilize their rule.

Prosecution ensued as soon as the Umbrella Movement ended. The authorities made thorough use of the legal means at hand to incarcerate the movement's leaders. Joshua Wong, for instance, served two brief prison terms for his movement involvement. Even before a final conviction was announced, the prolonged court process itself was already a mental torment for those indicted as well as a deterrent against further movement engagement. The last related trial was announced in April 2019, more than four years after the Umbrella Movement's conclusion. The verdict was harsher than expected, as all nine defendants were found guilty, with four immediately sent to prison and five others given probation or social service orders.

Another case of how the SAR government relentlessly weaponized legal means against dissidents was related to the 2016 Mong Kok disturbance, also nicknamed the "Fishball Revolution" (named after a popular street food). The incident originated from a dispute over government agents' attempt to suppress food peddlers during the Lunar New Year holidays in the name of public hygiene. Edward Leung Tin-kei, then a twenty-four-year-old charismatic by-election candidate, urged his supporters to resist the police. Since Edward Leung vocally advocated for Hong Kong's self-determination, and his catchy campaign slogan "Liberate Hong Kong, Revolution of Our Time" (*gwongfuk hoenggong sidoi gaakming/guangfu xianggang shidai geming*) smacked of the intention of proindependence, the prosecutors evoked a long-defunct charge of riot crime against him. In 2018, Leung was sentenced to six years in prison.

Repression also came from other administrative measures. Edward Leung and the five other activists were barred from joining the legislative election at the end of 2016 simply because election officials did not see them as bona fide supporters of OCTS. Nevertheless, the election ushered several young and proindependence candidates into Hong Kong's Legislative Council. The authorities cited the technicalities of the swearing in ceremony to unseat six freshly elected opposition legislators in 2017. The following year, the SAR government ordered the disbanding of the first openly proindependence organization, the Hong Kong National Party.

Taking advantage of the prodemocracy opposition's disarray, the SAR government forcibly pushed forward several controversial revisions, such as outlawing filibusters from opposition lawmakers, allowing PRC officials to exercise their duty in Hong Kong's new high-speed rail station, and criminalizing disrespectful behaviors during the singing of the national anthem. The prodemocracy camp was so demoralized that they failed to mount a strong resistance to these regressive changes. Adding to their woes, prodemocracy parties were defeated in two back-to-back by-elections in 2018, yielding seats to their pro-Beijing rivals.

The seeming failure of the Umbrella Movement and its subsequent reprisals brought about profound pessimism among prodemocracy activists and their supporters. Chung Yiu Wa, one of HKFS's leaders, pensively reflected on the desperate need to cope with the circumstance as "darkness shrouded the society." *Time Maybe Is Not on Our Side* was the book title of his collected essays. Even if the former student activists were able to establish themselves in business and academia in the future, he wondered whether it would be too late to recover "lost ground" (Y. Chung 2021: 56, 79–80). As citizens seemed to lose faith in democratization, prodemocracy media outlets suffered from an acute decline of subscribers to the extent that they struggled financially to pay their employees (Tam 2020: 536). Kin-man Chan, a sociology professor and one of the three OCLP initiators, talked about the prevalent powerlessness in the wake of the Umbrella Movement. He found some solace when his trial was able to rally some erstwhile supporters (K. Chan 2020: 12). Both Kin-man Chan and Benny Tai later received a sentence of sixteen months in jail.

"Be Water Revolution"

As Chan and Tai were escorted directly from the courtroom to prison, another political storm was brewing in the city. In February 2018, a murder took place in Taipei, and the Hongkonger suspect escaped back home without being caught. Ignoring the Taiwanese government's repeated extradition requests, the SAR government cited this unsolved case to launch a legal revision in February 2019. Yet, the ELAB defined the self-governing Taiwan as part of the PRC's territory—which the democratic island could not accept—and, as such, the extradition would proceed as a fugitive transfer between the PRC's territories. More shockingly, the legal draft allowed Hong Kong residents, expats, and transit passengers to be transferred to the PRC court system, which was notoriously known for slavishly toeing the party line. This seemingly technical amendment threatened to dismantle the firewall that has enshrined the city's rule of law and judicial independence. Not surprisingly, the city's lawyers, prodemocracy politicians, human rights activists, and students immediately rose to oppose the ELAB. Foreign consulates lodged démarches to express their grave concerns. Businesspersons and Chinese mainland migrants also expressed their opposition because of their personal experiences in the PRC's courts. Opponents denounced the ELAB as the "extradition to China" (*sungzung/songzhong*) bill, playing with the homophone for "funeral." The SAR government made some minor adjustments but insisted on enacting the ELAB to facilitate the transfer of murder suspects to Taiwan.

In hindsight, the SAR leaders probably intended to make use of the post-Umbrella window of opportunity when the prodemocracy opposition was at its nadir to engineer a far-reaching legal revamp for the goal of expediting the integration of the city and the mainland. Apparently, the government underestimated Hongkongers' deep-seated sense of insecurity. While the city's residents ostensibly benefited from China's growing prosperity and perhaps shared a sense of national pride with the global rise of the PRC, they were tenaciously attached to a legal system inherited from the British era that promised fairness and equality before the law. The PRC's staple practice to persecute political dissidents with trumped-up criminal charges also raised worrying concerns. For thirty years, hundreds of thousands of Hongkongers have annually gathered on June 4 to commemorate the tragedy of the Tiananmen massacre, shouting the slogan "ending one-party dictatorship"; that seemingly harmless act of mourning could have easily landed them in prison in the mainland. As the commentator Joseph Lian (2022: 78) pointed out, transporting American colonists "beyond seas to be tried for pretended offences" was among the cardinal grievances against the British monarchy that revolutionaries listed in their 1776 Declaration of Independence. With their personal freedom at stake, Hongkongers launched a citywide resistance campaign.

The protest movement flared up in the early summer of 2019, as the government planned to put the ELAB to a second reading. On June 9, over a million Hongkongers peacefully demonstrated only to receive a condescending rebuke from the authorities. To prevent the immediate passage, crowds gathered again to block the entrances to the Legislative Council on June 12. The police resorted to using 240 tear gas canisters and other weapons, and the arrestees were summarily charged with the crime of "rioting." The escalated use of force nearly created a tragedy of a fatal stampede (Citic Besiegement Team 2020), and the legislative session was forcibly adjourned. Outraged by the recalcitrant responses, the demonstration on June 16 purportedly attracted two million participants. Although Carrie Lam, the SAR leader at the time, announced a temporary ELAB suspension on the eve of the second demonstration, the so-called Be Water Revolution was already born. The name derived from the city's beloved martial arts star Bruce Lee, who famously characterized the essence of the combat technique as "formless and shapeless like water." Yet, who first evoked this rather Orientalist kung fu philosophy at that critical moment probably will remain forever unknown, but the slogan became widely adopted among participants. In the following, I use Be Water Revolution and anti-ELAB movement interchangeably.

Departing from the city's protest tradition, the Be Water Revolution was remarkable in many ways. First, there was no figurehead leadership in this prolonged campaign. Although CHRF initiated two major demonstrations in June, its representatives were not able to speak for the movement. While many student organizations (Tong and Yuen 2021) and professional groups (Ma and Cheng 2021) initiated protest actions of their own, most of the tactical discussion and decisions were anonymously made over online platforms, chiefly public channels on Telegram and chat rooms on LIHKG (a popular Reddit-like forum in Hong Kong) (Liang and Lee 2021; Urman, Ho, and Katz 2021). In my dataset of journalistic reports on 1,770 protest events from February 5, 2019, to July 5, 2020, 63% of them did not have an identifiable initiator or sponsor, which includes the following cases: anonymous calls to action on the internet, premediated actions by undisclosed participants, or spontaneous reactions. Regardless of their origins, I classify them as "no main stage." As mentioned earlier, the "main stage" refers to the podium erected in Admiralty during the 2014 Umbrella Movement. As the movement collapsed amid widespread dissatisfaction, the main stage became a discredited symbol of ineffective leadership. As the protest wave surged in the summer of 2019, "no main stage" became a popular slogan, as established political and civic leaders found themselves unneeded and unheeded in crowd scenes.

The Be Water Revolution self-consciously pursued a strategy of spatial dispersal, aiming at outwitting police deployment and encouraging more broadly based participation. Previously, Hong Kong's prodemocracy movement was fixed in conventional localities. The annual Tiananmen commemoration inevitably took place in Victoria Park, while the July First demonstrations traveled alongside the same thoroughfare on Hong Kong Island, usually from Causeway Bay to Central. The Umbrella Movement represented a breakthrough by occupying Admiralty, Causeway Bay, and Mong Kok simultaneously. By contrast, the Be Water Revolution was geographically decentralized, with suburban districts such as Yuen Long and Tsuen Wan emerging as hot conflict zones. There are eighteen administrative districts in Hong Kong, and we can identify Central and Admiralty (Central and Western District), Causeway Bay (Wan Chai District), and Mong Kok (Yau Tsim Mong District) as the conventional protest area, and the remaining fifteen administrative districts as the emerging area. In my journalistic database, 60% of protest events took place in the emerging area. With a more even geographic distribution, many Hongkongers experienced an acute "politicization of everyday life" (T. Tang and Cheng 2022).

While the Umbrella Movement unfolded as a massive act of civil disobedience, the Be Water Revolution further evolved toward a more radical direction. To use a three-part classification: (1) "peaceful protests" are those conventional assemblies and demonstrations that do not aim to create major disruptions or cause harm or damage; (2) "disruptive protests" are actions intending to cause disturbances without using force, such as strikes, blocking traffic, paralyzing a governmental agency with crowds, and so on; and (3) "violent protests" involve the use of physical force to cause personal harm or property damage. In the dataset of 1,770 protest events from February 2019 to June 2020, there were 1,158 peaceful (65%), 501 disruptive (28%), and 111 violent ones (6%). Protesters initiated many bold actions that were previously unthinkable, such as storming the legislative council (on July 1), a general strike (on August 5), blocking the airport (on August 12 and September 1), a weeklong barricade to paralyze the citywide transportation system (starting from November 11), and a sustained armed clash with the police in two universities (Chinese University of Hong Kong and Hong Kong Polytechnic University, from November 11 to November 29).

Yet, despite the escalating self-assertive tactics among the protesters, the Be Water Revolution supporters remained unwaveringly united, and many moderate prodemocracy citizens chose to tolerate these violent acts (F. Lee 2019; Yuen 2023). "Do Not Split" and "Five Demands, Not One Less" (withdraw the ELAB, retract the indictment of riot crime, release the arrestees, launch a commission of inquiry over police abuse of force, and direct elections of the chief executive and all Legislative Council members) continued to be the most frequently heard slogans. Poll surveys indicated that a majority of Hongkongers were sympathetic to the movement cause. In December 2019, 54.6% of respondents agreed that demonstrators should continue their actions (K. Wong, Zheng, and Wan 2022a: 148). Another study indicated that up to 44.2% of respondents were willing to tolerate protesters' use of violence, and the figures were higher among youths (51.8%), college graduates (48.2%), and people with higher incomes (51%) (K. Wong, Zheng, and Wan 2022b: 165–66). Perhaps, the best measurement of Hongkonger's preference consists in the resounding victory of the prodemocracy camp in the district council election on November 24, 2019. With a record high voter turnout (71.2%), prodemocracy candidates received 57.4% of the popular votes and won 86% of the total directly elected seats. This landslide vividly demonstrated the political spillover of a popularly supported protest movement (Shum 2021).

Finally, the Be Water Revolution's scale of mobilization is astonishing in other ways. In a city of 7.5 million residents, four demonstrations and rallies purportedly have attracted more than 1 million participants (on June 9, June 16, August 18, and January 1). Studies have found that 45.6% of polled residents took part in the protest activism, and the figure easily surpassed worldwide antidictatorship and antiausterity protests, which were said to have

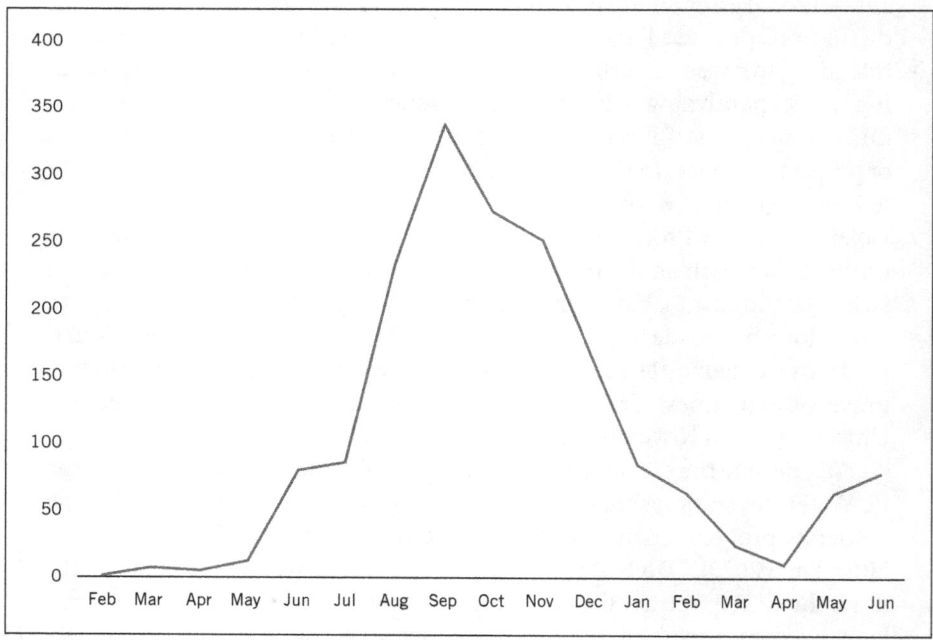

Figure I.1 Protest events, 2019–2020 (by month).

drawn up to 25% of the population at most (E. Cheng et al. 2022: 630). The escalated confrontation posed a headache for the SAR government; if they proved unable to contain the widespread disturbances, Beijing might decide to roll in its tanks to squash the protest. In mid-August, the U.S. president Donald Trump publicly warned about PRC's amassing of soldiers at the border and the prospect of a Tiananmen-style crackdown[1]—which luckily did not happen.

Figure I.1 presents the monthly distribution of protest events. Protests immediately emerged with the government's announcement of ELAB, in February 2019, and entered an ascendency phase with the pending legislative review in June. After the two University Battles in November, which alone led to the arrest of 1,377 people,[2] the movement's momentum suffered a mighty blow. With the outbreak of the COVID-19 epidemic, epitomized in the Wuhan Lockdown on January 23, 2020, the SAR government imposed social gathering bans, making collective actions increasingly difficult. The final blow came from Beijing's harshly imposed National Security Law (NSL), effective on June 30, which basically outlawed any space for protests in the city.

The Morning After

The SAR government's recalcitrance was the root cause of this prolonged resistance campaign. It was only on September 4 that the ELAB was finally withdrawn, and Carrie Lam's promised investigation over police violence and social dialogue was perfunctorily executed. One month later, the SAR evoked the Emergency Regulations Ordinance to impose a mask ban, further fueling public anger. The mask ban's legality was contested in court, and the judges finally upheld its constitutionality in April 2020, then, ironically, the ensuing pandemic forced the government to issue the mandate to wear a mask in public places.

While the Be Water Revolution began with the fear of being extradited to China, it gained steam because of the escalating public outcry over the excessive use of police force. Hong Kong's police, which used to take pride in being "Asia's Finest" for its professionalism, visibly shifted toward a "paramilitary internal security mode" (L. Ho 2020). From June 2019 to February 2020, the police shot 16,191 tear gas canisters, 10,100 rubber bullets, 2,033 beanbag bullets, and 1,880 sponge grenades.[3] A study on movement participants found that more than half of respondents reported having been attacked by tear gas at protest sites (69%) and experienced the shooting of tear gas near their homes (52%). These experiences with police violence are positively correlated with the acceptance of using radical protests (F. Lee et al. 2022: 439). Besides the use of more lethal weapons, Hong Kong police applied tougher measures against protesters. Starting in mid-August of 2019, no permits were granted to demonstration and rally applicants. In November, the police began to use preemptive control by arresting people before protest actions even started. In cases where police did not have sufficient grounds for arrest, they took note of participants' identity card number—an effective way to deter further involvement.

The apparent evidence of the police's connivance and collusion with progovernment mobsters wrought indignation. At the peak of confrontation, many of my informants were convinced that the PRC law enforcement agents were doubling as the city's police and that female protesters were sexually violated in the detention centers. Indicative of such prevalent distrust over police, a survey in November 2019 revealed that 59% of respondents said they were afraid of police at protest sites, whereas only 29% were fearful of demonstrators (Hong Kong Public Opinion Research Institute 2019: 3).

The Be Water Revolution ended under the triple pressures of reinforced policing, COVID-19, and the NSL. As the protest wave receded, Hongkongers faced a ruthless reprisal from the authorities. As of June 30, 2020, 9,216 persons have been arrested, 1,972 were indicted, and 141 were convicted.[4] The NSL, with its vaguely defined crimes of subversion, terrorism, secession, and collusion with foreign forces, further accelerated the legal crackdown. According to the Hong Kong Democracy Council, an overseas advocacy group based in Washington, DC, there were 1,900 political prisoners in Hong Kong as of October 8, 2024. Their punishment was unusually harsh. For instance, 214 people received prison sentences longer than one year, and 59 were imprisoned for possessing a laser pointer, which the police viewed as offensive weapons. Of the prisoners, 110 were minors, or under eighteen years old, with an average sentencing of twenty-seven months.[5]

While Hongkongers might have succeeded in preventing the ELAB's passage, the NSL, directly imposed by the PRC's rubber stamp National People's Congress with the deliberate circumvention of Hong Kong's legislature, amounted to much more serious damage to the city's rule of law. Under certain circumstances, Hongkongers could be sent to the mainland for trial. The law also made it possible for PRC security agents to openly operate in the city; they were not accountable to SAR government officials. In March 2024, Hong Kong's legislature swiftly approved another national security bill, outlawing the disclosure of "state secrets" and connection with foreign political organizations. With these changes, one could confidently say that the PRC's promise of a fifty-year high degree of autonomy for Hong Kong has prematurely expired.

The national security regime was no less than a wholesale transplant of the mainland's apparatus of repression. As a counterrevolutionary measure, it was less intended to contain the protest wave—which was already in decline with the onset of COVID-19—but more as a radical reset of Hong Kong's semiautonomy. Drastic changes soon followed. Citing reasons of national security, Beijing directly disqualified four popularly elected lawmakers in November 2020, and the remaining prodemocracy lawmakers resigned in protest. Using COVID-19 as a pretext, the SAR government postponed the legislative election to 2021, which proceeded under a new rule that significantly reduced directly elected seats. As prodemocracy candidates were not allowed to join this unfair election, the voter turnout was reduced to 30%. There were 389 prodemocracy district councillors following the electoral success in November 2019, but the threat of legal prosecution forced them to quit en masse. As of August 2021, more than 250 of them have resigned or forfeited their position due to arrest.[6] In January 2021, the SAR government arrested forty-seven political activists who were previously involved in a primary election of the prodemocracy camp for the alleged crime of subversion. The list included prodemocracy veterans and rising stars—clearly as an attempt to wipe out the city's opposition leaders.

In addition to political cleansing, Beijing set its eye on the media. After two consecutive arrests of Jimmy Lai, the founder of *Apple Daily*, the prominent prodemocracy newspaper with the highest daily circulation ceased to operate in July 2021. Other independent media outlets followed suit or transferred their operation to overseas destinations. On the eve of the NSL's imposition, many political organizations disbanded themselves to avoid political troubles. Using the pretext of investigating foreign money, the SAR government forced numerous civil society organizations to surrender their financial records. As such, veteran organizations that made up Hong Kong's prodemocracy movement, including CHRF, Alliance in Support of Patriotic Democratic Movements of China (the sponsor of the annual Tiananmen vigils), Hong Kong Confederation of Trade Unions (HKCTU), and others were forced to declare their dissolution. University student self-governing bodies were no longer recognized by the school administration, and many of them ceased to be active. The summer of 2021 witnessed a rapid mass extinction of Hong Kong's civil society.

The national security regime ushered in a radically sanitized Hong Kong that apparently was to the liking of Beijing's dictator. The only city that continued to commemorate the Tiananmen incident for thirty years was now forced to remain silent on the exact day (June 4). In fact, some have interpreted Hong Kong's recent changes as the city's own Tiananmen moment (V. Hui 2020). Facing the rapid slide of "mainlandization," the city's affluent middle class opted for migration, and their decisions were made easier because of friendlier immigration rules in Australia, Canada, and the United Kingdom. Three years after the NSL's enactment, Hong Kong experienced an atypical population decline.[7] Unsurprisingly, many emigrants were motivated by a deep-seated sense of political insecurity (Lui, Sun, and Hsiao 2021). It was also expected that vacancies in nursing, teaching, and other professions would soon be filled with Chinese migrants from the mainland, thereby further obscuring the city's distinctive identity.

With ratcheted up repression, a mass exodus of the prodemocracy middle class, and prospective tighter integration with the mainland, does this spell the end of Hong Kong's prodemocracy movement? Over various online chat rooms and channels, there have been heated discussions regarding the decision to stay or leave. Albert O. Hirschman (1970) famously theorized three typical responses (exit, loyalty, and voice) toward political decline. However, in the case of Hong Kong's ongoing autocratization and coercive assimilation, things are more complicated. Those who have chosen to stay face a prohibitive cost of voicing their dissenting opinions, but they have not simply endured the injustice with stoic silence (loyalty). Symbolic acts of defiance still emerged from time to time. For instance, after Queen Elizabeth passed away in October 2022, more than ten thousand Hongkongers lined up to pay their tribute at the British consulate, some even wearing yellow masks and black shirts—unmistakable insignias of the Be Water Revolution.[8] From street graffiti to cupcake design, a series of "furtive and fugitive resistance" used coded language to express the prodemocracy commitment anonymously (Meek and Hua 2023). Moreover, in late 2022, several international game hosts misidentified "Glory to Hong Kong," a protest song created during the Be Water Revolution, as the official anthem of the territory rather than the PRC's "March of the Volunteers." To no avail, the SAR government filed a formal demand to Google for correction of the search engine, whose page rank algorithm consistently indicated the protest song as Hong Kong's national anthem.[9] Many Hong Kong netizens experience gleeful schadenfreude at the self-inflicted humiliations of SAR officials.

The same goes for those who have left. Contrary to Hirschman's assumption about the powerlessness of exit, overseas Hongkongers have formed a dynamic web of diaspora activism with connections spreading across different continents. They have worked hard to preserve their distinctive culture and identity, building locally based community ties and advocating for human rights in the host societies. In addition, social movements should not be narrowly equated with street protests only. Even when demonstrations and rallies were no longer feasible, activists were still engaged in a number of what I called "postmobilization activism." In Hong Kong's case, they included participating in courtroom trials, assisting the imprisoned and their families, and other seemingly harmless activities such as operating independent bookstores and publishing community newspapers. True, these efforts per se were not likely to slow down the rapid democratic backsliding in Hong Kong, but they were helpful in mitigating the harms brought about by repression and sustaining an invisible community of resistance within the city and abroad. In short, Hong Kong's Be Water Revolution has certainly concluded, but the final chapters of the city's prodemocracy movement remain to be written.

Global Geopolitics

Hong Kong's recent political upheavals can be approached from different angles. Since the British possession in 1841, the city's viability has been predicated on being a trading post (P. Hui 1999), an embarkation port of the Chinese diaspora (Sinn 2014), a contending site between nationalists and communists (S. Tsang 1997), and a listening post during the Cold War (Roberts and Carroll 2016). In other words, Hong Kong thrived on a delicate balance between contending powers, benefiting from its unique positioning as a Western city adjacent to China (Carroll 2022). The same equilibrium explains the stagnation of the city's democratization after the handover. On the one hand, the West, led by the United States and the United Kingdom, was reluctant to push harder for the city's democracy as it might negatively affect their trade with China. On the other hand, the PRC was not strong enough to wean off its financial dependence of Hong Kong as a conduit of foreign investment, and, as such, it had to tolerate what it saw as the fastidious demands of the city's prodemocracy forces. As Ho-fung Hung (2022a) points out, the international political economy was at play in shaping the city's future. As PRC rulers were emboldened by their economic success and perceived the West's relative decline, particularly after the 2008 financial tsunami, they saw no reasons why they should continue to honor the original pledge not to meddle in the city's internal affairs. A more assertive China began to apply its global playbook to Hong Kong, including economic statecraft (enlarging the Chinese state-owned enterprises' presence), patron-clientelism (securing the loyalty of political and economic elites with rewards), and symbolic domination (controlling the media and promoting patriotic education)—a Chinese project of "internal colonization" (C. Lee 2022).

Geopolitical forces were undoubtedly continuing to shape the city's future. Situated in the stream of evolving world politics, Hong Kong's Be Water Revolution took place after the U.S.-led West was increasingly concerned about trade disputes, intellectual property infringement, military coercion over Taiwan, and human rights violations in Xinjiang and right before the COVID-19 outbreak and Russia's full-scale invasion against Ukraine. In these incidents, the West has hardened its attitude toward the PRC, which explains the slew of pro–Hong Kong initiatives, including the U.S. Hong Kong Human Rights and Democracy Act (2019) and Hong Kong Autonomy Act (2020), Canada's Lifeboat Scheme to Hong Kong residents (2021), and the United Kingdom's expansion of eligibility of British National (Overseas) (BNO) passport application (2022). In response to the political crisis triggered by the NSL, Taiwan also unveiled its Humanitarian Aid Program in 2020.

The Be Water Revolution was born in an era of accelerated international rivalry, and its emergence further acted as an independent force to reshape the existing geopolitical landscape. Hong Kong's case was not exceptional in highlighting the intricate two-way interaction between protest mobilization and geopolitical competition. Prodemocracy protests in Serbia (2000), Georgia (2003), Ukraine (2004), and Kyrgyzstan (2005) expanded the frontier of the democratic West and, at the same time, alarmed Russian and Chinese autocrats about the contagiousness of "color revolutions" (Bunce and Wolchik 2011; Wilson 2006). Ukraine's Euromaidan protest in 2014 led to Russia-assisted armed separatism and the occupation of Crimea, paving the way for their full-scale war in 2022. Taiwan's Sunflower Movement of 2014 was primarily driven by a potent national identity, which not only successfully forestalled a comprehensive free trade agreement with China but eventually paved the way for the ascendency of a proindependence government in 2016 (M. Ho, Huang, and Lin 2020; Rowen 2015). More recently, #MilkTeaAlliance, initially a Twitter meme that evolved into a cross-national network connecting prodemocracy activists in Hong Kong, Taiwan, Thailand, and Myanmar, facilitated a broadly based resistance movement against the expansion of Chinese authoritarianism (D. Chan 2023; Dedman and Lai 2021; Wasserstrom 2023).

Recognizing the delicate dialectics between social contention and geopolitics means that we need to rethink two conventional wisdoms. First, a "state-and-society" framework has been the bedrock assumption for students of social movements, directing their attention to the interactions between incumbent political leaders and protesters (Gamson 1975; Skocpol 1979; Tilly 1978). The entire literature on political opportunity structure is explicitly built on this premise (McAdam 1982; Tarrow 1989). Not that this scholarly framework is problematic per se; on the contrary, it has proven useful in analyzing the majority of social protests that do not reverberate beyond national borders. However, for truly transformative and history-making protests—in the Sewellian sense of "eventful" (Sewell 2005: 81–123)—like the Be Water Revolution, we must be mindful of the insufficiency of a state-and-society framework and pay more attention to the supranational processes that could be a catalyst for and a consequence of street protests.

Second, international politics students have long framed states as unitary actors whose action is primarily geared to a reified notion of "national interest." Conventional perspectives emphasize how hegemonic power, military might, and economic strength structure geopolitical relations. Yet, these discussions remain essentially state centered, with scant attention to civil society actors. Studies have looked at the existence of transnational advocacy networks (Keck and Sikkink 1998) and how social movements conduct international marketing (Bob 2010) and make strategic use of international organizations (Bob 2015). From another direction, great power competitions are likely to spill over to the realm of civil society, with dictatorships expanding their influence campaign beyond borders (Youngs 2022). By launching prolonged and challenging protest actions, prodemocracy Hongkongers were determined to push the envelope to the extent that Beijing could no longer rely on its SAR deputies and resorted to imposing a draconian NSL regime, further worsening the PRC's already fraught relationship with the West. During the heyday of protests in 2019, there was fearful speculation among prodemocracy Hongkongers that their existential issue might be used as a chess piece by the Trump administration to extract more concessions on trade from China. Such a scenario did not materialize, and, instead, Hongkongers successfully inserted their campaign into the agenda of the United States, the United Kingdom, and Taiwan, which all incurred Beijing's opprobrium for their pro–Hong Kong policies. As such, the Be Water Revolution belongs to the rare set of contentious politics in which bottom-up protest activism changes geopolitical structures.

An Actionist Sociology

To untangle the myriad of threads between street protests and geopolitical implications, this book examines the Be Water Revolution participants to understand how the numerous and anonymous Hongkongers contributed to this epoch-making campaign as well as how they responded to the full-scale state repression that enveloped them. I decided to structure my research in an agent-based account because, after all, it is Hongkongers' deliberate choices that set forth the previously unthinkable protest wave. Should we ignore such subjective origins of what Piven and Cloward (1977: 24) call "mass defiance," the resulting institutional disruption could not be adequately explained. Movement agency is the key focus that guides this book's investigation, as I intend to unearth the sources of creativity and enthusiasm that made possible such a spectacular protest rally like the aforementioned Hong Kong Way. Throughout the Be Water Revolution, numerous episodes that were previously unexpected and unthinkable unfolded. When the moment was ripe, participants in Hong Kong engaged in ways they were individually capable of; the accumulated result was perceived by Beijing as a mounting threat to their authority over the city.

Why did proverbially materialistic and rootless Hongkongers decide to join a life-and-death struggle to defend their hometown? What motivated so many young people to engage in physical confrontations with the police, many of them preparing a farewell letter to their loved ones before going to the street? What encouraged law-abiding citizens to tolerate or even assist violent behaviors such as erecting barricades, throwing petrol bombs, and vandalizing storefronts and public property? The key to solving these puzzles has to do with a fuller and more grounded understanding of Hongkongers' own agency.

The actionist sociology, or the idea of foregrounding social actors in major transformations, can be attributed to the French sociologist Alain Touraine. Opposing the functionalist perspective of society as an orderly system as well as the rational-choice model of individuals as calculating agents, Touraine aims to bring back actors that are capable of producing and transforming themselves—the capacity that he identifies as "historicity" (Touraine 1988: xxiv). In his conception, social movements play a central role in the struggle over historicity because they can lead to "a breakup of the political system" (66).

To make actionist sociology more operational, I borrow James M. Jasper's (1997: 64–67) idea of agency as "artful creativity." Movement participants are endowed with their own biographical sources, moral judgment, and skills, which enable them to initiate protest actions. People make protest, but they do not make it just as they please. But the constraints should not be conceptualized as "structural" but rather as an inherent condition of social actions. Jasper (2004) views social movements as a series of strategic choices in which participants must recurrently respond to a number of dilemmas and trade-offs. Different from rational choice theory, what is at stake is more than individual interests, incentives, or the decision to participate. Since social movements aim at changing history, a fundamental task of researchers is explaining how changes happen, as people no longer accept their habitual subordination but join in a revolt, or, in Jasper's own words, "When strategic players manage to break with expectations and make another choice, taking their opponents by surprise" (Jasper 2004: 7).

Central to Jasper's writings (1997, 2014) is a rejection of the mainstream approach that applies excessively structuralist and static concepts (resources, opportunity, frame, and so on) to the understanding of the dynamics of protests. Such a conceptualization typically underestimates the inherently fluid and indeterminate nature of collective action. As such, he emphasizes how people's cultural inheritance, biographical backgrounds, and even aesthetic tastes play a role in how they devise their own protests. Jasper's actionist perspective, or what he calls "sociology of strategic choice," leads him to reject the well-established theory of political opportunity structure because there is no such thing as opportunities objectively existing in themselves; they emerge only with the participant's own perception. In the same vein, resources become handy in social movements only insofar as people have the capacity to utilize them in the right place and at the right time (Jasper 2012).

Jasper further attempts to unpack the conventional notion of "agency," as it is often assumed to be unitary, preexisting, and fixed. "Players" can be simple or compound, and they possess varying capacities and multiple goals. Moreover, players' access to "arenas" (defined as a spatial bundle of rules and resources) cannot be taken for granted. In this view, social movements emerge when players enter an arena, and, to pursue their goals, they can also switch to other arenas (Jasper 2015). The upshot is that we need to embrace a more fluid and dynamic conceptual strategy than the dualistic structure-and-agency perspective.

In short, actionist sociology explicitly aims to provide a culturally sensitive microfoundation of protest actions, an interpretative account of participants' own worldview and decision-making, and an interactive and open-ended view of social movements and their opponents. Following these theoretical threads, this book proposes the notion of "collective improvisation" as the key feature that undergirds Hong Kong's Be Water Revolution.

Collective Improvisation

Improvisation, a fundamental aspect of human agency, is the acquired capacity to promptly adapt to new circumstances. Through our command of language, we consistently construct grammatically accurate and meaningful sentences that we have never utilized previously. The *Oxford English Dictionary* provides two definitions of improvisation. The first one is more narrowly focused on artistic production, "composing or performing music, poetry, drama without preparation," while the second one generally refers to "doing anything spontaneously . . . or on the spur of the moment; the action of responding to circumstances or making do with what is available." Both have to do with a trained competence to act unexpectedly.

In the study of contentious politics, Charles Tilly (1978: 151–53) introduces a theater-based concept, "repertoire of collective action," to make sense of why people in a certain period of time tend to use a limited set of actions to express their discontent. He suggests that cultural familiarity and action effectiveness are the primary considerations when choosing a repertoire. Implicit in this seminal concept is the recognition of "the clustered, learned, yet improvisational character of people's interactions as they make and receive each other's claim" (Tilly and Tarrow 2007: 16). In other words, people inevitably improvise to varying degrees when protesting.

One direction of repertoire research seeks to understand its long-term standardization to the extent that demonstrations, sit-ins, and other actions have become "modular," or the elementary forms of protest making (Tilly 1998: 12–13; Tarrow 2011: 38). This line of investigation complements the literature that points out the gradual institutionalization of social protests in established democracies with the emergence of a rule-based policing system (della Porta 1995; della Porta and Reiter 1998). As such, social movements become a permanent feature of democratic polity and diffuse to different sectors; at the same time, protests become routinized, less violent, and more predictable in their outcomes (Goldstone 2004; M. Ho and Ting 2023; Meyer and Tarrow 1998; Soule and Earl 2006).

Another research direction is interested in the issue of tactical innovation, which shares more affinity with the research questions in this book, as I seek to make sense of why so many Hongkongers departed from their habitual ways of protest making and embarked on an uncharted course. Doug McAdam (1983) notes that new ways of making protests typically have caught the authorities off guard and propelled an escalating wave of protests; in the long term, however, they have invited government countermeasures, thereby constraining their disruptiveness. Radicalization and its neutralization are a reciprocal and relational process (P. Chang 2015; della Porta 2018).

How do protest tactics evolve? How can an existing protest repertoire expand to incorporate new genres? The existing literature offers two contrasting explanations. The first perspective assumes social movements are largely organization based and leadership directed (Gamson 1975; Tilly 1978; Zald and McCarthy 1987). In an attempt to correct previous understandings of protests as unstructured mass responses, scholars, since the 1970s, have generally adopted an organization-centered view. Movements are more likely to take place when people are connected and unified (Granovetter 1978; Oberschall 1993; Useem 1980). Movements are sustainable only if they form "leadership, administrative structure, incentives for participation, and means for acquiring resources and support" (McAdam and Scott 2005: 8). "Development of leadership teams" (Staggenborg 2020: 15) is a key process in movement organizing. In this view, spontaneous participation will eventually give way to stable organizations. In the era of Fordist capitalism when business was dominated by hierarchical enterprises and politics by mass political parties, it appeared natural that social movements would eventually evolve into formal and professional organizations.

This organization-centered view has been taken for granted by researchers in the tradition of resource mobilization and political process theory, but, from the very beginning, there have been dissenting voices. Whether organizational leadership is able to play the role of initiating a social movement is not universally accepted. Studies have found a disconnect between organizational resources and innovative actions (Kriesi et al. 1995: 123; Koopmans 1993). Organizations are intrinsically conservative because they tend to be preoccupied with their own survival and often choose to restrain grassroots militancy (Fantasia 1989; Piven and Cloward 1977). Concomitantly, there is a growing recognition that unprepared, unplanned, and unscripted protests are often more innovative and unpredictable (Snow and Moss 2014).

The second perspective starts with the assumption that grassroots participants are innately innovative and resourceful. With the secular decline of mass membership organizations (Putnam 2001; Skocpol 2002), the number of large-scale massive protests initiated by political parties, labor unions, or civil society organizations became fewer. Noticeable global protests in the first two decades of the twenty-first century, including anti-globalization protests (Fominaya 2014a; Pleyers 2010; J. Smith 2008), the Arab Spring (Bayat 2017; Ketchley 2017; della Porta 2020), the antiausterity protests in Europe (Fominaya 2020; della Porta 2015), and Occupy Wall Street in the United States (Gerbaudo 2012; Gitlin 2012) proceeded without a leader or a command-and-control center. It was clear that citizens across the globe have become easily disgruntled, being more prone to take protest action, without prodding from organizational leaders (Krastev 2014; Carothers and Youngs 2015).

Analyzing the rise of decentralized movements, Jeffrey Juris (2008) points at the confluence of changes in norms (participatory democracy), organization (networking rather than hierarchy), and technology (the internet). However, the subsequent discussion diverges into two streams. One strand of research is exclusively preoccupied with technological factors alone. Digital communication is said to reduce transaction costs, thus ushering in an age of the "power of organizing without organizations" (Shirky 2008). The internet brings about the so-called politics of captivation, as some protest issues quickly emerge and grasp the national attention (Kang 2018). Social media makes possible a distinctive logic of "connective action," replacing the traditional "collective action" led by organizations (Bennett and Segerberg 2013). With digitally enabled communication, "instant insurgent communities" can be formed everywhere, thus making organizational leadership obsolete (Castells 2012).

The second category of literature exhibits an ideological leaning toward anarchism, which reflects an exuberant faith in the power of grassroots participants. It tacitly assumes that repressed people possess a clear-eyed understanding of themselves and their situations, and, when provided with a chance for democratic decision-making, they are consistently capable of generating the most suitable strategic choices. Such bottom-up sources of innovation are identified as "horizontalism" (Graeber 2013) or "multitude" (Hardt and Negri 2017), and both share a profound distrust of centralized leadership. Writers in this school celebrate the birth of "leaderless movements," which are said to be nimble, creative, and immune from being co-opted by the authorities. Furthermore, they reject the instrumental logic of conventional movements and insist on seeing participation itself as a valuable opportunity for people to envision a free society (Pleyers 2010: 37–57). Such belief is often identified as "prefigurative politics," which entails a blurring between the strategic and the expressive (Gerbaudo 2017: 64–70; Maeckelbergh 2011). In the case of Hong Kong, quite a number of observers maintain that the creative use of digital media facilitated the "leaderless" movement (Leung 2019).

In general, I find both existing approaches unsatisfactory in explaining the innovative strategic choices. The conventional model of organization-led movements is clearly outdated, but that does not mean preexisting organizations and leaders have become completely useless; in fact, they continue to fulfill some essential functions that could in no way be delegated to or replaced by anonymous participants. The second perspective of leaderless movements is also inadequate, suffering from a utopian technical determinism or a naive populism. More recent studies have indicated that digital communication does not unilaterally empower movement protesters but can serve as a high-tech tool to consolidate dictatorship (C. Chang and Lin 2020; Tufekci 2017: 223–60). When it comes to digital activism, entrenched elites continue to enjoy organizational and material advantages over their less privileged challengers (Schradie 2019). Naive populism is mistaken in its assumption that all individuals are equally and effortlessly capable of making strategic decisions. The widespread involvement of ordinary individuals requires specific conditions, including intense emotional priming, reflective learning, and collaborative networks. The absence of these prerequisites elucidates why large-scale decentralized movements infrequently occur.

This book proposes "collective improvisation" as the central process undergirding the widespread decision-making in Hong Kong's Be Water Revolution. Elaborating on my previous work (M. Ho 2018, 2019), I define collective improvisation as "peer-produced strategic responses without prior planning." Improvising movement tactics requires a sufficient number of like-minded participants, or what Hongkongers cordially call "fellow travelers" (*tungloujan/tongluren*) to work on the same goal so that ideas, talent, money, and labor can be tapped from many sources. Open-source communities have long circulated the so-called Linux law, "Given enough eyeballs, all bugs are shallow." When confronted with the frightening prospect of being sent to trial in the PRC courts, the open-source synergy from Hongkongers resulted in not merely troubleshooting a computer program but mobilizing large-scale and spatially dispersed protests, devising new tactics, donating resources to the movement cause, and opening new fronts to challenge the authorities. Their joint product was an unprecedented resistance campaign spanning the divides between street protests and logistic support, offline activities and online communication, mobilizing and postmobilization activism, and actions in the home city and the responses from overseas diasporic communities.

Peer-producing Hongkongers were connected with each other in different ways, including through personal ties such as kinship, friendship, classmates, alumni, neighborhood, coworkers, and newly forged comradeship at conflict sites, in addition to their anonymous interactions on online platforms. They were willing to work together because of a strong and spontaneous outpouring of emotions: anger at the recalcitrant government incumbents, indignation at police violence, grief for those who lost their lives, a sense of guilt because one has not been able to do more, and so on. These affective energies helped bring about a brand-new imagery of Hong Kong as an independent nation (Carrico 2022) with shared experiences of suffering and common aspirations. An anonymous poem beautifully captured the essence of such collective improvisation:

> *In a leaderless movement,*
> *If you just make the first step,*
> *You'll see there's something you can do, for everyone. (Bauhinia Project 2021: 44)*

Even though such visionary moments of collective effervescence were ephemeral and ultimately ruthlessly put down by stepped-up repression, they stand as a testament to the remarkable achievements that can be accomplished by the collective agency of Hongkongers when they unite as one.

Within the local context, the essence of collective improvisation during the Be Water Revolution is encapsulated by two slogans: "Brothers climb the mountain and each has to contribute his effort" (*hingdai paasaan gokzi noulik/xiongdi pashan gezi nuli*), meaning that movement participants are all aiming for the same goal, and they are doing it in their own ways; and "Do not snitch and do not split" (*bat dukfui bat gotzek/bu duhui bu gexi*), which essentially emphasizes an ethics of solidarity when confronting the same adversary so that moderate participants are obliged to tolerate radical actions. While it is true that these laconic slogans are ambiguous, with multiple possibilities of interpretation, they serve to expand the space for creative responses among previously uninvolved citizens (F. Lee et al. 2020). For the richness of these newly invented protest phrases, see the Glossary.

A quote from an interviewed activist who contributed to the Hong Kong Way suffices to highlight the essence of collective improvisation:

> In this protest, there were many people who promoted the ideas, some who paid money, and others who donated resources. That is the secret to why this resistance lasted that long and overcame so many difficult conditions. Because we insisted on the same belief, the power of this idea sustained multi-dimensional participation.

Collective improvisation is capable of making eventful protests that are not anticipated by participants and the authorities, yet this does not guarantee its final victory. In nondemocracies like Hong Kong, as long as the ruling elites stay cohesive and the repressive apparatus remains operative, there is little chance of overwhelming the government.

Collective improvisation shares some similarities with Tilly's notion of "repertoire" in that both stress the performative and creative features in protest-making. As Tilly (2008: 15) points out, "Participants in contentious politics commonly dramatize their claims rather than treating them as routine transactions." The concept highlights the fact that while protesters self-consciously depart from the everyday routine to make their voices heard, their actions remain within the more or less identifiable confines and often involve a selection of preexisting options. This insight originates from Tilly's historical survey of how the French made protests over the centuries, as "they followed available scripts, adapted those scripts, but only changed them bit by bit" (xiii). By contrast, my notion of collective improvisation is less concerned about the long-term conventionalization of protest-making but rather about movement practices expanding, proliferating, and mutating in a relatively short period of time, thereby ushering in an unexpected episode of contention.

There is another reason why this book chooses to be anchored in an actionist sociology, which has to do with unfavorable circumstances when the Be Water Revolution kicked off. As previously mentioned, the post-Umbrella Hong Kong witnessed growing restrictions on political freedom, and the city's prodemocracy movement appeared stagnated and disarrayed, whereas the pro-Beijing camp was making steady strides in organizing new immigrants from the mainland into a formidable voting bloc. Other evidence of the PRC's enhanced cyberwarfare capabilities showed that China was on the defensive during the 2014 Umbrella Movement, as Facebook and other social media outlets were dominated by promovement messages. Taking stock of how the Middle East and North African dictators collapsed during the internet-empowered Arab Spring, the Chinese government stepped up its cyberwarfare capabilities to the extent that its domestic digital public sphere transitioned from a relatively unsupervised outlet of dissidents to a tool to drum up proregime patriotism (Lei 2018). The PRC became capable of conducting information campaigns beyond its physical border. Five years after the Umbrella Movement, the PRC not only seized the Hong Kong crisis as an opportunity for promoting patriotic education within its own borders but also successfully propagated its narrative through various online media platforms for the international audience. In August 2019, Facebook, YouTube, Instagram, and Twitter (now known as X) (all banned in mainland China) decided to take down and disable thousands of channels because they were suspected of being a part of the PRC's disinformation campaign against the Hong Kong movement.[10]

The PRC's sharp learning curve in digital technologies highlights the formidable challenges faced by prodemocracy Hongkongers. How did the city's prodemocracy movement defy these manifest adversities and miraculously resuscitate itself to the extent that Hong Kong's overlords in Beijing felt compelled to renege on its international pledge to allow autonomy in the city until 2047? The most likely explanation for this puzzle has to do with the radical change in Hongkongers' agency and their collective improvisation, which evolved into a highly subversive weapon to the Chinese party-state behemoth.

Finally, one might as well characterize the government's responses to escalating protests as a sort of "collective improvisation," but I prefer to reserve this term for protesters' agency. True, the incumbents react to collective actions through a calculus of the cost of concession and that of disruption (Luders 2006), which is constantly shifting as the protest wave unfolds. While the government leaders can be situational in dealing with challengers, their responses are typically not collective or impromptu but bureaucratic and leader centered, which makes little room for the adaptation of novel practices. As such, throughout the Be Water Revolution, we witnessed the persistent ratcheting up of repression, from using more lethal weapons, evoking the emergency ordinance, and banning social gathering to enacting national security legislation. Clearly, once the government leaders opted for the repression option, it was difficult to change gears, even when the protest momentum had receded.

Plan of the Book

This book adopts an actionist perspective to understand the rise and the long afterlife of Hong Kong's Be Water Revolution by offering a closer look at why and how numerous average citizens chose to be involved in this high-risk and consequential protest movement. The making and unfolding of this extraordinary movement agency are the focus of this book.

Chapter 1 examines the immediate prehistory of the Be Water Revolution and analyzes how the discouraging failure of the 2014 Umbrella Movement incidentally paved the way for a larger uprising five years later. Many novel and experimental movement ideas incubated in the Umbrella Movement's occupation zones saw their full-scale implementation later. Post-Umbrella movement networks in neighborhoods or in professional occupations helped maintain connections among like-minded prodemocracy Hongkongers who could swiftly respond as soon as the ELAB threat emerged. Protesters evolved because they took stock of the lesson of a failed student-led movement, and such reflection and learning took place amid strong emotional outpourings of anger, guilt, and sorrow in the early summer of 2019.

Deviating from the city's tradition of a peaceful and civilized prodemocracy movement, the Be Water Revolution was noted for its assertive defiance, including guerrilla-style barricades, throwing petrol bombs, and vandalism. Chapter 2 looks at how collective improvisation made possible the teams of street militants as well as the invisible logistic network that sustained these radical actions. It was largely due to these submerged and embedded networks of collaboration that the SAR government came to face the greatest challenge to its rule.

Chapter 3 zooms out to survey the dynamics of protest, paying attention to how the Be Water Revolution's actions diffused and invented new tactics. As zones of engagement proliferated, the authorities were encountering greater pressure on multiple fronts, and these site-specific struggles helped broaden the movement's appeals. Yet, the power of collective improvisation had its inherent limits, and its creativity and militancy inevitably became exhausted as long as the government's repressive capabilities remained intact.

Chapter 4 analyzes the expressive and ideational dimensions of movement agency. As the Be Water Revolution proceeded as a last-ditch effort to preserve the city's autonomy, a new political imagery was born and gained currency among protest participants. Aspirations of self-determination emerged and were powerfully expressed in songs, declarations, and visual imageries circulated on online platforms. Highly symbolic language and protest repertoire also reinforced the sense of belonging to a community with the shared fate.

Being a first-class world city, political struggles in Hong Kong are bound to have international reverberations, not only because the city's political future was intimately connected to global geopolitics but also because overseas Hongkongers eagerly responded by improvising their supportive actions. Chapter 5 unpacks how they reconnected with home-based activisms, collected movement resources, and lobbied host governments, and, in so doing, global diasporic communities came into being, helping carry the torch of the city's prodemocracy movement outside of Hong Kong.

COVID-19 and NSL hastily put down street protests in Hong Kong, but the Be Water Revolution did not come to an end. Activism was diverted to new arenas, such as pandemic-related protests and building a prodemocracy economy. Rather than withdrawing into so-called abeyance structures, which primarily aimed at survival in a harsh environment, Hongkongers launched a number of initiatives such as supporting action for imprisoned activists, community newspapers and independent bookstores to maintain participant ties, and overseas-based news media to satisfy the need for independent journalism. Chapter 6 examines the plethora of these postmobilization activisms and shows how they minimized the harms brought about by political repression.

Finally, the Conclusion discusses the future trajectory of Hong Kong's opposition movement in comparison with the historical precedents of Taiwan's independence movement and post-Tiananmen overseas Chinese dissidents. I also elaborate on the significance and applicability of collective improvisation to other contemporary eventful uprisings around the globe.

For my primary dataset, I draw from 189 in-depth interviews with movement participants and two major journalistic outlets (2019–2020). I also carried out multiple-sited field observations and explored the wealth of published materials devoted to the Be Water Revolution. For more detailed explanations on methodology, see Appendix 1.

1

Evolving Protesters

Fei was a twenty-two-year-old female student in Taipei at the time I interviewed her in 2022. She had to leave Hong Kong because her progovernment father reported her movement activities to the police.[1] Afterward, she found herself being constantly followed in the street and her bank accounts frozen. Fei left her native city without telling her parents and had to support herself by working at a compatriot's store in Taiwan. Fei's drastic life turn originated from a shopping trip in 2019, in which she received a leaflet warning about the impending ELAB. Out of curiosity, she and her friends joined the rally in front of the Legislative Council on June 12. Witnessing the police crackdown, Fei knew she had the obligation "to stand up and to speak out so that the government hears our opinions." It was also a moment of epiphany, as she began to relearn what had happened to Hong Kong in the preceding years. She started to work with neighborhood activists to distribute leaflets and occasionally volunteered as one of the "scouts" (*saaubing/shaobing*) to report on police deployment. Fei took care to avoid standing too close to the conflict areas, but, nevertheless, she was arrested once and threatened with the criminal charge of unlawful assembly.

Fei described her premovement life as a "Hong Kong pig" (*gongzyu/gangzhu*)—a local idiom to describe those apolitical Hongkongers. "I rarely cared about politics, and my life was mostly about sports and going to school." Similarly, other self-confessed "ex–Hong Kong pig" interviewees spoke of their innocent years of political apathy, as their social media pages were merrily full of pictures of food, shopping, and international trips. To be clear, this swinish existence does not necessarily mean an inbred conservatism of bowing to governmental authorities, nor are they thoroughly indoctrinated by the CCP, because they know perfectly well that they lead a freer life than their mainland compatriots. "Hong Kong pigs" are realistic and cynical, embracing a rather resigned recognition of the futility of political dissent. According to Fei, a "Hong Kong pig" could lead a carefree life as long as they did not pay attention to outside changes. Her movement participation led to deep soul-searching:

> You can never go on sleeping like (mainland) Chinese. Once you are awake, you can never pretend you are still sleeping. A bird in the cage will always try to break free unless it does not know how to fly. If I could go back in time, I wish I could have done more for the movement and to be on the frontline.

The transmutation from a "Hong Kong pig" to a determined participant was a dominant narrative among many first-time protesters in the Be Water Revolution (see also Hong Kong Cherishers 2020: 214). However, such Saul-to-Paul conversion only made up for a minority of the participants in the citywide uprising. One survey on rally protesters on July 12, 2019 indicated that there were only 23.4% of them who did not take part in the Umbrella Movement (Chinese University of Hong Kong Centre for Communication and Public Opinion Survey 2020: 32). As for the other three-quarters of participants, a more pertinent question is about their *altered attitude* toward movement participation, rather than the change from apathy to engagement. Why did rule-of-law conscious Hongkongers decide to tolerate or assist law-breaking protest actions? How come they chose to depart from their age-honored routines of protest-making to join the unconventional activities of general strike, human chain, and so on? These questions have to do with the evolution of protesters.

Hongkongers commonly referred to their protest participation as "dreaming" (*faatmung*). Protesters commonly used this term when sharing their personal experiences at the conflict site in order to avoid the legal consequences. However, there is indeed something dreamlike or surreal about the protest actions in the Be Water Revolution because Hongkongers would not have done them in normal circumstances. This chapter investigates the making of movement agency, of first-timers and veterans, and how its emergence made possible the widespread collective improvisation during the Be Water Revolution. As Barrington Moore (1978) has pointed out, injustice has always been the moral root cause for mass revolts. Following this insight, this chapter further asks questions about the subjective processes of making sense of injustice as well as their consequences. I begin with the ambivalent legacies of the Umbrella Movement.

Occupy Zones as Movement Incubators

The existence of a "free space," where the subordinate can freely exchange their ideas and learn from their peers, has long been identified as a key factor for movement insurgency.[2] According to Francesca Polletta (1999), these free spaces facilitate network building, form indigenous leadership, and explore future-looking identity and tactics. In occupy protests around the world in the 2010s, people typically usurped a public space in their confrontation with the authorities. Many observers have noticed the explosion of spontaneous activities like independent media, yoga practice, soup kitchens, people's libraries, environmentally friendly gardening, and so on, because participants literally intended to enact the vision of their ideal society. These "protest camps" operate as a free space, giving free rein to participants to initiate their own actions (Frenzel, Feigenbaum and McCurdy 2014; Glasius and Ishkanian, 2018; Näre and Jokela 2022; Pickerill and Krinsky 2012).

With its seventy-nine days of roadside occupation, Hong Kong's 2014 Umbrella Movement also witnessed lively and experimental encampment zones (M. Ho 2019: 154–62; Yuen 2018). What has endearingly been called "Harcourt Village" sustained a beloved communal life of sharing and caring—a living utopia surrounded by the city's hypercompetitive capitalism. The protest camp emerged as an incubator for new strategic ideas and identities that have not been thought of or practiced before. One participant described her personal experience during the Umbrella Movement as follows:

> While we were in the occupation zones, we were fantasizing about what we could do. There were some things we wanted to do but did not put into practice then. We also initiated some campaigns on a small scale. For instance, we often screened documentaries on worldwide protests in the occupation zone, but we did not have similar screenings and discussion elsewhere. There has been talk about "letting flowers blossom everywhere" (*pindei hoifaa/biandi kaihua*) at that time, but the truth is we failed to bring the movement momentum to communities.

One of the reflections born in this social laboratory was that protesters should not constrain themselves to the occupation zones only but rather spread demands for democracy to different communities. Particularly when the Umbrella Movement persisted into its second month, participants found themselves struggling to fill in the occupation zones with enough people. In so doing, occupy protesters became defensive by limiting their impact spatially. Recognizing this problem, students launched an "Umbrella Community Day" by setting up flyer distribution booths. However, these outreach initiatives were not successful because they came too late and easily became targets of progovernment mobsters. After the end of the Umbrella Movement, there emerged a spin-off campaign to organize neighborhoods with the slogan "support the Umbrella Movement by going to communities" (*caangsaan lokkeoi/chengsan luoqu*). Its proponents maintained that activists should move beyond occupying the streets to "reoccupy our communities."

As such, when the 2019 protest took place, demonstrators avoided occupying a site permanently; when overwhelmed by the police force, they quickly withdrew and regrouped at another site. "Be Water" became an oft heard plea to those reluctant protesters who refused to concede. In this way, the 2019 movement proceeded in a more spatially scattered pattern; geographic decentralization not only maximized the pressure on police deployment but also facilitated the participation of suburban citizens. Chapter 3 describes in depth how this spatial dynamic played out.

Newer actions that first appeared in the Umbrella occupation zones proliferated elsewhere. My journalistic dataset indicated that thirteen art exhibitions, sixteen TV or documentary screenings, and three concerts were held from June to December 2019. Perhaps, the most well-known reinvented repertoire inherited from the Umbrella Movement was the "Lennon Wall." In 2014, Lennon Wall referred to a section of a concrete staircase in the government complex that was covered with handwritten Post-it notes. Given that students formed the majority of those involved, it was unsurprising that they utilized their everyday stationery to embellish the occupied zone. Over time, this transformed into more than just a decorative act, becoming a hub for spontaneous expression and artistic endeavors. The accumulation of countless Post-it notes formed a striking mosaic, effectively visualizing the collective demands of the people. In 2019, Lennon Walls became ubiquitous, popping up in many localities across Hong Kong. While there were still handwritten Post-it notes, new Lennon Walls were decorated more with designed posters that were prepared by professional visual artists and downloaded and printed by local volunteers. They became street galleries for the movement. The art house–style presentation in Kwai Fong, for instance, came to be known as the "Lennon Museum of Fine Arts," while the "Lennon Tunnel" in Tai Po was famous for its gigantic scale. Localized Lennon Walls served many functions. They became community bulletin boards constantly updating the movement's progress and symbolizing local resistance. In short, they emerged as powerful statements with which local residents reclaimed their neighborhoods (Li and Whitworth 2022).

Umbrella Movement participants also initiated an operation of "supporting small stores" (*caang siudim/cheng xiaodian*), encouraging promovement citizens to stop at mom-and-pop stores whose businesses were devastated by the occupation. The purpose was to leverage consumer power so that people with small businesses would not be alienated from the ongoing protest. During the Be Water Revolution, this seminal idea fledged into a form of economic warfare in which protesters profusely patronized promovement stores and boycotted progovernment ones. Known as "yellow economic circle" (*wongsik gingzaihyun/huangse jingjiquan*), this project of a citywide solidarity economy was devised to sustain the protest activism over the long haul (Li and Whitworth 2023; D. Chan and Pun 2020).

In sum, the ideas of more evenly spreading the campaign spatially and building an economic front were already brewing in 2014. These suggestions emerged naturally from the participants' experimentation in the occupation zones and were only half-heartedly attempted. Noticeably, none of these novel ideas emanated from the Umbrella Movement student leadership; partly because of the existence of an increasingly dysfunctional command center, these novel tactics were not fully implemented. They were fully adopted only when collective improvisation was activated during the Be Water Revolution.

Lessons from the Defeat

The perceived disappointment of the Umbrella Movement resulted in a lingering sense of frustration, embarrassment, and humiliation. Many movement leaders and followers underwent a deeply traumatic experience and much soul-searching afterward. What emerged later was a shared conviction that they pursue a different strategy to avoid making the same "mistake."

One of the issues has to do with the limit of civil disobedience. Prior to the Umbrella Movement, there had been criticisms of ritualized repertoires among Hong Kong's prodemocracy movement. Proponents of "joyous resistance" (*faailok kongzang/kuaile kangzheng*) advocated for an assertive style of protest-making to exert pressure on the authorities (Ng and Chan 2017). Taking inspiration from the OCLP, the Umbrella Movement adopted the principle of civil disobedience, as its massive sit-in marked a major breakthrough in Hongkongers' law-and-order habitus. However, throughout the 2014 protest, there emerged dissident voices that demonstrators should go beyond civil disobedience by masking their identity, fighting back against police, disrupting government agencies, and challenging the symbols of Beijing's sovereignty over Hong Kong. Supporters of this movement strategy had been identified as "militants" (*jungmoupaai/yongwupai*), and these tendencies remained marginalized in that episode. In 2014, spontaneous initiatives to interrupt the National Day ceremony, blockade public servants from entering their offices, storm into the Legislative Council, and other escalating attempts were forcibly intercepted by the movement leaders, who denounced these tactics as "irresponsible hit-and-run." The movement's picket members threatened to arrest these masked activists and turn them over to the police, while, at the same time, pro bono lawyers announced that they would not offer legal services to these perpetrators. Vandalism of public property was strictly prohibited then. Militants were seen as unwelcome troublemakers, suspected as disguised agents provocateurs, or "ghosts" (*gwai/gui*) in the local parlance.

This unresolved tension between militants and the leadership of the Umbrella Movement persisted even as the police cleared the final occupy zone. Nevertheless, in the years that followed, there was a noticeable increase in sympathy toward the militants. This shift was partially influenced by the government's harsh legal actions against leaders of the Umbrella Movement and the OCLP. These punitive prosecutions seemed to highlight the apparent ineffectiveness of civil disobedience, contributing to the growing support for militants. On the other hand, the militant tendency grew with the meteoric rise of Edward Leung in the legislative by-election in February 2016. Leung represented young insurgents who have long chafed at mainstream prodemocracy politicians' moderation. As an eloquent and charismatic speaker, Leung advocated a brinkmanship strategy called "the edge of violence" (*boulik binjyun/baoli bianyuan*), meaning that protesters should continue escalating the tension to the point that the incumbents lose their poise by resorting to counterproductive repression. Should that scenario happen, the prodemocracy movement could gain wider support and pressure the government into more meaningful concessions.

Leung secured a decent 15% of by-election votes. His disqualification from the subsequent election and sentencing to six years in prison for his involvement in the Fishball Revolution elevated his status to heroic leader. In a 2017 biographical document *Lost in the Fumes*, Leung candidly revealed his depression and self-doubt behind the public persona, which further endeared him to the younger generation. Leung was serving his prison term while the Be Water protests were raging in Hong Kong's streets. But, in a sense, he was not entirely absent because his signature slogan "Liberate Hong Kong, Revolution of Our Time" was the constantly heard battle cry among demonstrators, and his advocacy of more assertive protests had become a reality. Therefore, partly due to Leung's larger-than-life influence, the willingness to accept, support, or even engage in disruptive tactics became more widespread.

The second unresolved issue is related to the disappointing decision-making core during the Umbrella Movement. Replacing the OCLP leaders, the HKFS emerged as the widely recognized public face of the movement, and its televised negotiation with government officials was one of the most riveting moments during the entire incident. As the occupy action dragged on, the HKFS was increasingly mired in agonizing indecision, being reluctant and unable to call an end to the dwindling protest and, at the same time, struggling to contain the agitation by impatient militants. In the end, the HKFS, together with the main stage in Admiralty, came to symbolize ineffective leadership. Such lingering discontent led to a walkout wave, as four university student associations voted to leave the HKFS in early 2015.

A pervasive feeling of self-blame among the former HKFS leaders existed because they had missed a valuable opportunity and wasted the trust of Hongkongers. After the eruption of the Be Water Revolution, an interviewed student leader revealed his gut reactions in the intervening five years:

> We are constantly thinking of the question: if we were given the chance to do it over again what would be a better way to proceed? This question has been deeply on the minds of many people.

Another former HKFS leader appeared resigned to the verdict of defeat. As he reasoned, "The Umbrella Movement's failure turned out to be a 'success' in stimulating the rise of anti-ELAB protests." A centralized leadership was prone to make mistakes because it assumed too many responsibilities. "Since there is no main stage now, the responsibility is on everyone."

Another former Scholarism participant shared the same reflection:

> The main stage took a long time for discussion. If you were not a legislative council member or an HKFS core member, you would not know what happened. You were just a participant who could not decide anything. But in the anti-ELAB movement, everyone has the right to make a decision and can do something without asking for permission.

As frustrated student leaders grew settled with their diminishing role, Hong Kong's political opposition experienced further fragmentation. As said before, the prodemocracy movement was stuck in a deep divide before the onset of the Umbrella Movement (Ma 2011). The occupy protest gave rise to a wave of electoral participation among youthful participants. The 2015 district council election witnessed a surge of so-called Umbrella Soldiers (*saanbing/sanbing*) who refused to join existing prodemocracy parties. The 2016 legislative election saw newly emerged insurgent candidates, whose electoral success edged out many prodemocracy veteran politicians. Consequently, when the Be Water Revolution happened, prodemocracy lawmakers found it hard to assume the mantle of movement leadership, even though they went to great lengths to resist the ELAB in April and May 2019.

As the Be Water Revolution flared up in June, prodemocracy politicians found themselves marginalized on the sidelines. Younger generation lawmakers who intimately understood the frustration of young protesters attempted to negotiate with the police on their behalf, and the result was that they suffered equally from police violence. Elder opposition politicians sought to restrain what they saw as reckless radicalism to no avail. Leung Yiu-chung, a British-educated Marxist and a prolabor lawmaker, was manhandled by a masked protester as he decided to stand in the way of the ramming of the Legislative Council on July 1 (22 Hongkongers 2019: 136). Symbolically, that memorable scene came to signify the fading away of these prodemocracy veterans.

While established political leaders suddenly found themselves unneeded in the Be Water Revolution, younger generation leaders also felt the same centrifugal force. As the leader of Demosisto, the political party that evolved out of Scholarism, Joshua Wong was released from jail on the morning of July 17, the second prison term for his involvement in the Umbrella Movement; in the afternoon, he made an appearance in the Legislative Council and spoke to the protesters there. On July 23, as protesters gathered outside, he used a microphone to direct the crowd to besiege the Police Headquarters in Wan Chai, and later the protest evolved into a spontaneous action to paralyze neighboring government agencies. Wong was then severely criticized for his attempt to assume leadership. Even though he was merely a twenty-two-year-old college student then, Wong was perceived as too old school and too established among the protesters. Afterward, he learned not to assume such a high-profile role in subsequent gatherings, and his Demosisto redirected the effort to international lobbying and online campaigns (see Chapter 5).

In short, the bitter ending of the exhausted occupy protest was a painful lesson for participants who decided to pursue a decentralized and disruptive course. As a participant reflected, "Occupy is like a mirror. . . . We are actually doing the opposite of what we did five years ago" (Ibrahim and Lam 2020: 60).

The Umbrella Legacy

Newer organizing efforts emerged immediately after the forced eviction of the Umbrella Movement, as participants attempted to embed the democratization project in their everyday life. What have generally been referred to as "post-Umbrella organizations" (*saanhau zouzik/sanhou zuzhi*) mushroomed throughout the city. The generic term covers a number of heterogeneous organizations initiated by Umbrella Movement participants. Some of them were more or less personal vehicles of those who intended to join the 2015 district council election and the 2016 legislative election. While these organizations were centered around would-be candidates, they tended to prioritize Hongkongers' interests, or the so-called "localist" tendency. The second type of post-Umbrella organizations were also neighborhood based, but they were primarily geared toward what geographers would call "place-making" (Huang 2018), or activities that nourished the shared sense of belonging in the hope that democracy could be first realized in a community before its citywide upscaling. These community activists typically began with communal issues to encourage resident participation, and they also held film screenings of works like *Winter on Fire* (2015), a Ukrainian documentary about the Euromaiden protest, and *Ten Years* (2015), a Hong Kong dystopian film about the loss of political freedom. Last, various professions from lawyers, medical doctors, financial workers, insurance agents, psychiatrists, and university professors initiated their own efforts in recruiting like-minded colleagues.

The flurry of these postoccupy organizing efforts attests to the inspiring power of the Umbrella Movement, despite its discouraging collapse. In hindsight, they were instrumental in consolidating and expanding prodemocracy networks beyond the brief period of street mobilization. Candidate-centered organizations challenged the entrenched hegemony of proregime politicians in their electoral districts and helped foster a new crop of prodemocracy contenders who eventually prevailed over their conservative rivals in the district councillor election of 2019. Neighborhood organizations were not explicitly political in the beginning, but, as they delved more deeply into community concerns, residents came to realize that a number of their day-to-day issues, such as their public housing management and tap water quality, resulted from the lack of city democracy and rampant collusion with big business. Finally, professional groups had their role to play in promoting democratization. While most of the officially recognized professional organizations, such as the Law Society of Hong Kong, were conservative and progovernment, the newer organizations were more likely to initiate proactive actions according to their professional norm. For instance, the Progressive Lawyers Group launched initiatives to promote the rule of law and human rights education by dispatching practitioners to high schools for pro bono lectures. Moreover, these groups were able to make use of Hong Kong's semidemocratic functional representation to maximize their dissident voices. In the 2017 election of the city's top executive by twelve hundred electoral council members, the prodemocracy camp managed to secure more than three hundred seats. Although prodemocracy electors failed to affect the predestined selection of the Beijing-picked loyalist Carrie Lam, it nevertheless demonstrated the power of bottom-up organizing.

As years went by, many of these post-Umbrella organizations became less active, partly because participants gradually reverted from public engagement to private concerns, and also as a result of the lack of ostensible progress on the part of Hong Kong's prodemocracy movement. Yet, despite these decreasing activities, they provided an infrastructural network, paving the way for the swift escalation of the anti-ELAB movement. For instance, one neighborhood-based activist revealed:

> Some of our community participants are marketing specialists, and they can quickly produce leaflets to be distributed on the street the next day. We also have lawyers and businesspersons whose offices can be used as storage for movement supplies, like bottled water. If there is a participant arrested in a certain district, we can also mobilize our local friends to come to the police station.

Profession-based groups also utilized their specific leverage. For instance, Hong Kong's financial workers who had hands-on knowledge of the mainland market and politics intimately knew the potential harms of ELAB, and they mounted a concentrated lobbying effort targeting the financial sector lawmakers. Finally, when the Be Water Revolution flared up, calls for a general strike, such as that on August 5, were primarily made up of these professional groups whose members were often not unionized. These preexisting professional networks also provided the impetus for the brief campaign for new labor unions in early 2020 (Lin 2021).

After the Be Water Revolution erupted, many post-Umbrella organizations adopted a self-effacing strategy. Some of them were formally registered, and they did not want to risk their legal status in the increasingly tense confrontations. Some were perceived as partisan, or "too yellow," according to an interviewee, because of their previous electoral participation. For example, core members of Umbrella Parents, a prominent post-Umbrella organization, were active in sponsoring rallies in the name of mothers (June 14, July 15, and November 28) without using the group name because they wanted to appeal to more parents beyond the prodemocracy camp. Hence, it is easy to underestimate the role of these candidate-centered, neighborhood-based, and professional organizations that laid down a crisscrossing submerged network of mobilization. Like other contemporary worldwide protests, a preexisting network of interconnected activists has been a critical key to the movement emergence (Fominaya 2014b; Gunning and Baron 2014: 165–66). What appears to be a spontaneous outburst is more aptly described as a result of accumulated network building.

Inspired by Taylor's (1989) classical study, many analysts look at these post-Umbrella organizations as a "structure of abeyance," or a necessary act of hunkering down during the adverse situation as activists withdrew from public appearance and formed inward-looking closely knit groups (H. Chung

2020; F. Lee et al. 2019; F. Lee, Chan, and Chen 2020; Ma and Chen 2021; G. Tang 2023). My reading of these initiatives departs from this interpretation for several reasons. These organizations began as proactive attempts to carry out the unfinished project of the Umbrella Movement, and participants believed their actions were extending the front lines of democratization, rather than as a defensive measure for self-survival. True, Hong Kong's prodemocracy movement suffered several disheartening defeats, and the regime was waging ruthless lawfare against Umbrella leaders. But most post-Umbrella organization enthusiasts did not feel personally threatened to the extent that they should suspend their activities and withdraw to their own small circle; instead, they sought to reach out and build a more broadly based coalition. In a nutshell, these post-Umbrella organizations were not structures of abeyance but intentionally planted seeds that ended up facilitating the city's next insurgency.

Deadly Shocks

As an extreme repertoire, suicide protests are not infrequent in the East Asian context: the South Vietnamese monk Thich Quang Duc's self-immolation against the government's persecution in 1963, the Japanese writer Mishima Yukio's dramatized hara-kiri for his right-wing nationalist cause in 1970, the South Korean worker Jeon Tae-il's suicide for poor labor conditions in the same year, and the Taiwanese dissident Nylon Cheng's suicide for freedom of speech in 1989 are among a few iconic cases. In China, the waves of Tibetan suicide protests in 2008 and the spate of young worker suicides at iPhone-producing factories in 2010 (J. Chan, Selden, and Pun 2020) also caught worldwide attention. However, as a precarious lifeboat in China's great upheavals in the twentieth century, Hong Kong did not encourage its denizens to cultivate local attachment; instead, as a transshipment center, the city excelled in expediting the flow of money, goods, and people without friction. Observers noted that migration constantly remained a popular option, and the "willingness to sacrifice their lives for Hong Kong" was seen as insane (Matthews, Ma, and Lui 2008: 12).

With the ELAB being framed as a death knell for the city's legal and political future, such an acute sense of threat brought about politically motivated suicides. My journalistic database documents six suicide protests in 2019. The first three cases happened within two weeks in June, and all the victims left protest notes before killing themselves. On June 15, Marco Leung Ling-kit, in a yellow raincoat, mounted the scaffold in a commercial building in Admiralty and unfurled a banner handwritten with "Withdraw the ELAB. We are not rioters. Release wounded students. Carrie Lam to Step Down. Help Hong Kong." His solo protest immediately attracted spectators and resulted in a standoff with the police for hours. Marco Leung fell to the ground when firefighters unsuccessfully attempted to subdue him.

Leung's tragic death immediately cast a prolonged and sorrowful shadow over the nascent protest movement, sparking off waves of would-be imitators. While psychiatrists were offering consultation services, graphic designers produced and distributed brochures and zines about mental health, and numerous neighborhood citizens volunteered for ad hoc search teams to prevent similar attempts, the government officials stood callously without any response. Leung's yellow raincoat soon became a potent protest symbol, and what he wrote on his banner later evolved into the Five Demands.

Furthermore, the police's aggressive use of force also resulted in several incidents of deaths. These episodes were especially explosive as Hongkongers were used to a mild style of policing and low casualties in protest occasions. On August 31, riot police stormed into the Prince Edward Station and severely beat up anyone whom they suspected as demonstrators, and the brutal scene video recorded in numerous passengers' mobile phones sent a shock wave across the city. Despite the government's repeated denials, many people continued to believe the police secretly disposed of several severely wounded victims. On September 22, the naked body of the fifteen-year-old girl Chan Yin Lam was found in the ocean. Chan was a trained swimmer and had joined the protest before her family reported her missing. This news broke on October 11, giving rise to the suspicion that Chan may have been detained and tortured by the police. A progovernment TV channel later released an interview of Chan's mother who claimed her disturbed daughter died by suicide, but the mother was widely believed to be an impersonation by a fake actor, further adding fuel to the speculation of a botched cover-up. The death of Chow Tsz Lok, a twenty-two-year-old university student on November 11, was another scandalous episode. His mysterious fall from a parking tower was suspected to be related to a police roundup operation, which also delayed the arrival of emergency ambulances. See Figure 1.1 for a graph presenting how these death tragedies and rumors stimulated mourning activities in Hong Kong.

These mourning activities took place in 1,775 protest events in my journalistic database, and they came in great varieties, including candlelight vigils (50), wreath laying (75), folding origami cranes (39), reciting Buddhist sutras (6), erecting a shrine (21), offerings for the dead (9), offering incense sticks for the dead (17), spreading joss paper (26), displaying a coffin (3), pasting elegiac couplets (4), silent mourning (74), bowing (13), and playing funeral music (1).

While journalistic sources provide valuable documentation, they are inevitably incomplete. My field observation on October 19, forty-nine days after the Prince Edward Station incident, indicated the lasting and pervasive

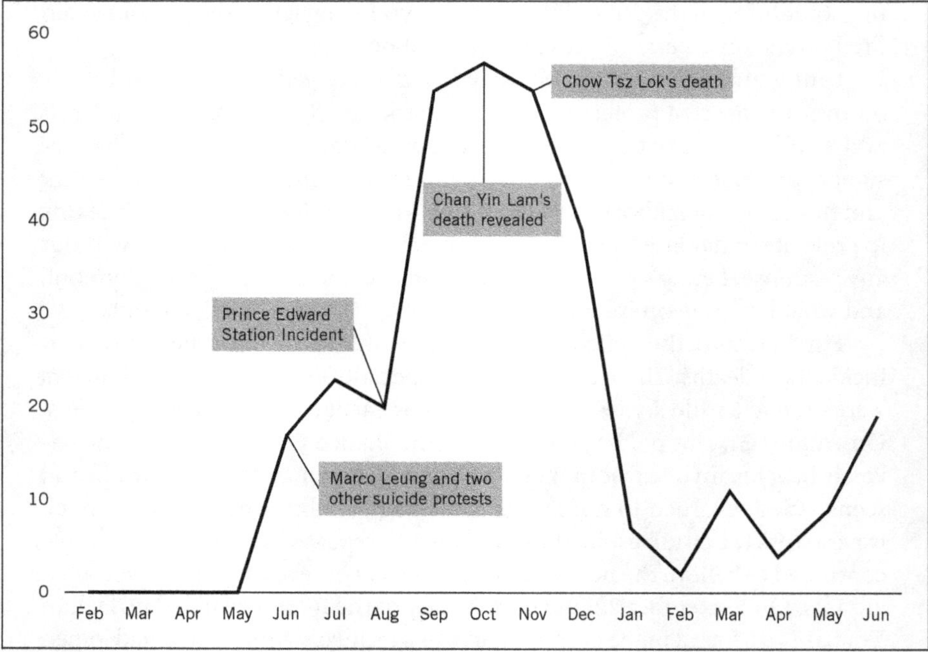

Figure 1.1 Mourning activities, from February 2019 to January 2020 (by month).

atmosphere of mourning. At the station's B1 Exit on the intersection of Nathan Road and Prince Edward Road, people laid down bouquets of white chrysanthemums, incense sticks, and candles. Plaques dedicated to "August 31 Martyrs" and other victims (including a picture of Chan Yin Lam) were set up. Taoist talismans and pictures of Jesus Christ and Lord Guan were pasted on the wall in the early morning, reflecting mourners' diversity in faith. At noon, more people gathered, some offering their respects and others distributing leaflets, while four seated middle-aged women donning ritual gowns were reciting Buddhist sutras. In the late evening, the makeshift shrine was already full of offerings including fruit, rice, roasted chicken, and so on. Night shift sanitarians cleaned what the authorities considered eyesores, and another cycle of funeral offerings began the next day.

Clearly, prodemocracy Hongkongers were genuinely grieving for a series of protest-related deaths, voluntary or not. The obsession with death manifested in different ways. Symbolically, it was about the impending death to the city's proud judiciary system, while, physically, they were witnessing the repeated loss of lives of young Hongkongers. This all amounted to the viscerally felt "moral outrage," or "a stimulus that causes an individual to come to terms with a reality that is quite opposed to the values and morals" (Lemonik 2013). It was with such a strong emotional state that Hongkongers launched their protest.

Emotional Outrage

Outrage at these deaths elicited strong emotional responses. Researchers have found the sense of guilt widespread among Be Water Revolution participants (Mok 2022; G. Tang and Cheng 2021). My interview data confirms the prevalence of such feelings. Typically, many senior citizens thought they had failed to secure the city's democratization so that their younger generation had no choice but to risk their lives and futures in risky street confrontations. A retired banker who devoted herself to providing money and resources for young protesters put it bluntly:

> Why should I help young people? I was simply too lazy and too stupid in the past. We did nothing except make money, and that is why I have a sense of guilt. In addition, after I die, I do not want my children and grandchildren to live in a Chinese city and become Chinese.

Separated by distance, overseas Hongkongers were also prone to feel guilty because they could not be present. With their eyes glued to the live streaming of ongoing protest activities, they easily became agitated and anxious. Some of the diasporic Hongkongers I interviewed flew back to join the demonstrations, and every time they had to leave for study or work in their host countries, they carried a burden of sorrow in their hearts. Even among those who left Hong Kong to escape arrest, there existed a wrenching feeling of survivor's guilt as if they had betrayed their partners. Several of the escapee students I interviewed long entertained thoughts of returning and surrendering themselves to the police because they could not bear the thought that many of their fellow protesters were languishing behind bars while they were able to enjoy freedom elsewhere. The urge to atone for one's guilt for not being able to share the same suffering weighed heavily on overseas exiles.[3]

Similarly, one interviewee referenced his remorse for not being able to help his fellow protesters:

> I constantly asked myself this question: I had many movement experiences and was well-prepared in thought. But when facing a dangerous situation, I did not have the courage to keep fighting. My first reaction was to flee from the scene for self-preservation rather than to help those who stood by my side.

Another student whose sensitive skin could not sustain tear gas felt regretful that he was prevented from joining the frontline protests. His strong dermatological reactions often required extra attention from first-aiders, leaving him to think of himself as a useless liability for the movement. He found it difficult to forgive himself for not having stormed into the Legislative Council with his friends, and for a while he often dreamed of the arrest of his close friends.

At its core, the sense of guilt implies one's moral culpability for other people's suffering. One way to relieve this psychological tension is to double down on one's contribution. Joining rallies and demonstrations, making donations, tolerating those disruptive protest acts, and so on, are common outlets for discharging negative feelings. As Hong Kong's church leaders and Christians chipped in to provide resources for frontline protesters, they were mockingly referred to as "buying indulgence" because they were insufficiently engaged in the past (H. Chan 2019: 63). Lau Kwong Shing (2020: 188–89), a professional illustrator, explained why he decided to create political artworks for the movement:

> It was Hong Kong's critical moment, and I could no longer pretend nothing happened and kept on doing what I wanted to do. . . . I overcame my internal struggles, and I could no longer bear it. I realized that I had to face greater risk and might be attacked by some people. I was aware that my company could sever the relationship and my job could be affected.

The film director Lam Sum attributed his motive to produce a movement-themed movie to the feeling of powerlessness in the wake of the June 2019 suicide protest wave:

> [I] could not stand idly by while vividly witnessing people being knocked off by the government as they dropped to the ground over and over. My profession is filmmaking, and I believe that films have the power to move people. (Ren and Chan 2022: 17)

Aside from the sense of guilt, the emergence of the Be Water Revolution was accompanied by a complex mixture of strong emotional responses. Anger at the officials' callous recalcitrance and mendacity, pride in being able to demonstrate solidarity at a critical moment, and the warm feeling of unity from joining together for a common cause. Emotions are more readily communicative than discourse. Once emotional outrage is activated, it immediately becomes a powerful stimulus for movement participation. A middle-aged participant recounted her memorable experience:

> On June 12, I was distributing resources in Admiralty. The police suddenly shot tear gas. Without protective gear, my sight became blurry and tears kept coming down. Three youngsters immediately accompanied me to a safe corner. As I calmed down, I noticed they were only middle school students with plastic wrap on their arms, which smacked of pepper spray. I never thought that a 17-year-old would tell me he would have never forgiven himself if he did not stand up to fight. They all brought their personal testaments in case they could not make it home today. During the lull, they took out their textbooks for study because they were preparing for the college entrance examination. I immediately shed tears at that sight. I kept thinking what I was doing at their age.

Another sixteen-year-old protester told of his sudden catharsis after narrowly escaping the police violence. He immediately asked a stranger whether he could lend him a shoulder and then he burst into tears, feeling completely drained:

> For the first time, I experienced anger triggered by fear. The demonstration in Shatin on July 14 taught me a lesson to protect myself with the necessary equipment. The second lesson was never to act alone, but to form a team. (Kwan 2020: 91)

Emotions were also easily contagious even to non-Hongkongers who were supposed to stay professionally neutral. According to a Taiwanese journalist, many of her fellow reporters dispatched to Hong Kong were genuinely shocked by what they witnessed. They met many Hong Kong informants who sincerely hoped their personal stories could be duly recorded and transmitted abroad. Before ending their business trips, many Taiwanese reporters embraced their Hong Kong colleagues in tears to bid farewell.

Students of contentious politics have long contended that movement emergence is always accompanied by a change in the social rules of feeling, from shame to pride, from loneliness to solidarity, from fear to indignation, and from sorrow to anger (Britt and Heise 2000; Gould 2002). What has been identified as consciousness-raising is inseparable from emotional arousal. Alongside rational persuasion, emotional mobilization has been identified as a central phenomenon (Aminzade and McAdam 2001: 33; Jasper 1999: 69). As such, thinking and feeling should not be seen as two separate realms, but intimately integrated in the same process.

In the case of Hong Kong's Be Water Revolution, the strong outpouring of guilt and other intense feelings constituted what Jasper (2018: 128) calls "moral emotions," which "operate as individual motivations, the ultimate goal of movements, indeed the very raison d'être of movements." Such a high-pressure crucible catalyzed a fundamental rethinking of the strategies of the prodemocracy movement, resulting in an unprecedented citywide uprising that was unthinkable in the past. For instance, Brian Leung, a student leader who decided to reveal his identity by removing the face mask in order to make a public speech during the eventful occupation of the Legislative Council on July 1, 2019, gained instant attention for his heroic act. But, in a subsequent media interview, he acknowledged having acted on the "impulse of the moment" (*jatsi cungdung/yishi chongdong*), and, if he "had thought about it for a second or for himself," he might not have done it (Standnews 2020: 46). Clearly, acts of collective improvisation are more likely to take place with the presence of strong emotions.

Conclusion

On December 11, 2014, nearly ten thousand people gathered in the occupy zone in Admiralty, the epicenter of the then seventy-nine-day Umbrella Movement, for the final night, as the police had announced there would be a forcible eviction the next day. Many new banners, "We will be back," were placed on the site, making it looked more like a farewell party. Less than five years later, a larger, longer, and more disruptive mass campaign indeed came back. But, as Hong Kong's protesters returned to the streets, they did not just repeat what they had been doing in the past; instead, they became more determined, more interconnected, and willing to try novel tactics. Taking stock of the previous failures, they managed to mount a citywide resistance without a command center. Newly founded neighborhood-based and professional organizations laid down a dense network of mobilization that could readily respond to the suddenly imposed ELAB threat. To exert greater pressure on the authorities, prodemocracy Hongkongers also discarded their prudish fixation on the "peaceful, rational, and nonviolent" (*woleifei/helifei*) style and evolved to engage in or tolerate disruptive or violent acts, cognizant that a "nice-looking" (*waaminleng*) rally could be entirely useless when facing an unresponsive and repressive regime. Finally, the evolution of Hong Kong's protesters took place in a powerful crucible where suicide, death, and police violence triggered a strong chain of emotional reactions that led many participants to end up engaging in what were unthinkable acts prior to the eruption of the Be Water Revolution.

With this understanding, the widely circulated protest slogan, "It is you who taught us that peaceful demonstration was useless" (*si nei gaau ngomun woping jauhang si mutjung dik/shi ni jiao women heping youxing shi meiyong de*)—first paint-written on a pillar of the Legislative Council and afterward proliferated in many street graffiti (Daddy Tian 2019: 141)—only captures half of the story. While the SAR government's headlong railroading of the ELAB and its ruthless crackdown were among the triggering factors, it also took embodied and emotional thinking and reflection on the part of participants to bring about the Be Water Revolution.

What enables participants in a movement to take independent actions without relying on directives from their leaders? Why do numerous proudly law-abiding Hongkongers opt for unlawful protests, risking their safety, careers, and even lives for a citywide political cause? This chapter delves into the radical transformation of movement agency at the heart of this process of radicalization. The development of an emotion-infused, daring, and desperate agency establishes the subjective foundations for collective improvisation. The movement cause needs to earn the support of a sufficiently large number of citizens, and it is better that they spread evenly across different strata, generations, locations, and professions. Moreover, they must be committed beyond a certain level and feel the urge to depart from their accustomed routine activities. Originally, the SAR government anticipated a cakewalk for its intended extradition revision, which unexpectedly triggered the largest incident of uprising since the city's transition to Chinese sovereignty. This unforeseen evolution will remain inexplicable should we fail to take into consideration the drastic remaking of Hongkongers' agency. The Umbrella Movement's long afterlife nurtured tactical visions and infrastructural foundations, but it still required a drastic and sudden mixture of threat, death, and affective stirring for the new protesters to make their debut on the stage.

2

The Logistics of Networked Militancy

Derek was a high school student when the Umbrella Movement erupted in 2014. His participation at the time was intermittent and minimal, but subsequent events like the Fishball Revolution made him more resentful of Beijing's interventions in his native city. Derek joined the Be Water Revolution when it flared up in June 2019, and, after personally experiencing pepper spray and tear gas, he chose to become a militant on the front lines. Starting in mid-August, Derek overcame his psychological barriers and began to throw petrol bombs and destroy progovernment company outlets, because he thought escalation was the only effective way to pressure the government.

Derek was once arrested but spared criminal prosecution because he was not doing anything illegal at that time. In fact, he exercised extreme caution when going to frontline protests. While protesters typically wore a black shirt, he deliberately wore unsuspicious clothes (or a "rainbow warrior robe" [*coihung zinji/caihong zhanyi*] in the protester lingo) when coming to the rally site and put on the protest uniform (black T-shirt) only when joining the crowd. He also had an extra casual outfit for his getaway so as not to be stopped by the police. Almost every Hong Kong citizen had a stored-valued transportation card (Octopus card), but Derek decided to purchase single-entry rides every time so as not to leave his travel records. In protest, Derek always brought a "ghost phone" (*gwaigei/guiji*): a mobile phone with a single-use sim card only carrying the Telegram app, the essential communication channel to keep Derek and his team members updated on information from online scouts.

Derek's petrol bombs were assembled in situ, as his team members carried the ingredients, such as petroleum, glass bottles, sugar, and clothes separately on the road in case they were intercepted.

Derek and his teammates were not fighting alone. It was a common scene that movement supporters were distributing protest gear like helmets and masks, which were often mentioned as "stationery" (*mangeoi/wenju*), at the gathering sites. Restaurant coupons and topped up Octopus cards were also freely distributed, and they were particularly important for cash-strapped young protesters. While most of these materials could be obtained at distribution booths managed by volunteers, Derek also had the experience of being quietly approached by strangers, whose cars were parked in the vicinity and their trunks contained all kinds of resources that Derek and his friends could utilize as needed. Anonymous providers were typically middle-aged and of middle-class background, usually called "parents" (*gaazoeng/jiazhang*), suggesting a quasi-familial relationship of care between senior providers and younger radicals.

"Parents" also assisted Derek and his comrades in other ways. Leaving the protest site in the late evening could also be problematic. Public transportation like metro and buses were out of service hours, and, even if they were available, the ride exposed one to police arrest or proregime mob violence. Often, they had to rely on private vehicles driven by parents, or the so-called school pickup (*zipfonghok/jiefangxue*). After a bruising confrontation with the police, militant protesters often avoided going directly back home but rather spent the night together in a "safe house" (often spare apartments owned by "parents").

This chapter examines the microfoundations of collective improvisation, or how militants and "parents" adopted innovative action collaboratively via interpersonal networks. These networks spanned across the divides between frontline protesters and logistics providers, between friends/acquaintances and strangers, between face-to-face interactions and cyberspace connections. As many classical and modern wars have shown, what decides the outcome of military confrontations is less about the soldiers' bravery or weapon sophistication than the continuous and steady supply of manpower and goods. How this intensive and exhaustive use of social ties was made possible in the Be Water Revolution is the focus of this chapter.

A High-Risk Protest

While the SAR government has long promoted its "global city" image, Hong Kong also earned the nickname of "city of protests" in the Western media (Holbig 2020: 328). Its annual June Fourth Tiananmen candlelight vigils and July First prodemocracy demonstrations were a case study of massive yet peaceful and orderly protest. Even facing mob violence, the 2014 Umbrella Movement leaders managed to stick to the principle of nonviolent civil disobedience. The anti-ELAB protest exploded into a citywide resistance mostly because the authorities decided to adopt highly repressive tactics to subdue opponents. On June 12, 2019, as the crowd gathered near the Legislative Council to forestall the passage of the ELAB, the police shot 150 rounds of tear gas and used novel lethal weapons such as rubber and beanbag bullets. As a result, thirty-two participants were arrested and at least seventy-two were injured on that day. Political protests in Hong Kong suddenly became "high-risk activism," as participants knew the "anticipated dangers in legal, social, physical, financial and so forth of engaging in a particular type of activity" (McAdam 1986: 67).

As a consequence of heightened repression, even peaceful participants began to be concerned about their personal safety. Because of the fear of arbitrary arrest and being sent to the mainland if they were suspected of being illegal immigrants, they needed to have their Hong Kong IDs with them at all times. The city's ID cards contain a radio frequency identification feature, which led many participants to wrap their cards with aluminum foil to protect against remote detection. If possible, cash transactions were preferable to swiping one's Octopus card, because they left no digital footprint. Crowdfunding was more likely to attract donations if the online platforms were hosted abroad as participants knew the SAR government and Beijing found it difficult to retrieve the user data. An interviewee made it a rule to carry her doctor's order for regular walks, because she thought it could provide a ready-to-use excuse for her presence at the protest sites. If these peaceful participants needed to go to great lengths to ensure their personal safety, one could imagine the extent of extra care for militants like Derek to avoid legal consequences.

The existing literature on high-risk activism revolves around two main questions. First, researchers are interested in why and how people choose to take part in these dangerous activities, knowing that their idealistic convictions can bring about grave consequences. Second, studies are interested in the small-group dynamics that sustain long-term participation.

As for the first question, studies indicate certain personal characteristics such as youth, being single, childlessness, and previous involvement as conducive factors for high-risk activism participation (Gundelach and Toubøl 2019; McAdam 1986; Wiltfang and McAdam 1991). Relational ties based on family, friends, and colleagues were found to encourage such participation (della Porta 1988: 160; McAdam 2003: 285; Nepstad and Smith 1999: 33). The second line of investigation is interested in the small-group dynamics because it assumes in-group solidarity and the concomitant insulation from the larger environment as the key component to continuing participation in high-risk activism (Einwohner 2006; Loveman 1998; Parkinson 2013). "Ideological encapsulation" in the case of clandestine political violence helped secure the long-term commitment of participants as they were already detached from mainstream society (della Porta 2013: 204–34). Similarly, a close-knit structure fortified with a religious belief helps sustain participation in high-risk activism (Nepstad 2004).

Both strains of literature tacitly understand high-risk activism as movements by a small number of radicals, whose beliefs or methods are at odds with mainstream values. Yet, this assumption is not entirely applicable to Hong Kong's Be Water Revolution, which is more appropriately characterized as a majoritarian movement. A poll survey in July 2019 indicated that a solid 69% of respondents opposed the ELAB, and only 19% were in favor.[1] Since the movement goals were rather consensual, participant numbers were larger, and they could always easily find support elsewhere (M. Ho 2023b). Rather than individual conversion into a radical cause, Hongkongers' movement agency was collectively forged in a powerful catalysis of moral outrage and emotional outpouring, as indicated in the previous chapter. Thus, instead of focusing on the question of recruitment, I call analytical attention to how and why different Hongkongers chose their roles (militants or supporters) in the campaign and their corresponding tactics for managing risk.

Younger Hongkongers tended to be more active in the campaign, and they were disproportionately targeted by the authorities. Among the 8,981 arrestees as of May 2020, 1,707 were minors and 5,640 were aged between eighteen and thirty, according to a media analysis.[2] In other words, those who were under thirty constituted nearly 80% of all arrestees. Militants who dared to use violence made up only a minority of all participants. In the rolling surveys of on-site participants from June to December 2019, between 3% and 20% of respondents took part in the actions "that resisted the police's forward advance," while between 38% and 57% "donated resources other than money" (Chinese University of Hong Kong Centre for Communication and Public Opinion Survey 2020: 46). For the sake of brevity, this chapter identifies the former as "militants" who were mainly engaged in confrontational activities against the police, and the latter as "supporters" whose functions were concentrated on logistic gathering and provisions. Following the insights on relational ties in the existing literature on high-risk movements, this chapter examines how militants and supporters managed to utilize personal connections for their respective protest activities.

Militant Teams

In the anarchist literature on leaderless movements, there exists a principled abhorrence of political and movement organizations because they are largely seen as a hindrance to instinctual rebelliousness among the subordinate. The highly seditious book *The Coming Insurrection* declares that "organizations are obstacles to organizing ourselves." Its anonymous authors anticipated the spontaneous emergence of a popular revolt, when "people find each other, get on with each other, and decide on a common path" (Invisible Committee 2009: 15, 101). Ironically, the anarchist assumption of the combat readiness among the grassroots was in part in sync with the outdated collective behavior theory that largely assumed disorderly protests naturally flowed from atomized and alienated individuals. Such a view was also shared by the Hong Kong authorities. Carrie Lam once claimed those demonstrators "have no stake in society,"[3] implying their marginalization was the root cause of their radical behaviors. However, even without a hierarchical organization, militants still needed trust networks to join the protest campaigns.

As a self-avowed militant, King claimed that he did not have "moral scruples," and he was not opposed to being called a "maniac for violence":

> I have done all kinds of things on the frontline. I smashed stuff, fought police, stormed the cordoned-off areas, and even intended to kill police to save people. . . . I was good at dismantling things, like removing the guard rails. There was one time when the police headquarters were sieged and I sealed its door. I welded it with silicon materials and the keyhole was fully stuffed. It was super sturdy!

Yet, King did not engage in these high-risk activities alone. He participated in a five-person team whose members knew each other since the 2014 Umbrella Movement. At the protest site, King and his team members carried military-grade walkie-talkies to stay connected with off-site scouts who were constantly monitoring the police deployment. For a safe retreat, King and his partners often planned several possible routes and hideouts in advance. Even with a radical antiestablishment mentality, violent protests still needed to be carried out with coordination.

Forming a team (*siudeoi/xiaodui*) whose members could look after each other in risky confrontations is of critical importance to the survival of militants. In fact, even among peaceful participants, the fear of random arrests loomed so large that many of them made it a rule to report one's own location from time to time. Militants' engagement in illegal activities, such as building makeshift barricades, storefront destruction, and throwing petrol bombs, needed close collaboration among trustworthy partners. On-site division of labor was also necessary for showcasing a defiant gesture. For instance, protesters used umbrellas to shield violent acts from ubiquitous surveillance cameras. To transform pavement bricks into a projectile weapon, team effort was needed. As a militant explained:

> Some people were in charge of digging bricks up, and other people broke them into halves because a whole brick was too heavy to throw. Then there should be other people who carried the finished products to the frontline.

Although the Be Water Revolution proceeded under the "no main stage" spirit, it was not composed of nomadic individuals but numerous teams that operated with their own decision-making independently.

There were some militant teams who were willing to grant interviews to the media. The Dragon Slaying Brigade (*toulung siudeoi/tulong xiaodui*) was probably among the most well-known. They were composed of a few dozen participants who could be mutually identifiable by secret insignia but avoided everyday contact. Rather than passively responding to the police's use of force, this brigade adopted a proactive philosophy by assaulting police and proregime mobsters directly.[4] Probably due to their high publicity, the brigade became the police's prime target. In December 2019, three of its members were arrested and charged with illegal possession of firearms. While waiting for the criminal trial, they joined a desperate speedboat escape to Taiwan in August 2020; all twelve fugitives on board were intercepted by the PRC Coast Guard and then sentenced to jail in China, which gave rise to the so-called #Save12HongKongYouth campaign.

In my interview sample, there are twenty-two self-professed militants, all of whom formed their own teams. Among the nine interviewees who revealed more information, the team's maximum size was 12, and the minimum was 5, with the average being 8.3. Clearly, there was a size limit for militant teams because they required mutual trust and intense collaboration. These teams were different from the numerous Telegram channels that they joined, and these online groups sometimes initiated actions and acted together, but they did not require that members know each other personally and shoulder the risk together. Not all team members were able to join every action. Before departing, there was often detailed planning and task distribution; when they were at protest sites, they often stayed close and looked out for each other. As the police were found to deploy undercover agents, militants often minimized interacting with unknown protesters for safety reasons. In other words, members of different teams rarely worked together.

Team members often originated from preexisting networks. Current or former classmates, friends, neighbors, and colleagues were often the core initiators, and new members were added by personal introduction. Some team members came from the same neighborhoods, facilitating their participation in the local area. Preprotest acquaintances and friendships constituted the foundation for trust in such high-risk activism. As an interviewed militant explained, some of his team members were originally internet friends only, but, afterward, they met in person several times and developed "real friendship." Only two of the militants I interviewed joined a team with unknown protesters they had met during the action. Initially, they used pseudonyms for self-protection; later, with more shared experiences in protest, they began to use their real names.

The reliance on preexisting ties among militants stood in sharp contrast to first-aiders, who were generally willing to collaborate with unknown partners. My interviewee sample includes six first aid respondents and only one of them routinely worked in a seven-person team whose members she knew before. According to another interviewee:

> On July 21, I first participated in the movement as a first-aider. I met other colleagues and then we formed a temporary team. We did not know each other before, and I did not want to know their identity and real names. An ad hoc team like this does not even bother to form a Telegram group. After that day, I did not contact them either. Later I joined some first-aiders' Telegram groups, but there was no coordination before major events. First-aiders just worked as ad hoc teams there. . . . I really did not care that much because the goal was to save people.

First-aiders, compared to militants, were less exposed to police violence and arrest because they typically operated at a distance from ongoing conflicts, and, therefore, they were less reliant on group support. On the other hand, militant teams came with a strong moral obligation toward mutual help. In the acclaimed film, *May You Stay Forever Young* (2021), which recounts the story of a collective effort to prevent the suicide attempt of a young female protester, two search participants had to quit the mission at the last minute because they felt compelled to join their teammates who were fighting the police elsewhere (Ren and Chan 2022: 245). Solidarity also brought about strong emotional attachment. My interviewed militants spoke of the miraculous feelings of facing the same danger together. "It is a very pure form of trust, just like children's innocent belief which you should never betray."

All of the militants I interviewed were high school or university students, or young full-time workers at the time of protest. When they were not engaged in protests, they often spent time together eating, drinking, singing at karaoke, or playing online games. Protest and nonprotest activities, in other words, reinforced their personal connections. In addition, as previously mentioned, militants often avoided going home after an intensive engagement with the police, and instead they often spent the night together in the so-called safe house. According to a militant, her seven-person team rented an apartment where they could store their "stationery" (protest jargon for their gear). Later, they often "ate, slept, or did strange things together" there.

The escalating protest also brought about intergenerational conflicts within families, especially when youngsters and their parents embraced different political views. To avoid conflict, some young militants chose to move out of their homes. There were also cases of eviction and cutting off family relationships by conservative parents (R. Lai 2023; Tsang and Wilkinson 2022). Voluntarily or not, these militants needed to find accommodations and the arrangements of temporary cohabitation were not uncommon among militant teammates. Unsurprisingly, intimate relationships developed out of these close daily contacts. Several of my interviewees reported that they had a boyfriend or girlfriend in their own teams. The mixture of romance and politics was well known, as evidenced by a then popular, albeit sexist, saying, "Girls will only marry frontline brothers and boys will only marry logistics sisters" (*gamsang zigaa cinsinbaa, gamsai ziceoi haukansi*).[5]

Trust networks in these militant teams made it possible for Hongkongers to wage a defiant challenge to the authorities. However, it is important not to idealize the connection among militant teammates as if it were a long-standing revolutionary comradeship. As the government stepped up the crackdown and more people were arrested, many militant teams decided to dissolve themselves and avoid subsequent contact. Many of my interviewees only had a vague understanding of the whereabouts of their former teammates. The news of their exile or imprisonment was often heard through the grapevine. If a member was arrested, it brought about mortal fear among other participants because the police were known to forcibly retrieve the arrestees' cell phone data. As such, the remaining members often took precautions for self-protection, including avoiding contact with arrestees even after their release. Finally, when militants chose to flee abroad (see Chapter 5), their decision was often made individually and deliberately kept as a secret from their former teammates. There were intimate couples who fled together, but they often ended up parting ways in the host countries. In short, the disruptive protests of the Be Water Revolution drew strength from preexisting connections and the subsequent bonding among militants, but these interpersonal ties appeared fragile in the face of ruthless repression from above.

Resource Mobilization: Institutionalized and Networked

Resource mobilization theory posits that the "aggregation of resources" (McCarthy and Zald 1987: 18), rather than subjective grievances, is conducive to the emergence of a movement. Because of its convertibility and fungibility, money is seen as a versatile resource for social movements (Edwards and McCarthy 2004; Edwards, McCarthy, and Mataic 2019). As a high-income city, Hong Kong offers a privileged site for observing how material wealth helps undergird a territory-wide antiauthoritarian struggle (M. Ho 2024). When the city's affluent middle class is consumed with a deep sense of guilt (see Chapter 1), there emerges a collective urge to contribute to the movement. A rolling telephone survey from May to December 2019 indicated that wealthy respondents were more likely to be sympathetic to the movement. Of those whose monthly family income was HK$60,000 (US$7,643) or above, 71.3% were promovement, and the figure declines progressively as one moves to lower income brackets (only 43.8% for those with a monthly income of HK$14,999 [US$1,911] or below) (Chinese University of Hong Kong Centre for Communication and Public Opinion Survey 2020: 165).

As an atypical "movement of the rich," the Be Water Revolution's financially comfortable constituencies rarely took the risk of being physically involved in a direct confrontation. In an interview, a retired banker claimed to have joined more than thirty rallies or demonstrations in a year. And yet, except for eye irritation caused by tear gas, he was never injured. He insisted on his bona fide credential as an "active participant" because:

> I continue to donate. Sometimes monthly, and sometimes one-off. . . . We are the so-called "peaceful, rational, and nonviolent" (*woleifei*), and being timid is our characteristic. We have nothing except money, and we just do what we are capable of.

With such a compensation psychology, the Be Water Revolution was unusually capital intensive, as far as social movements go. For instance, two leading organizations that offered legal assistance to arrested protesters accumulated a considerable amount of donations. The 612 Humanitarian Relief Fund stated a donation income of HK$236 million (US$31 million) as of May 2021,[6] and the Spark Alliance had an account with more than HK$70 million (US$9 million) when it was raided by the police.[7] In the latter half of 2019 alone, my journalistic database reported nineteen cases of crowdfunding initiated by alumni, NGOs, politicians, and netizens for movement purposes. In addition, since Hong Kong is a high-income city and its overseas migrants typically earn less than before, the direction of resource remittance is different from other diasporic movements (Moss 2022: 139). Rather than repatriating monetary and other resources from overseas migrants to their homeland, home-based Hongkongers actually collected money to sponsor the exiled protesters. For instance, Taiwan-based exiles tried to make a living by becoming online vendors, selling Taiwanese products to Hong Kong's politically conscious consumers who were willing to pay more (M. Ho and Chen 2021). The seemingly endless financial resources for the movement were often a talking point for PRC officials and their Hong Kong collaborators, who asserted that it was evidence of foreign powers working to "destabilize" China. But they were manifestly mistaken in insisting on the "secret funding" from abroad, whereas the domestic sources ought to pay the bill.

While cash flows could be made via above-mentioned institutional channels (registered organizations or fintech platforms), which proceed more or less without reliance on interpersonal ties, other logistic tasks such as collecting and distributing nonmonetary resources (protest gear, for instance), providing shelter and job opportunities, and performing care work for those affected continued to be done in the traditional fashion that required interpersonal collaboration. Moreover, some supporters were not entirely satisfied with such hands-off participation, and they found direct interaction with like-minded participants more psychologically meaningful and fulfilling. The aforementioned retired banker also once volunteered in a school pickup mission to transport protesters stranded in the airport on September 1, 2019. The emergency campaign was called "Hong Kong's Dunkirk Evacuation," because the World War II episode also relied on massive voluntary contributions to relocate soldiers mortally threatened by the advancing enemy. My interviewee spent five hours on a driving trip that normally took less than thirty minutes. Yet, he found it worthwhile as he was able to bring some stranded protesters safely back.

Institutionalized channels could not always address the emergencies that required on-the-spot interventions. For instance, when the news began to circulate on the internet, around 8:00 P.M. on July 21, that proregime mobsters armed with metal sticks were found roaming around near the Yuen Long metro station, neighborhood-based supporters near the Mei Foo station (a transfer hub for Yuen Long–bound passengers, see Figure 3.5 for locations) immediately launched an emergency response. Knowing that those protesters who just concluded their rally downtown could face physical danger should they board a Yuen Long–bound train, Mei Foo supporters swiftly collected available clothes and urged transfer passengers to change their attire for their personal safety. Two hours later, when physical assaults took place in Yuen Long station, Mei Foo supporters chipped in their money and encouraged protesters to take taxis home. The notorious Yuen Long incident resulted in forty-five injuries of gangster violence (for a detailed report of the Yuen Long incident, see C. Lau 2020), accelerating the accumulating protest cycle (see Chapter 3). The episode of Mei Foo activists' timely intervention is based on my interview data and is nowhere to be found in the media report.[8] As such, it is impossible to estimate the precise number of casualties that have been avoided. Nevertheless, this story demonstrates the abiding importance of preexisting ties for movement supporters whose contribution is largely in terms of resource collection. Furthermore, the presence of locally embedded connections facilitated emergency repurposing, when an unanticipated incident required immediate responses on the part of community participants. Mei Foo residents were able to launch their rescue operation because the middle-class neighborhood had sustained a vibrant post-Umbrella organization since 2014, thus creating a close-knit and embedded network of prodemocracy activists. This episode also indicated the dialectic relationship between social ties and movement participation, as interpersonal relationships enabled protest making and were reconfigured in the process (Diani 2001). In the same vein, collective improvisation was made possible by the preexisting ties; however, its innovative application also widened, deepened, and strengthened these connections beyond expectation.

Although supporters were less exposed to arrest and violent risks than militants, they still needed to make extensive use of their friendships, alumni, colleagues, and other social ties for the purpose of the movement. In particular, post-Umbrella professional and neighborhood organizations (see Chapter 1) bequeathed a crisscrossing network for resource gathering. An interviewed supporter shared his experience:

> I have friends in medical care, those who were willing to offer restaurant coupons, and people who could offer voluntary driving service. I have dentist friends who take care of those protesters whose teeth were damaged by tear gas bullets. I also know some managers who are willing to provide part-time jobs to protesters.

In addition, there were supporters who went abroad for the procurement of protest gear when both local and online supplies were in acute shortage, and these activists usually relied on their private networks of fundraising. The inbound shipment of such protest gear originally relied on commercial service and individual passenger delivery, but the SAR government later tightened its customs inspection of import items. As such, supporters had to devise new ways to circumvent the new regulations. An interviewed supporter who happened to know a company manager who imported 3M goggles and filter masks for interior decorating workers and lab analysts simply asked him to buy more with her money. Another London-based supporter who happened to live near Heathrow Airport had his room stocked full of protection masks, which were always ready to be picked up by Hong Kong–bound flight attendants.

In a nutshell, supporters utilized institutional approaches to contribute their share in order to minimize their own risks. But there were times and situations when they found it necessary to resort to preexisting networks to facilitate resource gathering, shipment, and distribution.

When Supporters Met Militants

When supporters intended to send their cash or in-kind assistance to militants, they had the option of relying on trustworthy intermediaries who could forward items to those protesters in need. These intermediaries included the local offices of prodemocracy district councillors, activist churches (such as the Good Neighbor North District Church), and the so-called yellow stores, or promovement shops and restaurants. There were several reasons for choosing such an indirect approach. Many well-intentioned supporters did not know militants personally, and some wanted to avoid the trouble of possibly being implicated. As a supporter explained to me, "They don't know me so they might think I could be a 'ghost' (an undercover agent)." In fact, fear also emanated from the reverse direction. Supporters were afraid of meeting "fake" militants who might legally implicate them.

Some supporters chose to be present at the rallies, and they personally distributed their purchased protest gear and restaurant coupons to unknown protesters. Such distribution could be quite random, inefficient, and wasteful, because protest sites tended to be fluid and chaotic, and a sudden police charge might necessitate the hurried abandonment of these precious resources.

In place of such anonymous interactions, some supporters knew militants personally. One supporter told me she often spent several hours in the evenings at her neighborhood Lennon Wall so that she had the opportunity to meet those militants who needed assistance. Because of her regular presence there, local yellow storeowners also recommended that militants go to the Lennon Wall to meet her. She explained:

> If they are hurt, I will take them to see the doctor. If they need additional jobs, I will ask friends and friends of friends to see who needs more employees. If they don't have enough money for tuition, each of us will donate some. Problems that can be solved with money are the easier ones. There are some self-regarded militants who are reluctant to take money, and then we'll have to find more jobs for them.

Preexisting ties also helped supporters to forward their assistance to unknown militants. A supporter who had a militant cousin decided to give her a monthly stipend of HK$5,000 (US$637) so that she could share the money with her teammates. This case indicates that the existence of one single tie can access the networks of both supporters and militants. Another militant spoke of a mysterious supporter whom one of her teammates knew, who was said to be a top manager in a land development company with many affluent friends. He gave financial assistance and offered referrals to medical doctors through his private channels. When some of her militant friends had their passports confiscated due to judicial persecution, this supporter even provided money for them to be smuggled out of Hong Kong.

Hongkongers who assisted militant protesters were often referred to as "parents" and some supporters apparently took the familial appellation seriously by offering more than material resources. Their involvement became holistic and personal as these supporters cared about not only their basic necessities but also their well-being and future. One supporter, for example, noticed that militants grew weary of eating fast food from free coupons, so she decided to cook homemade meals to alleviate their homesickness.

Some supporters took in evicted militants as boarders in their homes rather than relocating them to a spare housing unit or simply subsidizing their rent. An interviewed supporter once hosted a female activist who suffered from domestic violence from her abusive parents. During her two-month stay, my interviewee and his wife chatted with her, provided pocket money, and picked her up after the protests. Despite being short lived, their relationship resembled that of a foster family.

The award-winning documentary film *Revolution of Our Times* (2021) tells the story of a "rioter family" composed of a "Daddy" (a manager), a "Mommy" (a clerk), and around ten younger militants. "Daddy" and "Mommy" were militants themselves and they got to know each other when taking shelter together after a nasty fight. They formed a team by taking in stray younger participants. With the growing movement involvement, they began to live together and celebrated the MidAutumn Festival (a traditional family reunion day) and held birthday parties. During the University Battles in November, many of the family members were injured, and, subsequently, they decided to flee to Taiwan together. "Mommy" revealed that her greatest worry was how to secure visas and jobs for her "children." And there were moments when "Daddy" thought he might have become too devoted to his fatherly role because he kept reminding his "children" to maintain hygienic habits (Revolution of Our Times Team 2022: 117–72).

In sum, there existed a wide spectrum of supporter-militant relationships. They could be distant, anonymous, and indirect, but, on the other hand, some developed into a quasi-familial bonding, providing more warmth and mutual support than many participants' natal families.

A Cyberspace City

Many researchers have noted the prominent role of social media in Hong Kong's Be Water Revolution (Li and Whitworth 2024; Su, Chan, and Paik 2022; Urman, Ho, and Katz 2021). While digitally savvy Hongkongers were already used to online platforms such as Facebook, Instagram, WhatsApp, three platforms in particular—LIHKG, Signal, and Telegram—came into prominence in the 2019–2020 protest movement. LIHKG, which only admitted users with a Hong Kong–based email account (thus making it difficult for PRC cyber warriors and trolls), had a built-in feature of user voting, which facilitated strategic decision-making in the absence of centralized movement leadership. Signal, with its end-to-end encryption design and other privacy protection features, was more suitable to one-to-one online communication. Telegram became increasingly popular among Hong Kong's movement participants because of its channels (which only allowed admin posting) and groups (which allowed many-to-many conversations), which made it easier for militants and supporters to set up or join the online communication platforms according to their specific needs. As such, while LIHKG emerged as a de facto command center and Signal as the preferred private chat room, Telegram sustained an online catalog for all kinds of movement requirements or, more aptly put, a virtual logistic warehouse for the city's revolt.

Table 2.1 shows Telegram channels and groups that were particularly useful to militants and supporters, classified by their main functions. Eighty-six district/neighborhood-based platforms provided updated information specific to locality, such as local protest actions, yellow stores, transportation, and other emergencies. There are forty-seven platforms involving distribution of resources (protest gear, food coupons, accommodations, job opportunities, etc.). These became the digital meeting places where supporters and militants could come together. The same connecting functions were provided by twelve platforms specializing in medical support including emergency wound care, Chinese medicine, and psychiatric services, and six school pickup platforms. Finally, scouting referred to the monitoring of police deploy-

TABLE 2.1 TELEGRAM CHANNELS AND GROUPS FOR SUPPORTERS AND MILITANTS

	District/ Neighborhood	Resource distribution	Medical support	School pickup	Scouting
Channel/Group numbers	86	47	12	6	17
Maximal subscribers	46,799	22,477	147,654	81,763	237,870
Average subscribers	9,159	4,035	17,775	30,344	69,827
Total subscribers	787,692	182,063	213,296	189,663	1,187,058

Note: (1) In addition to many Telegram directories for movement-related channels and groups, the information here also includes those found by a manual search. (2) All channels and groups listed here were public, not private. (3) The data presented here represents the situation as it was around November 2020. Since the NSL became effective, many channels and groups decided to cease their operation, and many users terminated their subscriptions for safety reasons. As such, the figures presented in this table represent only a diminished version of the actual situation from the movement's heyday.

ment in the hope that the real-time information could facilitate better on-site decision-making on the part of frontline militants. There were seventeen scouting platforms on Telegram.

The figures in Table 2.1 reveal some insightful clues. Regional channels and groups were the most numerous, partly suggesting that citywide resistance was fluid and widely dispersed so that residents of different districts and neighborhoods needed to keep on top of the ever-changing situation. Scouting channels attracted the most followers because demonstration and rally participants, peaceful or not, were seriously concerned about their safety. Among the resource-distributing platforms, the most popular one (with 22,477 followers) was actually a job-matching site, indicating that the loss of one's livelihood was a grave concern among militants. Finally, the total subscribers of medical support and school pickup platforms (213,296 and 189,663, respectively) surpassed those of resource distribution ones (182,063). This also highlights that the militants' need for medical care and a safe getaway exceeded their need for protest gear.

In addition, there were also specialized Telegram channels for finding yellow stores, doxing (exposing police officers and their family members' personal data), sharing graphic designs, and so on. The rich varieties of these online platforms demonstrated that the Be Water Revolution proceeded in another digital universe. Mirroring what happened on the streets, there was another invisible city where supporters and militants were active in exchanging information, resources, and services.

Communication scholars typically emphasize that social media's design features (or "affordances") enable certain actions to take place in cyberspace. There is no denying the ease of establishing and managing channels or groups in Telegram, say compared to Facebook, thus making it the preferred digital catalog for all kinds of movement logistic demands. Yet, despite the technical convenience, offline actions are still needed to fully implement transactions between supporters and militants.

For instance, militants with material needs would not automatically use resource distribution channels simply because they were readily accessible in their cell phones. Their concerns about authenticity and personal safety were pervasive and reasonable. A channel admin asked his friends with a "reputation in civil society" to share and spread the information. He also invited other post-Umbrella organizations to promote his channel on their website. As such, digital availability still needed personal endorsement.

The delivery of required resources could also be problematic when militants and supporters only contacted each other via their Telegram accounts and when both sides were reluctant to reveal more personal information or to meet in person. One supporter told me that she typically used commercial drop-off and pickup boxes in public places. Once she put the goods inside, all she needed to do was to send the box number and access code to the receiving party. Whenever there was intense fighting, another interviewee, who managed a private group of around twenty school pickup drivers, was always monitoring another group of militants, who might report their urgent need to leave at any moment. His job was akin to being a taxi dispatch manager, manually matching the request and the transport service.

In short, while online communication made possible the mobile, instant, and nearly cost-free information flow that empowered both militants and supporters, there was a need for coordinating online and offline actions. In this way, the internet connection across different platforms extended, rather than replaced, preexisting interpersonal networks.

Conclusion

With the ELAB looming as the final nail in the coffin to the city's freedom and rule of law, along with the spate of suicide protests that generated emotional and moral outrage, Hongkongers stood ready to experiment with novel ways of protest-making. The need for individual mental fortitude aside, they still required social ties, preexisting or newly minted, in person or virtual, to launch a sustained and disruptive protest movement.

Improvisation means the generation of innovative responses to unfamiliar situations; however, such creativity does not come out of a void but rather from deploying one's capacities and resources in novel manners. Seen in this way, Hongkongers are particularly well positioned to launch the unexpected campaign. As mentioned earlier, a prodemocracy struggle in a high-income city with solid support from the affluent middle class means the movement can tap into a wealth of material resources. From the Umbrella Movement onward, the city has witnessed a progressive radicalization of political campaigns, and more and more prodemocracy activists grew used to the transgressive style of protest-making. Last, as Hong Kong is an international hub, Hongkongers are English-fluent, cosmopolitan, and mobile, which makes it easier to broadcast their messages on a world stage. As the following chapters show, these endowments became a vital asset when Hongkongers chose to launch their collective improvisation.

This chapter has examined the microfoundations that made the Be Water Revolution possible. People repurposed their preexisting relationships among classmates, friends, neighbors, and colleagues for the movement's purpose; these previously apolitical ties became trustworthy bonds among frontline militant protests and logistic provisioning on the home front. They also forged new ties as the eruption of a citywide insurgency provided ample opportunities for previous strangers to know each other and even form intimate relationships. The use of social media is an integral part of these movement network expansions rather than an outright replacement of face-to-face interactions.

The intensive and exhaustive use of social ties happened in a context where social protests suddenly became a risky endeavor in a city previously known for mild policing and political tolerance. Social ties, inherited or deliberately made, catalyzed movement participation by helping reduce the risk exposure of each participant. As such, Hongkongers improvised by making creative use of their interpersonal relationships and thereby cultivated creative and new protest tactics.

3

Flowers Blossoming Everywhere

Observers of Hong Kong's Be Water Revolution have noted its "leaderless" characteristics—no individual was entitled to speak for the whole movement (Au 2020: 30; He 2020; Y. Lai and Sing 2020). On the streets, militant protests were spearheaded by anonymous but connected "smart mobs" who applied guerrilla tactics by avoiding frontal engagement with the police (Ting 2020). On the logistics side, a multitude of online/offline, home-based/boundary-crossing networks facilitated resource gathering and distribution (see Chapter 2). As such, there existed a seemingly contradictory characterization that the movement was actually "leaderful" because organizing and decision-making tasks were broadly distributed among participants (Dapiran 2020: 75; Y. Lai 2022). This chapter seeks to move away from the semantic debate over whether the movement is leaderless or leaderful by taking a close look at the movement's decentralizing dynamics in terms of its tactical innovation, action initiation, and spatial choice.

Taking place in an era that celebrated networked capitalism and information society, the Be Water Revolution did not proceed with a singular person as its figurehead, nor was it coordinated with an organization as its command center. Evidently, what happened in Hong Kong deviated from the classical model of leadership-centered and organization-led social movements. A decentralized movement was clearly more creative, innovative, and resilient, and its swift evolution often intrigued Hong Kong's movement veterans. For instance, Shiu Ka-chun, an activist social worker and opposition lawmaker who was released from prison in early October 2019, was genuinely surprised to find a new style of protest-making:

> Everything is faster than expected, and after an initial shock, things have made several turnabouts. It starts with movement slogans and jargons, and then the implicit rules of action, and finally resentment against the police. Honestly, it is not difficult to catch up with the latest development intellectually, but it remains challenging to fully comprehend it. (Shiu 2022: 294)

Another human rights activist reflected on the novelty of such a decentralized movement:

> In the previous demonstrations, there were persons who chanted slogans through loudspeakers, and others followed by repeating; when it came to 2019, as long as someone shouted, others would respond, and there was no need for a loudspeaker. Anyone was allowed to shout anything, regardless of who she or he was. It was participation by all people.

However, Hong Kong's decentralized movement also deviated from the oversimplified account in the emerging literature on leaderless movements. Digital connection supplemented, rather than replaced, face-to-face interactions. Contrary to the anarcho-populist expectation of radical equality in participation, movement agency remained differentiated as it was largely determined by experience, skills, and resources. Neither were extant political and movement organizations entirely outdated as their established reputation and resources remained an irreplaceable asset to the protest mobilization. Finally, collective improvisation—the central process in the decentralized movement—was not an endlessly renewable energy; its innovative and mobilizing capacity was bound to be depleted in the face of determined repression from the authorities over the long haul.

"Flowers blossoming everywhere" was an often heard protesters' idiom during the Be Water Revolution, often without being precisely defined. The phrase carried multiple related meanings, including the spatial spread of protest activities to less familiar areas, the initiation of actions by new actors, and the adaptation of unconventional actions. As the following indicates, these processes all take place as a result of collective improvisation.

The Dynamics of Protest

The Be Water Revolution involved sustained mobilization over a prolonged period. Like the South Korean protest against then president Park Geun-hye (2016–2017) and the French Yellow Vest Movement (2018–2019), Hongkongers developed a weekly rhythm of participation, with smaller and peaceful events on weekdays and larger more confrontational ones during the weekend. In my dataset, 69% of weekday events were peaceful, a higher proportion than those on weekends (56%).

Figure 3.1 presents the distribution of protest events by week. There are five clear peaks in the 71-week cycle: (1) 38 events in the 16th week (June 10–16), (2) 84 events in the 24th week (August 5–11), (3) 120 events in the 28th week (September 2–8) and 117 events in the 29th week (September 9–15), (4) 111 events in the 32nd week (September 30–October 6), and (5) 107 events in the 38th week (November 11–17). There was a visible decline in the number of protests after the 38th week, which could be identified as the turning point of the whole protest cycle.

All these episodes of intensive mobilization took place in the wake of extraordinary events that shocked Hong Kong citizens. The first peak happened as the government sent the controversial ELAB for review and protesters intended to stop the legislature from passing the revision. On June 15, Marco Leung committed suicide in protest, further fanning popular indignation. The second peak was triggered by the Yuen Long incident on July 21, in which progovernment mobsters physically assaulted metro passengers who were suspected of taking part in prodemocracy protests while the police were conveniently absent for hours. This incident substantiated the suspicion that had been circulating for weeks that police were colluding with triad members, thus giving impetus to the general strike on August 5. The third peak was in reaction to the Prince Edward Station incident on August 31. On that eventful evening, police stormed into the metro station and severely beat those they identified as protesters. Like the Yuen Long incident, shocking images from cell phones instantly went viral; in this case, the violence came from law enforcement agents, and people came to believe that victims actually died and that their deaths were covered up by the authorities. The fourth peak originated from a series of interrelated outrageous revelations. On October 1, police shot an unarmed high school student protester with live ammunition, and the victim was nearly killed. Four days later, the government suddenly announced a mask ban in public spaces, further infuriating the protesters. Finally, the fifth peak witnessed the two famed University Battles, triggered by the first death widely believed to be due to police negligence. Chow Tsz Lok was a university student whose lethal fall from a garage tower was related to a police roundup in the area. Chow was pronounced dead on November 8, and his death unleashed a torrent of angry protests.

While Hong Kong's 2019–2020 protest cycle originated from opposition to the ELAB, its weekly fluctuation reveals the decisive impacts of short-term events. Clearly, two categories of incidents are of particular importance. First,

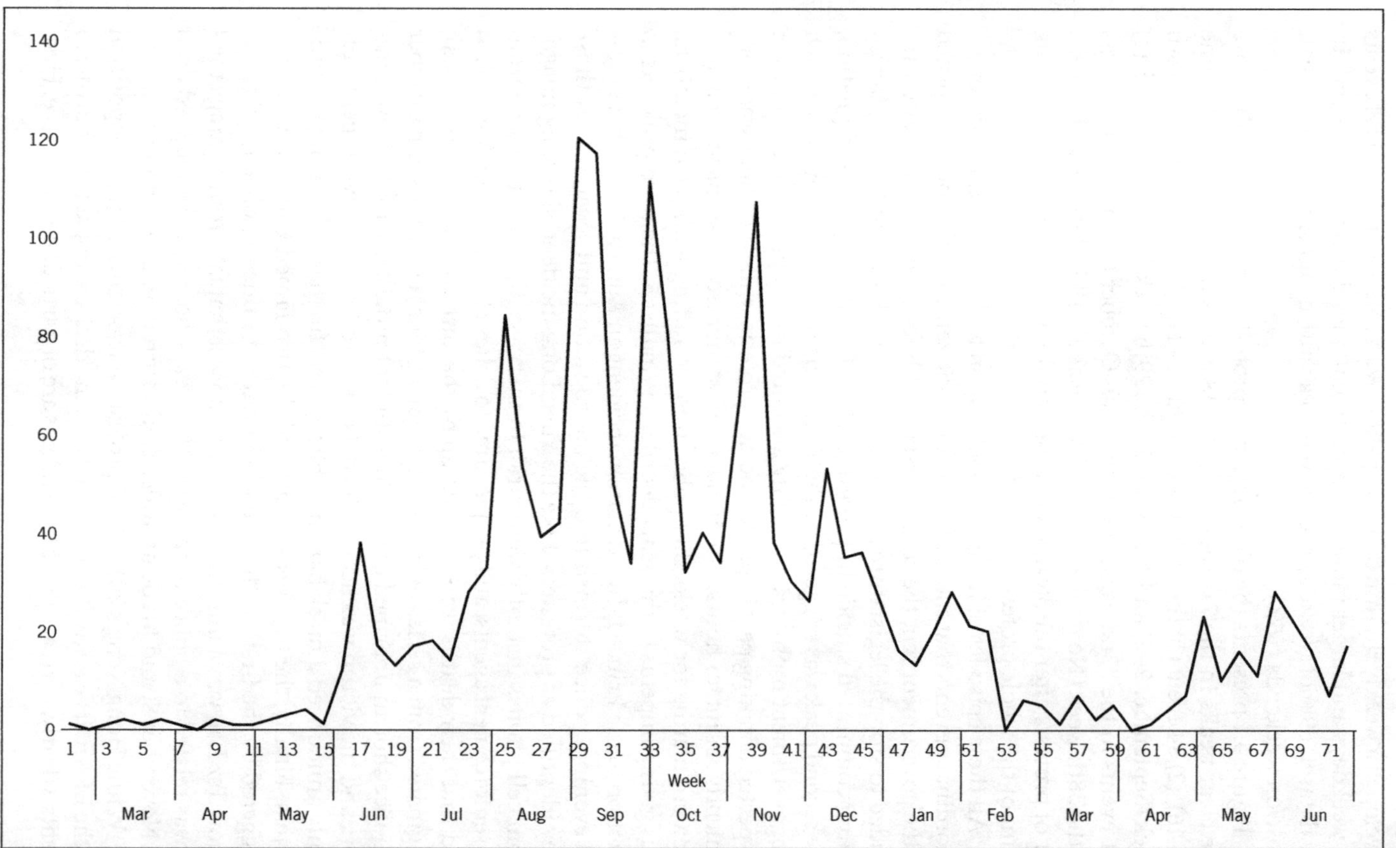

Figure 3.1 Protest events, from February 2019 to June 2020 (by week). *Note: The first week began on February 18, 2019, and the last ended on June 29, 2020.*

impending danger tended to encourage protest participation if people believed their action could make a difference. The imminent passage of the ELAB in June and the mask ban in October fall into this category. It confirms that the threat (defined as the cost of inaction) rather than the opportunity (as the cost of action) exerted a more powerful mobilizing effect (Goldstone and Tilly 2001). People took to the streets because they believed the situation had evolved into a case of now or never. Second, moral outrage (see Chapter 1), or a sensational revelation of systemic injustice, was obviously at play. Leung's suicide, the Yuen Long incident, the Prince Edward Station incident, the October 1 shooting, and the death of Chow all dramatized the fundamental flaws of an unresponsive and undemocratic government. Thus, heightened protests ensued as an expression of righteous indignation. The analysis so far indicates that the protest dynamics are less driven by a rationalist calculation of risk and cost and more as an emotionally charged, yet precisely tuned, response to the ongoing situation.

The decline of protest events was certainly due to the increasing crackdown and rising number of arrests, but it was also related to the fact that there was no more shocking incident of similar magnitude that could activate the power of moral outrage after the two University Battles in November 2019. The absence of such inflammatory episodes did not originate from more moderate policing, and, in fact, the opposite appeared closer to the truth. On the first two days of 2020, the police arrested 400 and 286 people, respectively. Yet, arguably, the police had executed the order of eviction more tactically by resorting to preemptive dispersion and thus reducing the use of force. Instead of acting after the crowd had congregated, the police sought to prevent the gathering of the crowd in the first place.

Knowing that grief and anger were among the strongest psychological triggers to participation, protesters sought to launch rallies in the name of memorializing those emotionally charged incidents to avert the declining trend. From mid-November 2019 to early July 2020, there were forty-six events that were nominally initiated for these purposes, including sixteen events to commemorate the first anniversary of the June 2019 demonstrations, ten for the Yuen Long incident, eight for the death of Marco Leung, four for Chow Tsz Lok, seven for other deceased protesters, and one for the Prince Edward Station incident. Most of these protest actions attracted few participants and thus failed to reverse the declining wave of protest dynamics. Previous studies have shown that protest events repressed by the state are more likely to inspire follow-up actions (Biggs 2005; P. Chang and Lee 2021). In the case of Hong Kong, protesters intimately knew the wisdom of not "letting a good crisis go to waste," and yet their creative improvisations to commemorate these tragic events were not entirely successful when the movement momentum was rapidly depleting.

The Peaceful, the Disruptive, and the Violent

From another perspective, the Be Water Revolution can be analyzed through the tripartite division of events: peaceful (conventional assemblies and demonstrations), disruptive (strikes and blocking traffic), and violent (vandalism). Figure 3.2 plots the weekly distribution of these three events.

There existed a clear pattern of gradual escalation of protest militancy. Peaceful protests appeared first and reached their peak in the 29th week (September 9–15) with 113 events. Although one "premature" incident of disruptive protest happened in the 4th week (March 11–17), their continuous presence began in the 15th week (June 3–9), and the climax came in the 38th week (November 11–17) with 76 events. Finally, violent protests were the last to emerge, in the 22nd week (July 22–28). As such, the Hongkongers' campaign was radicalized in a progressive manner. As the government remained adamant in pushing through the problematic ELAB, protesters had to attempt unconventional protests with greater militancy. It was the widely perceived ineffectiveness of peaceful means to stop the legal revision that invited more militant street actions to take place.

Since violent protests only made up a small minority (6%) of total events, whereas disruptive ones and peaceful ones were 65% and 28%, respectively, we can combine violent and disruptive protests as a measure of militancy. Correlation coefficient analysis also indicates that the intermediate category of disruptive protest is closer to a violent one (0.6859) than to a peaceful one (0.3994, both at $p = .05$) (see Table 3.1). In other words, disruptive protests were more likely to take place together with violent ones rather than peaceful ones.

While peaceful protests were the dominant form in most weeks, there were ten unusual weeks where the combined number of disruptive and violent protests surpassed that of the peaceful ones: the 23rd week (July 29–August 4), the 24th week (August 5–11), the 32nd week (September 30–October 6), the 33rd week (October 7–13), the 38th week (November 11–17), the 44th week (December 23–29), the 49th week (January 27–31), the 50th week (February 3–9), the 53rd week (February 24–March 1), and the 58th week (March 30–April 5). These ten weeks witnessed the uncommon surge of movement radicalism, and their temporal distribution reveals an interesting thread. The first five weeks were all located in the peak periods just identified, or adjacent to them, which can be explained by the heightened tension that encouraged participants to adopt more militant options. The other five weeks took place in the declining phase of the protest cycle, after the 38th week, indicating that these militant actions were more likely out of desperation; in other words, the violent turn appeared to be the swan song of a dying movement.

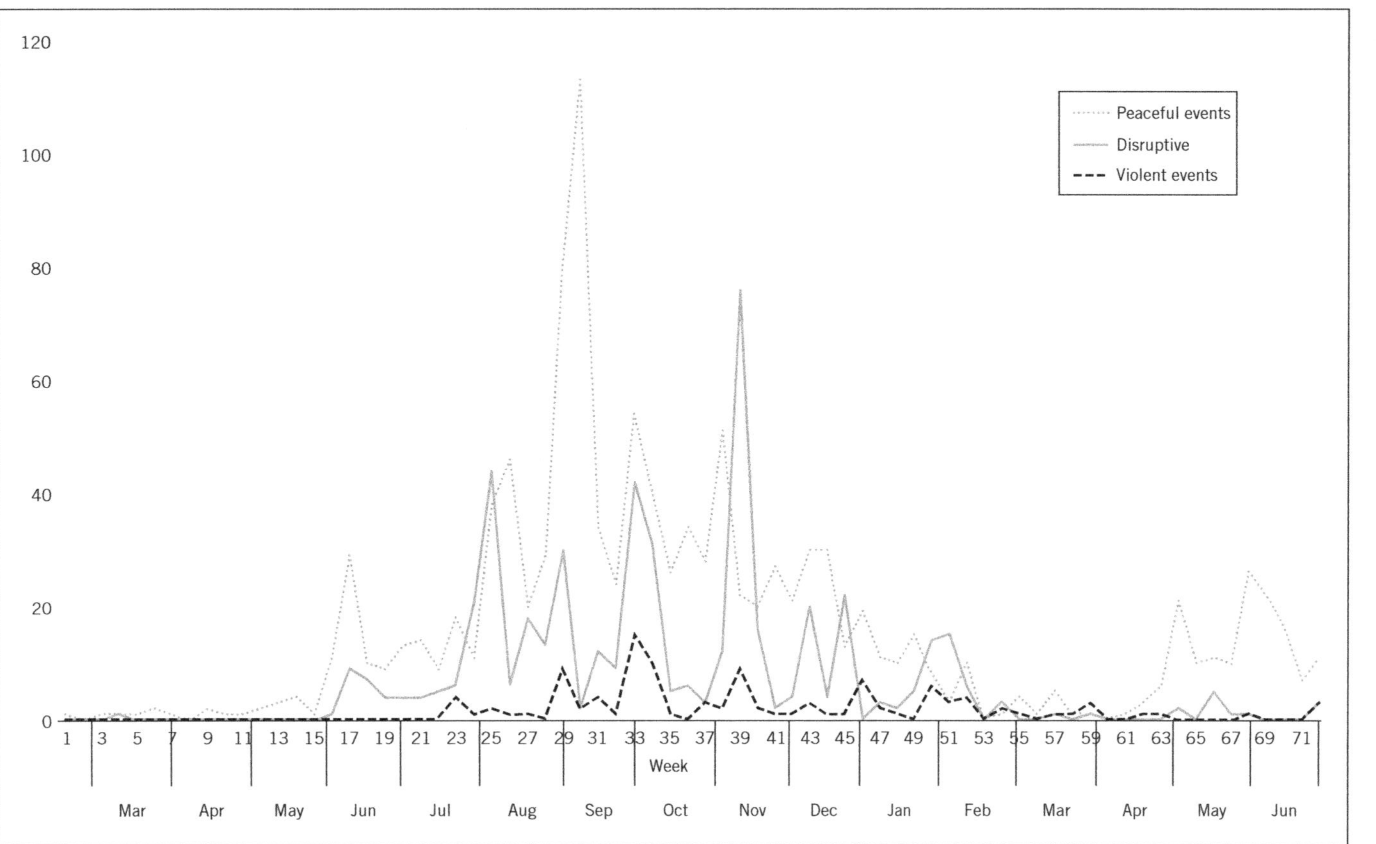

Figure 3.2 Three types of protest events (by week).

TABLE 3.1 CORRELATION COEFFICIENTS OF THREE PROTESTS (BY WEEK)				
	All weeks	1st to 37th weeks	38th to 49th weeks	50th to 71st weeks
Peaceful and Disruptive	0.3994*	0.5104*	0.1208	−0.0247
Peaceful and Violent	0.4575*	0.5547*	−0.0348	−0.1501
Disruptive and Violent	0.6859*	0.7507*	0.6370	0.5852
Note: *p = .05.				

Table 3.1 shows the mutual correlation among the three protest types. I use the 38th and 49th weeks as dividing lines since those eventful periods witnessed the two University Battles (mid-November) and the Wuhan Lockdown in the mainland (late January), which marked the beginning of the COVID-19 pandemic. Before the 38th week, all three types of protest demonstrated positive and significant dyadic ties, meaning that the more one protest type happened, the more likely the other two types would follow. Yet, these close relationships began to disintegrate in the declining weeks. Especially from the 38th to the 49th week, a negative association between violent protests and peaceful ones appeared. Beginning in the 50th week, both disruptive and violent protests discouraged peaceful protests. Although the correlations in the latter two periods were not statistically significant, the results suggest violence and disruption began to crowd out other more moderate actions, thus creating a vicious circle in which violent protesters became more isolated and easily singled out for police repression.

Observing the Italian protest cycle, Tarrow (1989: 324) concluded, "Violence was the product of the end of a period of mass mobilization." Although the magnitude of protest violence in Hong Kong never reached that of the Italian Hot Autumn of 1969–1970, the lesson is equally applicable in that the growing reliance on violent means marked the marginalization of the movement, not its strength. The finding here also dovetails with the first-person account of Hong Kong demonstrators. One interviewed participant revealed:

> There might be only four or five thousand "militants" in Hong Kong. The criterion is that they were willing to join violent struggles, using force in combat, throwing tiles or bottles, or using offensive weapons. Those who merely dismantled guard rails or blocked the road were not truly militants. . . . Militants' action needed to be sheltered by the on-site presence of peaceful participants; without them, militants found it difficult to carry out their actions.

In other words, once peaceful participants were no longer willing to join street protests due to the perceived high risk or because of the COVID-19 outbreak, militants became isolated and more easily targeted by the police.

The Power of "No Main Stage"

The majority of events were organized in the so-called no main stage (63%) fashion (see Figure 3.3), meaning that they were not initiated by known organizations or individuals. In lieu of a decision-making core, many protest events were anonymously proposed and discussed on internet platforms.

As the Be Water Revolution's protest cycle unfolded, initiators also experienced a concomitant change. Before the flare-up, preexisting political, civic, and student organizations nearly monopolized all the protests, constituting 94% of them from February to May 2019. Once the protest cycle entered the crescendo phase, not only had established organizations intensified their mobilizing efforts but also "no main stage" events instantly became the majority, and their dominance continued until the end of the cycle. In October, such anonymously organized events even accounted for more than three-quarters of the total (78%). By then, other established groups were past their prime, as their mobilizing capacities had reached their peak: June (political organizations and religious ones), August (civil organizations), and September (student organizations). August saw the high-water mark for civil

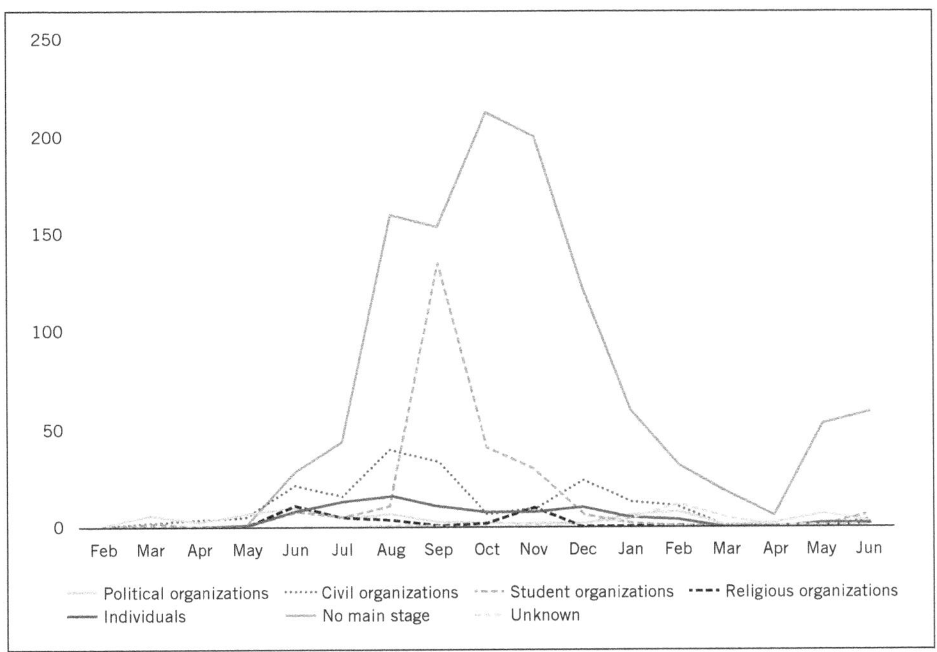

Figure 3.3 Initiators of protest events (by month). *Note: (1) The number of counted events here is 1,818, which is larger than the number of events (1,770) because it includes events cohosted by different organizations, and (2) civil organizations include advocacy, professional, and labor groups.*

organizations with the general strike on August 5 attracting the participation of many professional and labor groups, whereas middle school and university students launched their actions of a class boycott when the semester began in early September.

The resilience of such "no main stage" protests stood in stark contrast to the established organizations, which operated with more formal and informal constraints. Take, for instance, the CHRF, the umbrella organization that had been responsible for the annual July First demonstration since 2003. The CHRF was among the first to call attention to the problems of the ELAB. Yet, after the government stopped issuing permits for protest gatherings in late August, the CHRF refrained from sponsoring new events for a long time. For instance, the CHRF originally proposed a demonstration in Kowloon on October 20, but after their application was rejected by the police, several opposition lawmakers stepped forward by initiating the event under their individual names, which in the end purportedly attracted the participation of 350,000 people. One CHRF leader explained their difficult situation:

> Many young people want to besiege the Legislative Council. Our organization cannot and will not stop them, but we are not going to endorse them. We have our business to do. When we know many people want to join a demonstration, what we can do to protect them is at least trying to apply for the permit for the sake of legality. This is our duty as well as limitation. As for those actions that break the law, we can only appreciate these people who are willing to carry out things that we are not able to do.

Aside from legal constraints, formal organizations need to be accountable to members and are more reluctant to adopt a risk-taking option. My dataset of events shows twenty-eight strikes or refusals to report to work from June 2019 to January 2020, but none of them were initiated by labor unions. As one HKCTU staff member candidly explained:

> We are afraid of calling a general strike because what happened five years ago [during the Umbrella Movement] was a failure. . . . A political strike has a high threshold to meet. We are a general union with nearly two hundred thousand members. If we initiate a strike, there needs to be at least ten thousand workers to join us.

Peer-Produced Protests

Collectively improvised protests were more agile than conventional actions by preexisting organizations because they were less bothered by legal requirements and accountability to mass membership. Fear of failure also constrained leaders of established organizations. At the core of these anonymously initiated protests was the process of collective improvisation. A diverse range of participants, each with their own professional skills, niche knowledge, and personal experiences, contributed fresh ideas for action. These proposals were extensively circulated and debated on social media platforms such as LIHKG. Eventually, some of these ideas gained acceptance and were implemented. By adopting the principles of peer production, it became feasible to harness the creativity and imagination of a vast community of like-minded individuals. This approach also fostered a culture of embracing bold and experimental endeavors, as the reduced cost of failure allowed for greater risk-taking.

Indeed, the outcomes of these anonymously initiated calls for action did not always match expectations. However, events that failed to materialize received minimal attention and remained largely unreported. For instance, in response to a call to launch protests in all eighteen districts simultaneously on October 13, 2019, an interviewee responded to join the rally in Sun Yat Sen Memorial Park, the designated gathering ground for the Western District on Hong Kong Island. To her disappointment, she said, "There were only me, my husband, and the Sun Yat Sen statue. Those netizens did not show up." On that day, the journalistic database registers sixteen protest events spread across ten districts. As such, a flop in the Western District is almost imperceptible and inconsequential, except for the disappointment of some enthusiastic participants. The same goes for the proposed campaign to urge depositors to withdraw their savings to generate an acute bank run (the so-called #cashout campaign), circulating around mid-August. Although the financial regulator did not reveal the amount of cash withdrawal, it was certain that no banks in Hong Kong suffered from a money shortage. Nevertheless, even though such experimental movement proposals did not realize their stated goals, they should not be written off as a "failure." The pressure was clearly felt among bank managers and financial officials. One interviewed HSBC (Hongkong and Shanghai Banking Corporation) worker revealed that her boss had to report daily cash reserves to government regulators while bank employees practiced contingency plans routinely. By contrast, if these events were sponsored by known organizations, these suboptimal results would be accompanied by the problem of responsibility, which would have damaged their credibility.

In addition, collectively improvised protests appeared more capable of adapting to the ever-changing situation by articulating the justifications and the necessary restraints for radical actions (F. Lee et al. 2022: 441–442). As soon as vigilante violence against proregime mobsters (*siliu/siliao*) and vandalism, which was often euphemized as "renovation" (*zongsau/zhuangxiu*), emerged, there was a fear that resorting to naked force on the part of protesters would have alienated moderate citizens. Under an organization-led movement, leaders typically intervene to impose discipline to constrain the behavior of their followers. Without a decision-making core, the Be Water Revolution could only rely on collective improvisation to provide the rules of engagement to minimize damage. For instance, storefront destruction was later framed as a part of economic strategy in that protesters "renovated" the gangster-operated stores ("black stores"; the color black is often used to describe the criminal world), "decorated" Chinese stores ("red stores"; red represents the communist China), boycotted stores owned by progovernment businesspersons ("blue stores"; blue is often associated with the pro-government camp), and supported promovement stores ("yellow stores"; yellow is the symbol of prodemocracy movement) (*hak zongsau*, *hung zongsik*, *laam baamaai*, *wong bongcan*). Although it was not clear about the extent to which people who carried out acts of vandalism duly abided by this guideline, its wide circulation demonstrated that movement participants knew that force needed to be selectively applied to minimize the backlash.

The same tactical response from collective improvisation is also seen in the call for a "ceasefire" on September 11. Prior to that eventful day, Chinese media launched a propaganda campaign to portray the Hong Kong protest as "terroristic," ominously warning that major violent episodes would take place. To avoid being snarled in this trap, Hong Kong's movement participants proposed to suspend militant protests to avoid being associated with the September 11 attacks (Choy 2020: 217–20). According to the journalistic database, there were eleven rallies held on that day, and all of them remained peaceful. As a result, the Chinese media was unable to portray the Be Water Revolution as being in the same category as jihadist violence.

By empowering a multitude of actors with the "authority" to launch protests, a "no main stage" movement might run the risk of having conflicting schedules, thus diluting their strength. This became a potentially worrisome issue because different planners, organized or anonymous, tended to select the prime time of weekends for their own events. However, with a strong consensus of continuing the campaign, it remained possible for them to have prior negotiations to avoid scheduling conflicts. A CHRF staff member explained:

> In the beginning, everyone was closely observing the CHRF's schedule and filling the gap in between. Later on, when they saw our event announcement, they would cede the dates to us. Sometimes they contacted us and we negotiated for the best arrangement. After all, the CHRF had the greatest appeal, and everyone wanted to have maximal impact.

In addition, event planners also took unexpected emergencies into consideration. For instance, a demonstration in To Kwa Wan, a long-neglected working-class area in East Kowloon Peninsula, had been proposed in late July. But once the Yuen Long incident happened on July 21, a strong opinion emerged to delay the event originally planned on July 27 because a demonstration was going to take place in Yuen Long, which was widely seen as a much-attended rejoinder to the collusion of police and mobsters. As such, To Kwa Wan organizers negotiated with their Yuen Long counterparts to avoid the conflict, and, at the same time, they had online discussions and voting via a Telegram group in which "most of the participants favored a postponement." In the end, the demonstration in To Kwa Wan took place on August 17, four weeks later than the originally proposed date. In short, with a determined commitment to the movement goals and the existence of multiple channels of communication, a decentralized movement turned out to be capable of internal coordination and presenting a united challenge to the authorities.

From Core to Periphery

In a rising wave of protests, students of contentious politics identify a process of "geographic and sectoral diffusion" (Tarrow 1989: 285). Parallel to the shift from organizational initiatives to "no main stage" protests, there is also a discernible spatial dynamic from core to periphery.

Because of its history of colonization, Hong Kong is composed of three main geographic areas, Hong Kong Island, Kowloon, and the New Territories. Hong Kong Island has been the political and financial center, and, consequently, the prime choice for political protests, including the annual June Fourth Tiananmen Commemoration and July First demonstrations. During the Umbrella Movement, three spontaneously formed occupy zones were located in Admiralty and Causeway Bay (Hong Kong Island) and Mong Kok (Kowloon), the latter being a commercial hub with a distinctive working-class culture. The political significance of Mong Kok is enhanced by subsequent protests, including the 2016 Fishball Revolution, a violent resistance against a government crackdown on street hawkers.

Considering the previous protest evolution, I identify Central and Admiralty (Central and Western District), Causeway Bay (Wan Chai District), and Mong Kok (Yau Tsim Mong District) as the conventional protest area and the remaining fifteen administrative districts as the emerging area. The spatial distribution of protest events is presented in Figure 3.4.

In the first three months (February to April), protests took place almost exclusively in the conventional area (93%). When July came around, more

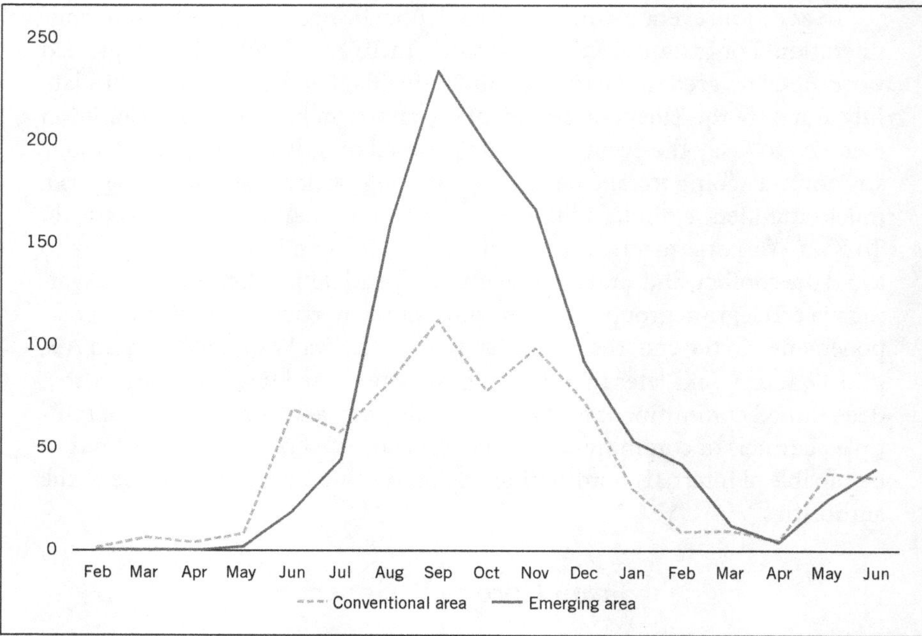

Figure 3.4 Locations of protest events (by month). *Note: The total here (1,809) is larger than the number of events (1,770) because it includes events simultaneously occurring in different areas.*

events happened there (56%), but, from August, the emerging area had taken the lead, and its dominance lasted to the end of the protest cycle. As a result, the periphery (1,091) witnessed more protests than the core (718). There is evidence that protests in the emerging area tended to depart more from the accepted norm than those in the conventional area. The proportions of disruptive and violent protests, respectively, in the emerging area were 32% and 8%, whereas those in the conventional area were 23% and 3%. The fact that the emerging area was more likely to see disruptive and violent protests suggests that spatial dispersal works in tandem with the adaptation of unconventional tactics. The spatial strategy worked to such an extent that the thinly populated Islands District also saw nineteen events. Sha Tin District, a bedroom community in the New Territories, developed in the 1970s, emerged among the hottest zones (150) on par with the Wan Chai District, trailing only behind the Central and Western District (353) and Yau Tsim Mong District (215), thereby earning the endearing nickname, "the capital of Hong Kong" among participants.

The decision to launch protests in new areas also meant localization, since most Hongkongers did not live in the conventional protest area, and, therefore, it helped encourage more broad-based participation. Tactically, it was also a spatial innovation in many ways. First, protesters knew that the police force was heavily concentrated in the city center, and protests in the suburban areas created a logistic headache for law enforcement. Second, as the number of arrestees increased due to more coercive policing, familiarity with the location helped protesters find escape routes when needed. As a University of Hong Kong student interviewee observed, "We know Central and Sai Wan well, and our students are more likely to join the protest here. We know which roads police are going to block and the location of safe houses." Last, a more geographically dispersed movement could tap into specific grievances that were known only to local residents. As mentioned earlier, there was a major demonstration in To Kwa Wan on August 17. One of the event initiators explained the reasons why a large-scale protest occurred in this unlikely place:

> We used to be a residential area, but since Tsim Sha Tsui and Central already have too many mainland tourists and some of them are diverted here. Neighborhood stores are gone and replaced with souvenir shops and pharmacies so that our shopping options become fewer. Streets are getting more crowded. At 6:00 A.M. every day, the tourist groups arrive, and the tour guides' loudspeakers wake everyone up.

To Kwa Wan residents' local grievances were also shared with people in Sheung Shui, another neighborhood troubled by tourists. Both places witnessed locally based anti-ELAB actions that sought to highlight their specific concerns. Residents were intimately familiar with their community issues and only they could frame the problem of the lack of democracy from a local perspective. In addition, as the Be Water Revolution unfolded, protesters could easily find local sites that could mobilize fellow citizens. For instance, a suicide protest occurred in Fanling and Chow Tsz Lok fatally fell from a parking tower in Tseung Kwan O, and both suburban towns saw a number of protest gatherings in the name of mourning. As the police escalated their use of force, police stations throughout the territory were constantly besieged by angry protesters, especially those in Yuen Long (for the Yuen Long incident), Mong Kok (for the Prince Edward Station incident), and Tin Shui Wai (where a female protester was subjected to immodest exposure during her arrest in August). With the anti-police resentment surging, police residences in Wong Tai Sin, Shang Shui, and Chai Wan also attracted protesting crowds. Whether it was based on long-standing complaints or newly emerging issues in the course of the Be Water Revolution, protesters found new ways to localize the movement, thereby accelerating the trend of spatial decentralization (see Figure 3.5).

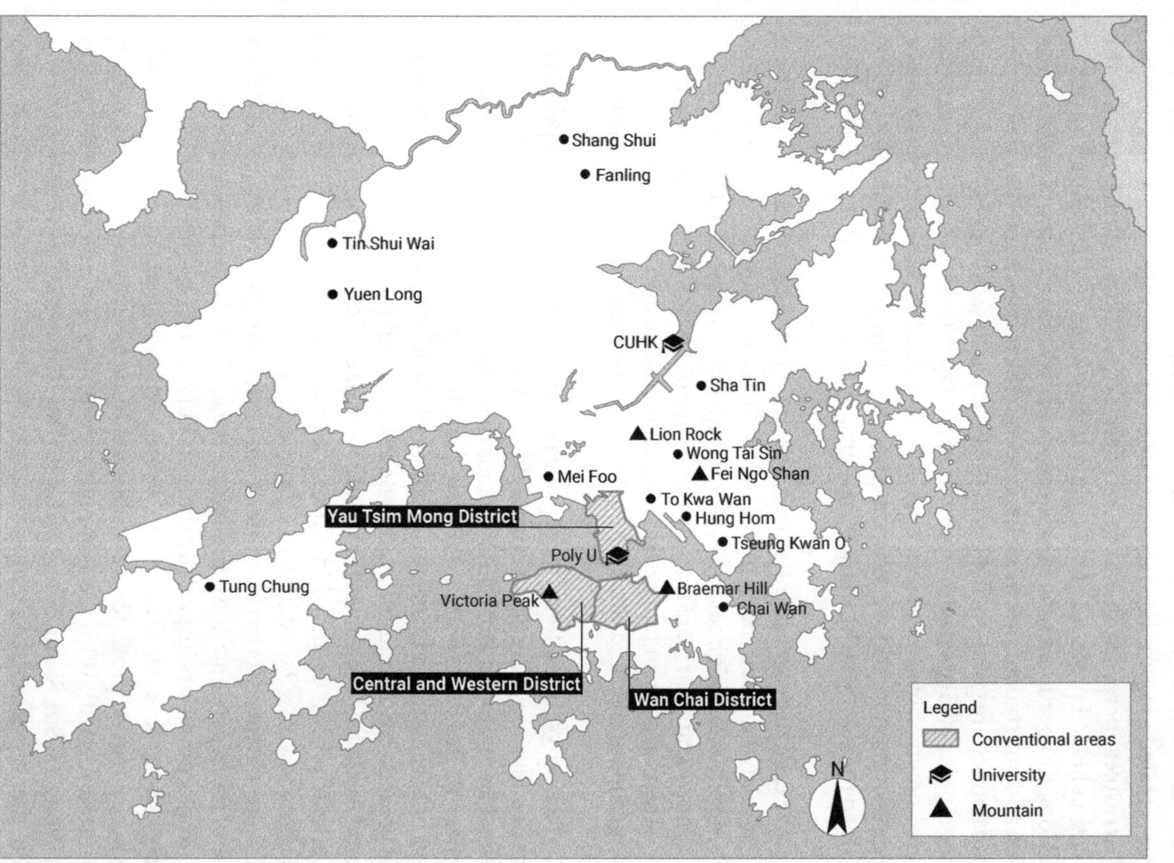

Figure 3.5 A map of major protest sites.

Spatial Tactics

The Be Water Revolution also invented spatial tactics that increased local participation. A campaign known as "Shouting Out the Window" began in mid-August, urging supporters of the movement to shout movement slogans at 10 P.M. every night. This proposal explicitly made use of urban density in Hong Kong, where most citizens lived in concentrated yet anonymous residential towers. As such, it took a few determined participants to chant slogans loudly to create the desired result of boosting the local morale. An interviewee told the author that she was genuinely surprised to hear the yelling from her next-door neighbor, and, from then on, they began to greet each other when meeting in the doorway.

Dispersed Lennon Walls, where movement supporters decorated the public space with handwritten Post-it notes, pictures, or design posters, also emerged as symbolic sites of local resistance. They served many functions. As community bulletin boards that were constantly updated with the movement's progress, they provided the latest information and encouraged local residents to join the upcoming rallies or demonstrations. Hong Kong's senior citizens were used to watching proregime television news and thus accepted their biased report against the movement. Lennon Wall volunteers intended to provide alternative information that could redress the imbalance. On the other hand, for returning frontline protesters, they represented a warm welcome after a bruising engagement with the police. Since many of them were adjacent to a metro station or a bus terminal, volunteers often gathered there to greet and help these protesters. Lennon Walls went beyond being static exhibitions; they required daily monitoring by local activists who had to collaborate closely to update information on the walls while remaining on high alert against potential police raids and assaults from proregime mobsters. As time passed, they formed a neighborhood-based team that became highly knowledgeable about the local surroundings and solidified by a strong local attachment. As one interviewed Lennon Wall activist shared her emotional experience:

> Originally, I planned to leave Hong Kong, and I thought Hongkongers were cold to each other. I have lived in Sai Wan for twenty years without knowing my neighbors. Because of the participation in the Lennon Wall, I began to interact with my neighbors and small restaurants so that I relearnt my community. This is a place full of love. Every time I reflect on the change I have been through, I always feel like crying.

In short, these spatial tactics served to reinforce local attachment by reconnecting Hong Kong's previously distant urbanites. As they joined hands with their neighbors for the same movement cause, they also facilitated the

Be Water Revolution's taking root locally. Particularly in the suburban centers in the New Territories, participants rallied in their familiar neighborhoods and managed their Lennon Walls, and a movement-inspired sense of belonging began to sprout. Even after the protest wave receded, the aroused sense of local identity still remained and gave rise to a campaign of community newspapers (see Chapter 6). This decentralizing trend echoes the findings that peripheral actors often emerge as tactical innovators in a protest wave (D. Wang and Soule 2016). As the protests spread out geographically, the more likely it is that the movement will attract additional participants, thereby creating stronger pressure for the government.

Tactical Innovation and Decaying

The emergence of novel tactics accompanies a quickened pace of mobilization. Newer protest-making methods encourage the participation of those who were not previously involved and aids the movement in attracting more participants. Typically, the law enforcement authorities find it hard to contain protesters when they deviate from the expectable routine. By departing from the site occupation and peaceful methods characterized by the Umbrella Movement, the Be Water Revolution created a major headache for Hong Kong police, who had to adapt to the increased militancy and creativity among protesters. In response, police first deployed water cannons armed with a toxic colored liquid (euphemized as "specialized crowd management vehicles"), in late August 2019, to disperse protesters. As such, tactical innovation invites countermeasures from the authorities, thereby containing its disruptiveness (McAdam 1983). Radicalization is a relational process in which protester innovation meets adaptive responses from the police; while protesters are able to react creatively, the effect of their responses tends to be neutralized over time (della Porta 2018).

Hong Kong's decentralized movement experienced a similar rise and fall of tactical innovation. A protest event comes with many activities, for instance, people might sing songs, read a declaration, and costume in a peaceful rally. Tracking the first appearance of all new activities provides us a measurement of the movement creativity. Figure 3.6 presents the timing of the first appearance of those 133 activities that are classified in my database. The expanding cycle witnessed the rapid emergence of new activities as shown in the sharp climbing curve from May to June. Yet, after the hot summer months, the ability to deploy previously unused activities quickly disappeared. From November 2019 onward, there were only five newly minted activities, including damaging law courts in November, "write with you" (*wo nei se/he ni xie*) (writing letters collectively to imprisoned protesters) in December, recruiting members in January, and distributing antipandemic supplies and threatening po-

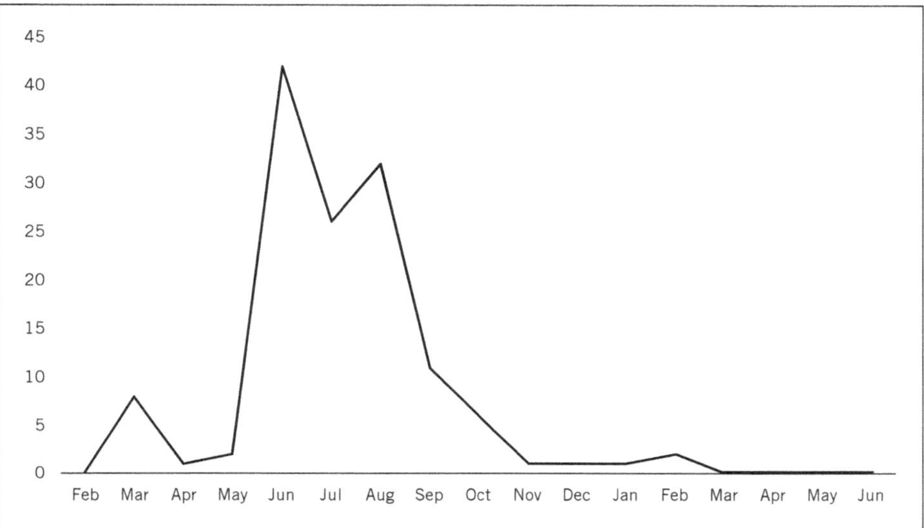

Figure 3.6 The first appearance of 133 protest activities (by month).

lice in February. Tactical innovation was disproportionately concentrated in the early half of the cycle. Once a protest action was invented, protesters tended to repeat the same action for a certain period of time before eventually abandoning it.

Out of 133 activities, two clusters are selected here for closer examination. The artistic and symbolic cluster includes creative communicative actions (large fixed bannering, human billboarding, displaying objects related to or inspired by the Lennon Wall, and collectively pasting posters), lighting actions (holding lanterns or releasing sky lanterns, laser beaming, cell phone lighting, holding lighting signs, flashlight beaming, and flashing car lights), artistic actions (dramatizing/dancing, singing songs, singing adapted songs, performing music, playing national anthems or displaying national flags of other countries, displaying drawings, and drawing pictures), and symbolic actions (covering one's right eye, wearing or displaying yellow raincoats, covering one's chest, placing dog food or playing the sound of dogs barking, placing the likes of homemade bombs, placing symbolic chairs for the officials, smashing progovernment singers' records, displaying the Goddess of Democracy, wearing the V mask, costuming, decorating statues with protest symbols, displaying other symbolic items, and staging other symbolic rituals).

This cluster of activities typically dramatized protesters' solidarity, commitment, and diversity with deliberately prepared props, clothes, and performances. They aimed at winning support and sympathy from a neutral audience by presenting a soft and inclusive image of the movement, especially with the international media and audience in mind (see Chapter 5). Some activities were expressive of the protesters' anger. Engaging in activities related to dogs (*gau/gou*) served as a covert expression of disdain toward the police, who were often contemptuously referred to as canines. Hence, when demonstrators amplified the sound of barking dogs through loudspeakers, those present instantly recognized the underlying message. Figure 3.7 shows this cluster reached its zenith in September 2019.

The other cluster to be examined includes activities of serious violence including chemical assaults (pouring flammable or unknown liquids, throwing petrol bombs, smoke grenades, and paint bombs, throwing back tear gas cans, and installing bombs), hurting people (opponents, police, and journalists), and setting fires. They are intended to cause physical harm for the purpose of intimidation. As can be seen in Figure 3.8, serious violence climaxed in November and quickly dissipated. That serious violence reached its climax two months later than those artistic and symbolic activities is also indicative of the stepwise pattern of radicalization mentioned earlier.

Two activity clusters represented the polar opposites among the full panoply of choices. Yet, whether peaceful or aggressive, these actions quickly fell into disuse after peaking, suggesting a swift declining utility for protesters. Also of interest is an uptick in the number of artistic and symbolic activities

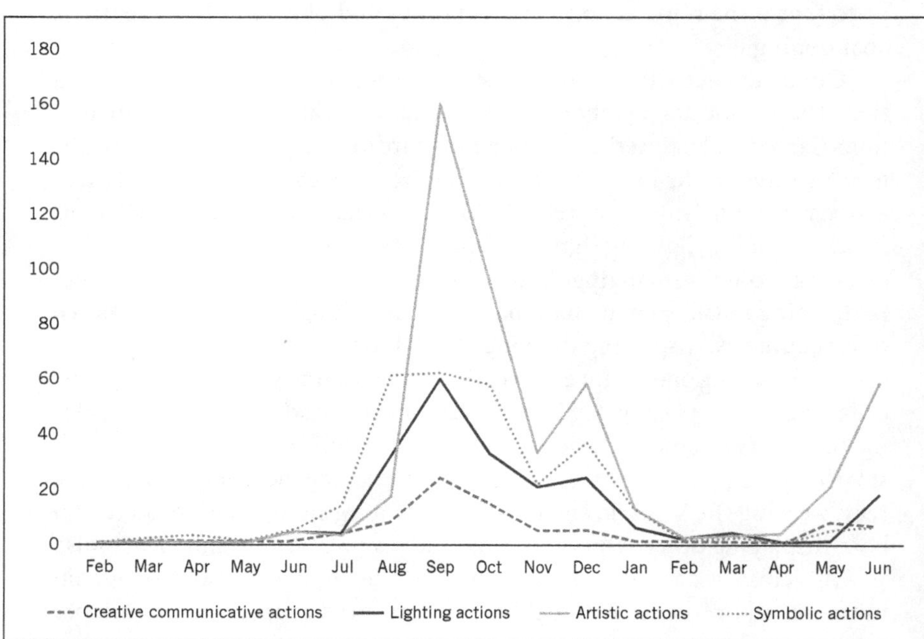

Figure 3.7 The artistic and symbolic clusters of activities (by month).

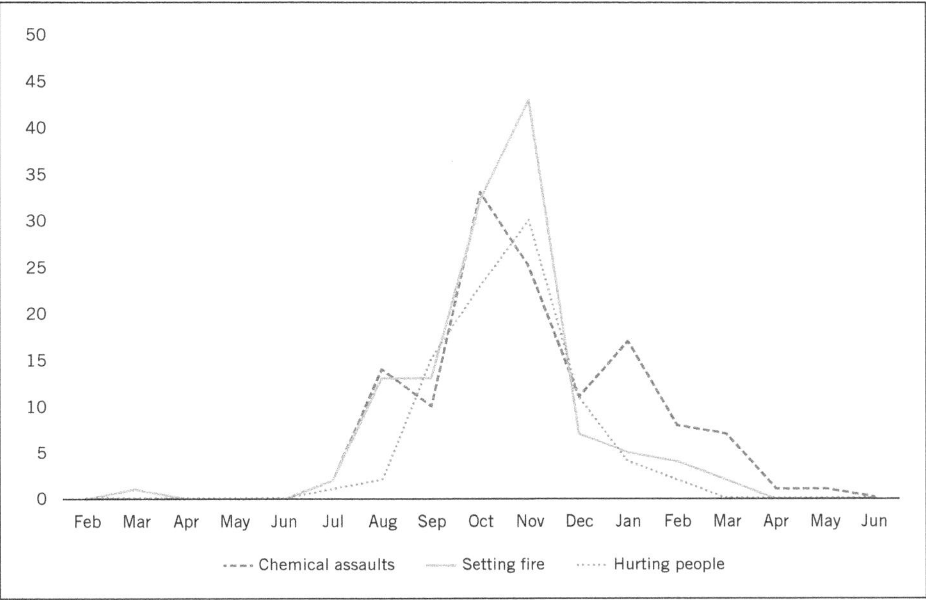

Figure 3.8 The serious violence cluster of activities (by month).

in both May and June 2020, without the parallel changes in serious violent activities. This has to do with the impending NSL, which threatened to punish what has been vaguely described "terrorist acts." As such, protesters concentrated their efforts on peaceful protests to resist the imposition of the draconian legislation.

Hong Kong's decentralized movement apparently undergoes the same dynamics of expansion and contraction without movement organizations playing a leading role. The absence of organizational leadership underscores the fact that intramovement competition for support and resources is not a universal feature explaining the movement growth and decay. Without prior coordination or a decision-making core, collective improvisation emerges as the driving force of innovation and diffusion. Such protest dynamics driven by mass peer production is rare because it requires an unusual scope and intensity of citizen participation. The Hong Kong case indicates that once a sufficient number of citizens decided to take their own initiatives in the heated contention, diffusion and innovation could equally happen without the sponsorship of preexisting organizations. What Shirky (2010) described as "cognitive surplus" was apparently the key process at play here, as a large number of committed citizens volunteered in their own way. While digital communication certainly facilitated the dispersal of decision-making, it would be an oversimplification to reduce the emergence of collective improvisation to technical factors only. What was needed is the political awakening of citizens who are determined to contribute their ideas, resources, and efforts. The involvement of numerous heterogeneous amateurs made it possible to tap an extraordinarily large pool of talent and experience with the result being a novel pattern of mass innovation that pushed the protest wave beyond conventional boundaries.

The Rise and Fall of "With You" Protests

The emergence of a series of "with you" protest actions and their variations is illustrative of such decentralized innovation. It began with a mass rally at the airport on July 26, called "flying with you" (*wo nei fei/he ni fei*), whose Cantonese pronunciation was very close to "peaceful, rational, and nonviolent" (*woleifei*). Apparently, the strategy of choosing the transport hub as the protest site prevented the police from using repressive weapons and was widely seen as a success to invite further adaptations. Among them, "shopping with you" (*wo nei shop*), or gatherings in shopping malls while protesting against progovernment stores, started on September 22, and these were staged in five different places simultaneously on October 5 and November 10. Peaceful gatherings in commercial venues could also take place with "folding origami cranes with you" (expressing one's concern for others; *wo nei zip zi hok*) and "singing with you" (*wo nei sing*). Starting on November 11, "lunch with you" (*wo nei lunch*) appeared as a way to facilitate the participation of white-collar workers, who were encouraged to make use of their lunch break for protest gathering. Journalistic reports show ninety-four cases of such lunchtime protests, with a high concentration in November (25) and December (36) and the number of participants ranging from two thousand to ten thousand. With the exception of one incident, "lunch with you" activities typically took place during weekdays as their main constituents were office workers.

The "with you" protests could also take a radical turn by disrupting the daily routine. On October 25, seven incidents of "going to work with you" (*wo nei faangung*) and "going to school with you" (*wo nei faanhok*) took place that were deliberate acts to create traffic congestion during rush hour. Such confrontational tactics further evolved into a citywide action to shut down the traffic flow, called "congesting with you" (*wo nei sak*). There were twenty-seven incidents of "congesting with you" on November 11 and seventeen incidents the following day. As Chenoweth and Stephan (2011: 10–11) point out, the tactics of nonviolence lower the participation barrier and more participation leads to tactical diversity. Here, the anonymously invented "with you" protests had the similar function of diversifying protesters and their actions.

In particular, the trajectory of airport protests ("flying with you") demonstrates the intensive engagement between tactical innovation and adaptive repression. Hong Kong's aviation industry workers were among the earliest supporters of the anti-ELAB protest. Employees of Cathay Pacific Airways and Cathay Dragon made an announcement encouraging their colleagues to take leave to protest in early June. Episodes such as a flight captain encouraging Hongkongers to keep fighting in a prelanding announcement and attendants refusing to distribute proregime newspapers were reported in the media. With such sympathetic insiders, protesters found it convenient to launch their action in the airport. Furthermore, since Hong Kong took pride in being a world city, political actions taking place in commercial airlines and the airport were bound to have international and domestic reverberations. From late July, protesters ingeniously posed as greeters in the arrival hall, holding placarding to welcome the persons named "Faan Sungzung" (opposing extradition to China) and "Loeng Zi" (conscience); at the same time, they distributed English-language materials to warn the international visitors about the legal risk of being extradited to China. The airport provided a more comfortable environment, "with air conditioning, free Wi-Fi, and one can also get a Starbucks drink," as an interviewed participant told me. In early August, airport protests grew in intensity, as more than ten thousand protesters practically blockaded its functioning, leading to the cancellation of all departing flights on the afternoon of August 12. Being a regional hub, the air traffic disruption in Hong Kong had perceivable consequences beyond the borders, as many connecting flights in other airports were delayed or canceled.

The advent of airport protests was made possible through countless exchanges of discussion, revision, and preparation, involving friends and strangers, spanning across online and offline cooperation. No individual or organization could lay claim as their initiator. Supportive flight crews and ground staff were certainly among the participants, but they did not mastermind these actions. The joint result of such collective improvisation was a large-scale and innovative action that was unthinkable as well as unprecedented. Such a form of collaborative peer production could equally function as a driving force for protest movements. By contrast, classical movements based on organizations, such as the sit-in protests in American civil rights movements, diffused due to the presence of experienced activists in different cities (Andrews and Biggs 2006).

Protesters deliberately chose the airport not only because it represented the city's international gateway but also because the police found it difficult to disperse participants with force, as they did in other crowded indoor spaces of shopping malls and metro stations. Nevertheless, the authorities eventually responded with an effective countermeasure. On August 14, the police obtained a court injunction to ban protest gathering in the airport. Later, people without the same-day flight ticket or boarding pass were not allowed to enter the airport. As such, when protesters staged a "flying with you 2.0" action on September 1, they decided to paralyze the ground transportation around the airport, with the result that the nearby transfer hub Tung Chung and the main highway was effectively clogged, but the airport continued its operation. When "flying with you 3.0" took place on September 7, all that protesters could do was but gather in five metro stations that were located further from the airport. One of my interviewees went to the length of booking a flight ticket and bringing his luggage in tow in order to join the latter events. But apparently, not every protester was capable of making such effort. Clearly, step-by-step, the government managed to tame the disruptiveness of such tactics by better insulating the airport from protesters. In addition to reinforced policing, the authorities stepped up disciplinary actions to dissident aviation industry workers. Citing safety reasons, the PRC aviation regulator threatened to ban Hong Kong's flights to and from mainland cities. Under such political pressure, Cathay Pacific underwent a major restructuring of its top leadership, and employees who were known to be involved in the protest activities were summarily dismissed. With these coercive measures, the authorities forcibly removed airport protests from the repertoire of the anti-ELAB movement.

Limits of Collective Improvisation

The preceding sections identify the following characteristics in Hong Kong's Be Water Revolution: (1) the progressive pattern of radicalization with the successive emergence and peaking of peaceful, disruptive, and violent protests; (2) in the ascending phase, all three protests mutually supported each other, while, in the descending phase, violence became marginalized and discouraged the presence of moderate participants; (3) spatial diffusion as protests without organizational leadership or those taking place in the periphery became numerically dominant; (4) the invention of new tactics accompanied movement expansion, and, yet, the innovation capacity quickly dissipated in the declining period.

These findings conform to the phenomenon of protest cycles found in the American civil rights movement (McAdam 1982) and peace movement (Meyer 1990), the Italian New Left movement (Tarrow 1989), and European new social movements (Kriesi et al. 1995). In his series of investigations, Sidney Tarrow (1989, 1993, 1994: 153–69, 2011: 195–233) provides an authoritative account of what he calls "parabolas of protest." A protest cycle is defined as "an increasing and then decreasing wave of interrelated collective actions and reactions to them whose aggregate frequency, intensity, and forms increase and then decline in rough chronological proximity" (Tarrow 1993: 297). Common elements endemic to a protest cycle include heightened conflicts, diffusion, and innovation that jointly disrupt the existing order. Yet, these classical accounts posited a distinctive logic of organizations. In particular, Tarrow (1989: 10) posits that the rising tide of protests is "not the result of pure spontaneity, but the competition between movement organizations and their old competitors for mass support." Once earlier protests successfully demonstrate the vulnerability of the institutions, they create incentives for follow-up efforts so that new organizations are likely to form, and old ones may radicalize their tactics (Tarrow 1994: 157). This interorganizational competition leads to "outbidding each other with violent attacks" (Tilly and Tarrow 2007: 100). In other words, the classical account of protest cycles assumes an underlying organizational dynamics.

While acknowledging the ingenuity and resourcefulness of decentralized movements, it is also important to refrain from uncritically idolizing their capabilities, as has been commonly seen in some literature. Within one month, airport protests were neutralized by highly adaptable authorities, and air traffic disruption never reached emergency levels. Collective improvisation was thus not a permanently renewable resource capable of indefinitely generating protest actions. Decentralized movements also found it difficult to maintain the protest momentum, even though they did not undergo the same process of organizational atrophy and collapse.

The reasons for their decline are as follows. First, organized or decentralized, protest movements were vulnerable to reinforced repression. Prolonged mobilization was attritional, favoring the governmental leaders with bureaucratic and constant resources at their disposal. Unless participants were willing and capable of escalating their protest to an armed uprising, routine police operations were usually effective in decimating the number of street protesters over the long run with mass arrest. In the wake of the two noteworthy University Battles in November 2019, the police arrested over ten thousand participants, and more than a quarter of the arrestees were criminally indicted, resulting in a severe hemorrhaging of protester ranks.

Second, diffusion to hitherto less active geographic areas had an inherent limit; beyond the saturation point, protesters ran out of new areas to explore new actions in. Both the "no main stage" protests (Figure 3.3) and those in emerging areas (Figure 3.4) plateaued in October and underwent a subsequent decline. The decline of novel actions over time (Figure 3.7) demonstrated that innovative capacity in a decentralized movement was ultimately a finite resource. Its creative explosion sparked off the high tide of contention; yet, such exceptional moments were difficult to sustain. Newly invented tactics had a short shelf life, and they quickly fell into oblivion once they became routinized. The observation here echoes what Tilly (2002: 118) says of the limited nature of the available repertoire since, at any given time, people "draw on previous experiences, incorporate readily available symbols, make selective references to shared memories" When making a protest. As Hong Kong's police stepped up its protest control by mass arrests and other coercive means, protest activities were channeled into less risky arenas, including political consumerism, union organizing, overseas campaigning, and so on. Yet, in spite of the ingenuity of these efforts, Hong Kong's anti-ELAB protesters effectively conceded the streets to the authorities and redirected their commitment to other forms of postmobilization activisms (see Chapter 6).

Last, while decentralized movements encouraged more broad-based participation and thus facilitated diffusion and innovation, the lack of leadership carried built-in flaws. While organizations in the ascending curve of a protest cycle were driven to compete for resources and allegiance, their fratricidal rivalry hastened the decline. By contrast, in lieu of organizational competition, decentralized movements can equally be incapacitated in the waning phase of a protest cycle. Tufekci (2017: 77–82) observes a phenomenon of "tactical freeze" in which earlier successes of a leaderless movement bequeath a debilitating legacy. As no one is authorized to represent the movement, decentralized movements cannot be institutionalized (such as in a political party or another organizational form), nor can they be stopped by a consensual decision. Decentralized movements can easily grind to a halt amid internal exhaustion and external repression.

Without organizational leadership, decentralized movements are capable of generating a powerful protest wave. Collective improvisation is equally capable of devising novel actions and diffusing them spatially. However, while decentralized movements might appear more creative, they cannot be sustained over the long haul. Inherent limits in spatial diffusion and the inability to adapt to a more conventional form of political participation are visible liabilities that contribute to the demise of a protest cycle. Aside from these internal developments, the steady and escalating application of repression from the authorities also raises the cost of collective actions.

The observation of a collectively improvised antiauthoritarian movement confirms the findings of classical studies of social movements in that ruling incumbents are usually able to withstand the challenge from below as long as there is no visible split among their ranks (O'Donnell and Schmitter 1986: 19; Przeworski 1986: 56; Skocpol 1979: 17). Chenoweth (2020) also points out that worldwide nonviolence resistance is becoming less effective due to more entrenched and adaptive regimes. As long as Beijing stood firmly behind Hong Kong's political leaders and the repressive apparatus remained intact, it was next to impossible for protesters to reap political gains. In the descending period of the anti-ELAB movement, there were stories of some radicalized protesters obtaining smuggled firearms, experimenting with improvised explosive devices, or going abroad for combat training (Yeung 2022: 151–52,

183, 247, 279). However, these scattered attempts of militarization stood little chance of overcoming a government armed to the teeth.

The Changing Roles of Organizations

Hong Kong's Be Water Revolution proceeded with a widespread anti-organization and antileadership sentiment, as protesters keenly felt that preexisting prodemocracy parties and movement organizations had failed in their stated missions. Movement decentralization, in a sense, meant that grassroots participants wanted to take back decision-making power and launched their own actions as they saw fit. As the name suggests, the Be Water Revolution aspired to be fluid, flat, and flexible. With the ELAB appearing as an imminent threat to the city's legal cornerstone, it became a widely shared perception that these prodemocracy veterans not only proved incapable of furthering the city's democratization but were also powerless to resist the erosion of civil liberties. While many ardent protesters genuinely believed these preexisting organizations had become hopelessly obsolete in a decentralized movement, the reality was more nuanced, as the CHRF, HKCTU, and other civil society organizations continued to play an irreplaceable role.

It is true that established organizations were constrained by their formal procedures, legal requirements, and membership accountability, so they were less likely to think and act outside the box. Organization-led protests were typically preplanned, scripted, and thus predictable. An interviewed CHRF activist revealed their modus operandi for staging an event:

> In the past, we usually had an agreement with the police. We would set up a stage at the terminus of the parade, which symbolized the end of the event. What happened afterwards was no longer our business. When the time was up, we simply declared that our demonstration was finished. . . . It was not that we tried to maintain distance with [other participants], but rather a division of labor. What happened after the CHRF's demonstration did not matter to us, but we would not prevent [them from taking other actions].

Yet, in spite of these constraints, the CHRF still managed to maintain its visibility during the Be Water Revolution. Before the flare-up in June, the CHRF was among the first civil society organizations to call attention to the pernicious effects of the ELAB. After the "no main stage" protests gained ascendency in the summer of 2019, the CHRF and other existing organizations continued to sponsor large protest events. In my journalistic database, there were eighteen incidents of rallies and demonstrations that attracted the par-

TABLE 3.2 THE TOP FIVE LARGEST PROTEST EVENTS

Dates	Events	Estimated participants	Initiator
June 16, 2019	"Denounce the Crackdown, Withdraw the Evil Law" demonstration	2,000,001	CHRF
August 18, 2019	"Stop Police and Gangsters from Destabilizing Hong Kong, Realize Five Demands" rally	1,700,000	CHRF
June 9, 2019	"Protect Hong Kong and Oppose Extradition to China" demonstration	1,003,000	CHRF
January 1, 2020	"Do Not Forget the Commitment, Walk Shoulder to Shoulder" demonstration	1,003,000	CHRF
July 21, 2019	"Independent Inquiry, Defend Rule of Law, Protect the Truth, Reassert Five Demands" demonstration	430,000	CHRF

Note: The participant numbers were based on the sponsor's estimate, which was typically higher than the police calculation. Critics contend that the numbers were inflated and thus incorrect. However, my interviewed CHRF organizers insisted that they deployed field staff to count the participants at both the beginning and the end of the demonstration routes so that their self-reported figures were reliable. Acknowledging that the participant number per se was a stake of the contention and also the impossibility to obtain a precise figure, I believe that the events listed here remain the largest in terms of scale. Also noteworthy is the fact that all five of these largest demonstrations and rallies took place on Hong Kong Island—the expected site choice for conventional protest-making.

ticipation of over a hundred thousand people; among them, only three did not have an identifiable person or organization as the initiator (the Yuen Long demonstration on July 27, the Hong Kong Way on August 23, and the Kwai Tsing-Tsuen Wan demonstration on August 25). Furthermore, the top five largest actions were hosted by the CHRF (see Table 3.2).

Being a veteran champion of Hong Kong's democratization, the CHRF established its reputation for being a credible and responsible force, and thus its events were always able to earn the endorsement of opposition parties and politicians. Precisely because it was mindful of legal technicalities, moderate supporters who were squeamish about joining an internet-initiated and anonymous protest would feel safer in a CHRF-initiated demonstration or rally. In addition, these larger events often served as important milestones, whose significance outweighed those numerous, albeit smaller "no main stage" events. Since the CHRF repeatedly highlighted the same core demands in these large protests, it also helped set the agenda of the Be Water Revolution, presenting a consistent message to the government and the international audience.

In addition, although existing organizations needed to work within many constraints, their staff (who were usually experienced and resourceful movement activists) had the freedom to engage personally without using the organization's name. For instance, many CHRF-affiliated individuals emerged as initiators for regional demonstrations and rallies, and they made extensive use of the CHRF's legal expertise in negotiations with the police. My interviewee described this strategy as "break up the whole into pieces" (*faa zing wai ling/hua zheng wei ling*). In this way, the established movement organizations proactively adapted to the seemingly irresistible demand for a style of flattened and spontaneous participation without appearing to have taken the movement leadership, and, at the same time, contributed their accumulated skills and human resources to the ongoing campaign. Yet, such self-effacing strategies often led to an erroneous impression that existing organizations became voiceless, passive, or, worse, useless.

The strategy of individualization played a significant role in the general strike on August 5, 2019, which reportedly saw the participation of three hundred thousand people. The concept of a general strike, capable of paralyzing the city's economy and pressuring the government to make concessions, had its roots in the Canton–Hong Kong Strike of 1925–1926, an anti-imperialist campaign against the British by Chinese nationalists and communists. Likely inspired by this historical precedent, the CHRF hastily called for a general strike when the ELAB was set to be reviewed in the legislature in early June. However, the planned industrial action did not materialize, leading to criticism from supporters of the movement. As the Be Water Revolution gained momentum, a Telegram channel emerged, urging a general strike on August 5. While the proposal garnered support from netizens, HKCTU chose not to lead the strike due to potential legal consequences. Nonetheless, HKCTU's younger staff, affiliated labor union officers, and their allies initiated a parallel campaign by organizing mass rallies in seven different locations. Experienced activists took charge of tasks like obtaining rally permission and managing the stages. Consequently, multiple protest actions occurred on August 5 with the seven rallies becoming the focal point of the general strike. This incident highlighted how existing organizations also engaged in collective improvisation. In hindsight, the citywide work boycott was an unconventional and audacious tactic that could originate only from brainstorming among anonymous netizens; its successful execution still required the involvement of activists with organizational experience.

Facing the growing radicalization in the wake of the 2016 Fishball Revolution, there had been discussion of the "collective aphasia" (*zaaptai satjyu/jiti shiyu*) among the opposition parties and the established movement organizations, which reflected their anxiety at being increasingly marginalized (Law 2016). Hong Kong's democrats had fought for the city's political future for a long time, but when mass enthusiasm surged, they found themselves unheeded and unwanted. As the Be Water Revolution quickly shifted gears to a decentralized pattern of mobilization, some observed that the existing organizations were no longer relevant in the escalating wave of confrontation. However, these pessimistic views turned out not to be true. The established organizations were indeed less innovative when it came to tactical imagination, but their activists certainly knew these constraints, and they reflexively accommodated the decentralizing trend. Rather than being hopelessly tied up by organizational procedures, they joined a number of improvised protests in their own capacity and creatively repurposed organizational resources, thus avoiding implicating their organization in legal trouble. In so doing, movement organizations changed from command centers to exchange platforms that found their rightful place in a seemingly leaderless movement.

In this regard, the characterization of Hong Kong's Be Water Revolution as completely leaderless and spontaneous is not entirely correct, and what is easily neglected is the continuing presence and contribution of existing organizations whose legitimacy and human resources were retrofitted for the purposes of this new movement. This observation is also corroborated in other contemporary global protests, including Egypt's Tahrir Revolution (Clarke 2014), Spain's antiausterity Indignados movement (Fominaya 2014b), and Ukraine's Euromaidan Revolution (Krasynska and Martin 2017). Social movements can be decentralized and proceed without organizational leadership, but it remains highly unlikely that they can be completely flattened to the extent that preexisting organizations are no longer relevant.

Conclusion

Social movements are a collective endeavor to make change, and the desired change can either be an improvement of the status quo or a resistance to its dreadful deterioration. Up until the 2014 Umbrella Movement, Hong Kong's political movement had been a proactive striving to realize democratization as promised in the Basic Law, but in the 2019–2020 opposition to the ELAB, it became a last-minute defense of threatened civil liberties and political freedom, which explains its determination, ferocity, and perhaps desperation. Regardless of their orientation, making changes requires that people stop repeating their normal routines, and the greater their departure from the expected, the more profound impacts they are likely to make. Any deviation from expected behavior, marching on the street, refusing to perform one's work duty, blocking traffic, and vandalizing storefronts, amounts to a challenge to the existing order, and the disruptive power grows when they become more numerous and more daring.

Yet, while obeying everyday rules can become habituated, breaking them for the purpose of making changes requires human ingenuity. A protest that is thoroughly routinized is at best ritualistic, while a creative one that has the potential of changing history is no easy effort. How the Be Water Revolution managed to break with the given expectations of social movements is the main focus of this chapter. I have sought to analyze how Hong Kong's protesters abandoned their time-honored peaceful tradition and ventured into the uncharted zone of disruptive and violent protests, invented new actor categories, diffused protest actions into suburban areas and neighborhoods, and experimented with novel tactics. Collective improvisation—in the sense of allowing different participants to contribute their ideas, resources, and efforts—is the underlying process for this movement creativity. However, contrary to oversimplified explanations in some of the existing literature, a decentralized movement that maximizes the participation of the greatest number is neither self-sufficient nor a cure-all. It is deficient because the existing movement organizations are not simply replaced by a faceless mass; they continue to possess critical resources such as credibility and experienced activists that can be redeployed for the movement's purpose. Neither is a decentralized movement endless in its creative capacity; there are inherent limits to spatial and tactical innovation. As long as the state's repressive apparatus remains intact, a decentralized movement is bound to experience the same attrition, exhaustion, stagnation, and, hence, inevitable decline as a conventional organization-led movement experiences.

4

Performing a New Community

Sauzuk, which literally translates to "hands and feet," is a term used more formally to refer to siblings both in Cantonese and Mandarin (*shouzu*), but it is rarely used colloquially. However, during the Be Water Revolution, *sauzuk* gained currency as a common expression in the prodemocracy camp, becoming synonymous with protesters, as they nearly became "brothers and sisters" for the like-minded Hongkongers. Consequently, street protesters were naturally *sauzuk*, so were those who were jailed (*jukzung sauzuk*), forced into exile (*laumong sauzuk*), or dead (*tingwok sauzuk*). One defining feature of the so-called yellow stores was that they hired *sauzuk* in need. During the two University Battles, participants launched a "besiege the PolyU and save *sauzuk*" (*wai leidaai gau sauzuk*) action to help those encamped protesters escape. Up to eleven hundred people were arrested on November 18, 2019, the highest number in one single day across the protest period. The unexpected redefinition of an uncommonly used term and its widespread acceptance demonstrated a growing affective transformation among promovement Hongkongers, who now felt united by a quasi-familial connection.

The term *sauzuk* seemed to transcend ethnic and class boundaries, bringing people together under a shared identity. On December 7, a rally was held to protest the forcible deportation of an Indonesian domestic worker Yuli, who covered the protest movement as a freelance reporter. Rally participants claimed Yuli as their *sauzuk*. An observer was intrigued by a student protester who tried to persuade his university president to join their ranks: "If the President can come out in support, you are *sauzuk*! If someone dares to hurt you, I will stand in the front" (Ma 2020: 325).

The sudden emergence of *sauzuk* into the daily lexicon of Hongkongers underscored the fact that a fresh sense of belonging began to sprout. In the crucible of the enduring protest movement, a political community was forged, where participants deeply recognized that their mutual bond had undergone a chemical transformation. This gave birth to a new collective identity among Hongkongers who shared a common political fate, brought together by intense street confrontations. Scholars have noted the existence of a growing nationalist sentiment before the Be Water Revolution (S. Chung 2023; Fong 2017; Wu 2021). The desire to maintain a distinct identity from China fueled a range of competing and overlapping narratives, including ideas of localism, city-state, self-determination, independence, and a return to British rule (Carrico 2022; Kaeding 2017; Veg 2017). Common to these yearnings was a decided rejection of Chinese nationhood as well as the determination to take back control over the city's own future. However, it was the unprecedented confrontation of the Be Water Revolution that powerfully galvanized this nationalistic aspiration through protest actions, songs, slogans, declarations, and artistic designs. This chapter delves into the behavioral, verbal, visual, and other forms of representation of this emerging ethos.

A Community of Suffering

The unforeseen escalation of the ELAB dispute and the subsequent widespread mobilization created numerous opportunities for participants to reassess and reaffirm their shared identity as Hongkongers. Especially during emotionally charged moments, many felt compelled to reexamine their connections with fellow citizens and took actions they might not have considered in ordinary circumstances. For instance, the wave of suicide protests in June triggered deep soul-searching among many of my interviewees.

In early July 2019, Katherine, a young office worker I interviewed, joined a spontaneous search team after a social media user announced the intention to follow Marco Leung by jumping from the same place. Katherine happened to work in the vicinity, and, before going to the office, she joined the rescue effort, which involved around ten thousand volunteers at the same time for the impromptu mission:

> I was so desperate that day and the weather was bad. The place we searched was where demonstrations usually took place. I kept thinking about what I could do besides finding the disturbed person. . . . We have been ignoring small people like them. I was thinking we should be able to contribute more from our daily life.

At that time, Katherine was about to leave her job at a foreign company for a civil servant position, but she decided to decline the offer and devoted herself to the movement by working as a community activist in her neighborhood. In November, she won the district council election by defeating a progovernment incumbent.

Another interviewee, Regina, was also troubled by the rising suicide epidemic, and decided to launch a personal zine project to "encourage everyone to live positively." Her inspiration drew from postcards distributed during the July First demonstration, which were simply titled "I am here" (*ngo hai dou*):

> The demonstration was full of strangers, but why should we be concerned about each other's safety? I was so touched and therefore I remembered that phrase. I really wanted to tell Hongkongers that we were still around even though some might have left. Whenever something happened, our emotional bond was there to stay.

Regina had just completed her graduate studies in the United Kingdom, and she personally knew that diasporic Hongkongers had many thoughts to share. Her self-financed zine *Ngo Hai Dou* invited more than twenty overseas Hongkongers to handwrite their thoughts for their compatriots back home. Regina was pleased that some unknown readers found solace in her literary output.

Knox, a Taiwan-based activist, was deeply affected by the final words of those suicide protesters, which became the spiritual source that continued to prod him in the campaign:

> I am different from other Hongkongers because I have acquired Taiwan's national ID card. Now I wake up every day and ask myself why I should be concerned about Hong Kong. This is a daily question I must confront. But the answer is very clear, and I am not hesitating. This is what I want to do, and the motivation remains very strong till now.

Finally, Lester's engagement commenced when he participated in an impromptu vigil for a protester who had died by suicide in his community. He played a role in arranging a makeshift altar adorned with candles and cards, despite his parents' progovernment stance and their belief that the deceased persons got what they deserved. He later embarked on a militant career by throwing petrol bombs on the streets. Nearly all his teammates were caught, but Lester was lucky to have fled abroad before his indictment.

In Hong Kong's Be Water Revolution, deaths from suicide protest and from suspected police torture and crackdown not only fueled the protest wave (see Chapter 3) but also helped cement a shared sense of belonging because people were motivated to mourn together. Rather than death per se, grieving with other people was a solidifying power for the shared emotional outpouring. As the aforementioned stories of Katherine, Regina, Knox, and Lester show, these collective sentiments are transformative for being capable of generating actions that one would not undertake under normal circumstances.

In addition to death, imminent danger also functioned as a powerful catalyzer to altruistic actions. As the occupation of the Legislative Council took place on the evening of July 1, many participants decided to evacuate upon learning of the police eviction planned at midnight. Four protesters doggedly decided to stay and faced the legal consequences of their own accord. At the last minute, some departing protesters chose to turn back at their own risk and pleaded with those staying to escape, which finally succeeded in averting arrest on that eventful night.[1] The dramatic interlude was minutely filmed and broadcast live by online media and it popularized the notion of "entering together and leaving together" (*cai soeng cai lok*), which was later repeatedly evoked in the subsequent protest actions.

The willingness to risk oneself for the sake of other compatriots turned out to be a powerful stimulus to the sense of community. In September, a nineteen-year-old university student assaulted a police officer who had subdued protesters on the ground. His action helped three protesters on the spot escape but caused him to be arrested and sentenced to ten months in prison. The "Righteous Mountain" (*ngok ji si*), named after his T-shirt with the Chinese character for mountain, instantly became a folk hero for risking one's safety to save others.

How the shared experiences of suffering reinforced a sense of belonging was best expressed by Brian Leung who delivered an online speech during a gathering on August 16. Leung was a localist opinion leader during his student era and later came to the United States for his graduate study. He was present during the consequential occupy action of the Legislative Council, and he chose to unmask his identity to encourage more participation. Afterward, Leung quickly left for the United States, and, in a speech that was delivered remotely, he defined a community as follows:

> Only when we see other's sufferings as those done for us, other people's sacrifices as those made for us, and every protest as a confirmation and recognition of those predecessors who have made an effort, can a community exist.[2]

Brian Leung's suffering-centered view of political communities succinctly captures the recent turbulent two months for prodemocracy Hongkongers, as the barrage of deaths, arrests, and injuries coalesced them into a people with the same purpose.

In a subsequent interview, Leung revealed his sources of inspiration:

> Now Hongkongers began to talk about *sauzuk*. I had the chance to meet overseas Hongkongers after the July 1 protest [in 2019], and then I realized what it meant to be *sauzuk*. The feeling of solidarity was really like brotherhood and sisterhood. Therefore, I really wanted to go back to Hong Kong to experience what they have been through. . . . I wanted to return to accompany them and share their sufferings, which was a very simple thought.

In short, being an activist himself, Brian Leung generalized the *sauzuk* experiences and elaborated a novel perspective on what it meant to be Hongkongers. His new formulation upended the existing stereotypical views of the city residents as mobile and unattached ("refugee mentality"), or apolitical and mercantile ("market mentality") (Matthews, Ma, and Lui 2008: 15–17), thereby bestowing a new layer of meaning to Hongkongers.

A Revolution in Rhetoric

A newfound sense of community is also evident in the evolving declarations and slogans as the Be Water Revolution unfolded. These statements were more than mere words but embodied actions, as participants solemnly read them out in public gatherings; and, in so doing, they ritually enacted the birth of a new community.

On the evening of July 1, 2019, as protesters stormed and briefly occupied the legislature for three hours, they recited an Admiralty Declaration, which contended that the recent protests were acts of civil disobedience mounted by people who genuinely loved the city. Hongkongers would "never cease pursuing universal values and the rule of law" and might choose to escalate their actions if the government refused to reform. The declaration also pointed to the lack of democracy as the root cause and requested immediate universal suffrage for lawmakers and the chief executive, echoing the core tenets of the Five Demands.[3] On July 21, as protesters gathered in front of the Central Liaison Office (which represented Beijing's presence in Hong Kong) some participants read out a document circulated online that reiterated the Five Demands and vowed to establish a provisional legislature if the government failed to respond.[4]

When Hong Kong's university students launched their class boycott campaign on September 2, the semester's first day, they held a rally attended by thirty thousand people. Among its event highlights, student delegates took to the stage and read their declaration in Cantonese and English. Taking cues from the U.S. Declaration of Independence, the statement began with a preamble that outlined a list of inalienable rights of citizens and the duties of the government. Since the Hong Kong government had abused its powers, students vowed to "take up the responsibility and to fulfil our destined roles by protecting our beloved homeland."[5] On October 4, as the government suddenly imposed a mask ban, protests simultaneously surged in many locations. In several evening gatherings, protesters narrated another text circulated online, titled *Declaration of Provisional Government*, which asserted that the SAR government had lost its mandate, and its authority would be immediately transferred to the provisional government.[6]

This analogous escalation in rhetorical militancy found a parallel in the street slogans chanted by protesters. The phenomenal rise of "Liberate Hong Kong, Revolution of Our Time," to the extent that the slogan became synonymous with the entire movement, deserves a closer look. The mantra was first coined by Edward Leung when he joined a legislative by-election in February 2016, but subsequently, it was largely limited to the insurgent localist camp. Moderate prodemocracy politicians and activists typically avoided using the slogan because it smacked of proindependence radicalism, which they saw as politically counterproductive. Yet, when street protesters began to spontaneously shout "Liberate Hong Kong, Revolution of Our Time" in July 2019, many of my interviewees who previously had reservations were genuinely surprised to find themselves perfectly willing to chant the slogan at the crowd scenes. A former Umbrella Movement leader mentioned two reasons for his personal change. First, with its growing popularity, it was no longer synonymous only with Hong Kong independence. Second, the slogan appeared to be the most "defiant" option among the existing ones, best symbolizing their strong will to resist.

Prior to the mainstreaming of this slogan, the most circulated idiom among protesters that envisioned the movement's goal was "a reunion without masks under the rice cooker the other day" (*taajat boudai ceoizaau soenggin*), meaning that protesters can finally gather together without using face masks to conceal their identities at the Legislative Council Complex (the building was often referred to as a giant rice cooker for its appearance). Clearly, the evolution of protest slogans went in tandem with the movement radicalization, as it shifted from the subjective needs among participants to the collective future of the city. Similarly, increasing assertiveness is also reflected in the three-part evolution of the slogans that addressed fellow Hongkongers: from "Add Oil" (*gaajau*) in two major demonstrations in June, "Resist" (*faankong*) in protests against the mask ban in October, and, finally, to "Revenge" (*bousau*) in the wake of Chow Tsz Lok's death in November.

Obviously, in the course of the Be Water Revolution, protesters began to freely employ the revolutionary narrative with thinly veiled allusions to overthrowing the government and asserting political independence. It was certain that Beijing and its Hong Kong collaborators monitored the growingly radical language with apprehension, while the movement's sympathetic observers and moderate supporters also had legitimate reasons for worrying about the unnecessary and potentially counterproductive braggadocio. How can we interpret this radical escalation in movement rhetoric?

It was clear that the turn to more aggressive narratives did not accompany a rise of protest violence. As Chapter 3 has pointed out, violent protests remained small and marginal, and, toward the declining phase of the mobilization cycle, they began to crowd out peaceful ones. Furthermore, the Be Water Revolution remained an antiauthoritarian struggle guided by the Five Demands until the very end. There was no sudden swerve into a nationalistic state-building campaign or an armed uprising. Without a corresponding turn toward violence and nationalism, how can we explain the increasingly visible disconnect between rhetoric and deed? True, detractors can easily dismiss these seditious assertions as irresponsible infantilism, but such a view cannot explain their widespread acceptance among movement participants.

Following J. L. Austin's theory of speech act, I think it is best to understand these declarations and slogans as performatives—utterances that are also actions rather than merely descriptive statements. Austin (1955: 10–11) contends that performatives have little to do with corresponding to the existing reality because their emphasis is to change the status quo. Therefore, there are bad and unsuccessful performatives, but a false one does not exist. In this light, these seemingly revolutionary narratives cannot be judged at their face value and literal meanings. If these statements merely aim at expressing the state of mind among protesters, they do not need to have the elaborate settings of mass rallies. It follows that the point is not about the acceptance of violence or nationalism among protesters or not. The fact that these declarations and slogans were enunciated in a highly ritualized manner suggests that they served a performative purpose. By dramatizing their rejection of the SAR government and defiance of Beijing, participants were enacting what a self-determining community would do under unusual circumstances. In short, rather than a statement of intent, these seemingly reckless declarations and slogans are no less than a potent assertion of agency: a necessary political baptism for a newly awoke people.

A Community of Identities

At the same time when prodemocracy Hongkongers were demonstrating their nascent agency through a number of "revolutionary" performatives, they also attempted to make sure that their own identities were seen and included in the new community. In fact, ever since the government introduced the controversial ELAB in February 2019, a wave of petitions by individuals and organizations emerged. Yuen and Tong (2021) found as many as 478 online petitions before the onset of the large-scale confrontation on June 9. Among them, 345 were launched by alumni of middle and elementary schools, 43 by tertiary institutions, 24 by professionals, 23 by religious organizations, 16 by residential communities, 14 by hobby and rights groups, and 13 by overseas Hongkongers.

Here, my research uses a different set of data based on the journalistic sources explained in Appendix 1. The observation period started in February 2019 and ended in July 2020, lasting seventy-two weeks in total. To count as promovement group statements, I exclude those made by single individuals, political parties or politicians, and advocacy groups. Reported statements that existed only in oral form or denounced certain individuals are not counted. I also choose not to include lawyers' defense statements and those general announcements without a specific group identity, such as the Admiralty Declaration mentioned earlier. Applying these selection criteria, I found 899 group statements emerging during the Be Water Revolution (see Figure 4.1).

This figure clearly shows two peak weeks of group statement activities. The first one took place in the 15th week (May 27–June 2), right before the intensive mobilization for the first large-scale demonstration on June 9. Among the 293 group statements in this week, 244 were initiated by alumni. The second peak took place in the 23rd week (July 22–28) as an immediate response to the scandalous Yuen Long incident on July 21. Among the 90 statements in the second peak, 21 were from government employees of various branches and 47 were from professionals. Since the infamous episode threw into sharp relief the moral abyss in which law enforcement openly abandoned their official duty to protect people and colluded with mafia gangsters, many professionals felt the urge to reassert their occupational ethics and condemn such egregious malpractice. The moral shock to Hong Kong's public sector workers was undoubtedly the greatest, profoundly calling into question professional pride in their competence and integrity. On social media, many government employees uploaded the photo of their ID cards with personal information covered by Post-it notes written with movement slogans. In an open letter to all Hongkongers dated June 24, civil servants of various departments stated:

> As civil servants, we feel extremely shameful about the government's actions. But as a member of Hong Kong, we will stand by in our positions to serve the citizens. In the face of unprecedented social turmoil, Hongkongers need to stay united. We also hope all civil servants can come forward to confront tyranny and stand with all citizens in safeguarding our homeland![7]

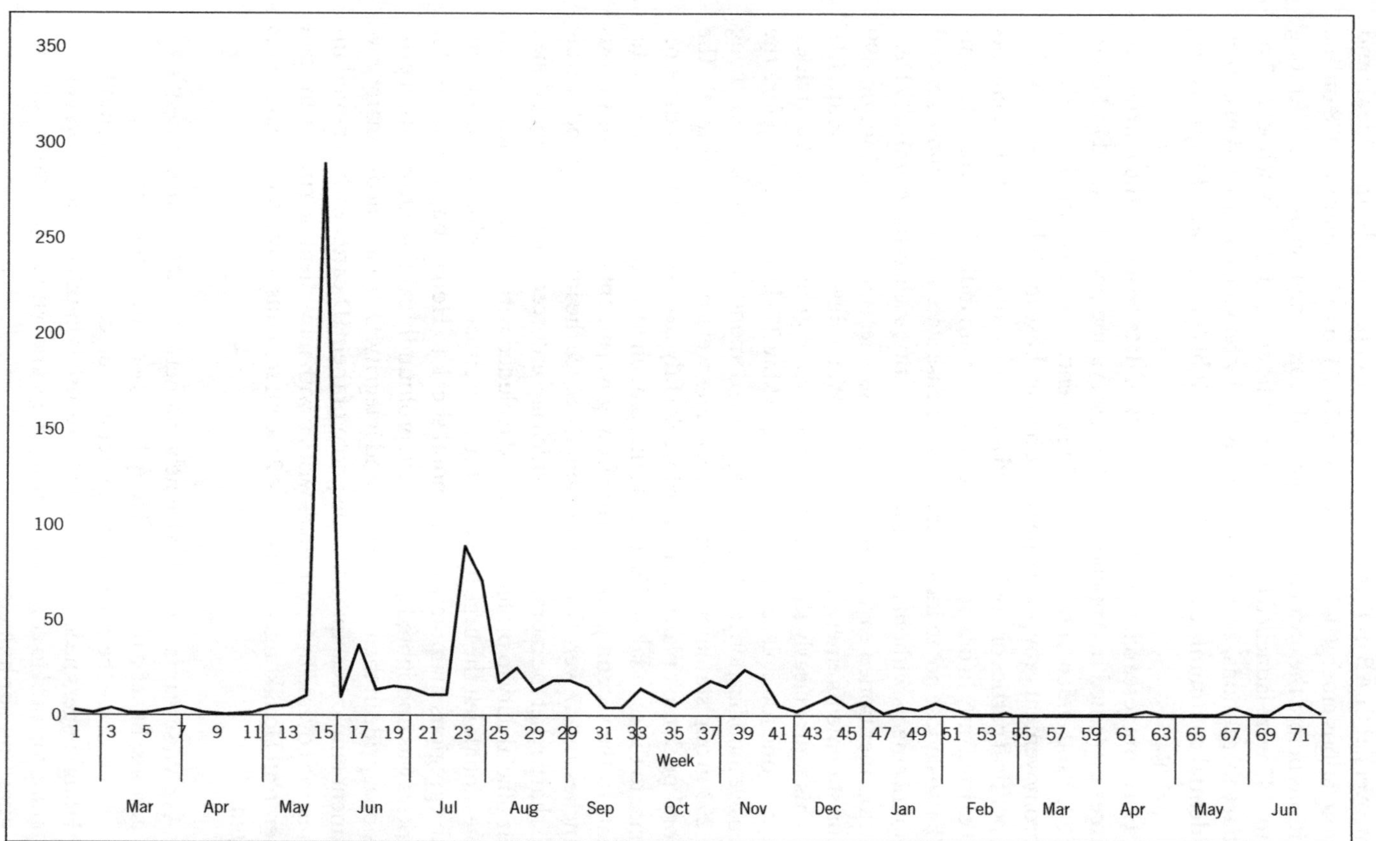

Figure 4.1 Group statements, from February 2019 to July 2020 (by week).

Among the total of 899 group statements 342 are by professionals, 285 by alumni, 82 by students and schools, 51 by civil servants, 47 by religious organizations, 24 by NGOs, and 12 by businesses and stores. The rest came from local communities, overseas Hongkongers, and others. Their monthly distribution is presented in Figure 4.2.

Paralleling the protest mobilization pattern examined in Chapter 3, there was a successive wave of group statements by different actors. The peak involvement of alumni and religious organizations arrived in May, civil servants and professionals in July, and students and schools in November. However, in comparison with Figure 3.4 on protest events, there is an obvious lack of synchronization between a group's statements and their protest actions. For instance, public statements by Hong Kong's religious organizations were concentrated in May and mobilizing for protest in June, whereas student protests peaked in September and their statements reached their climax in November. As such, issuing statements and staging protests appeared to be

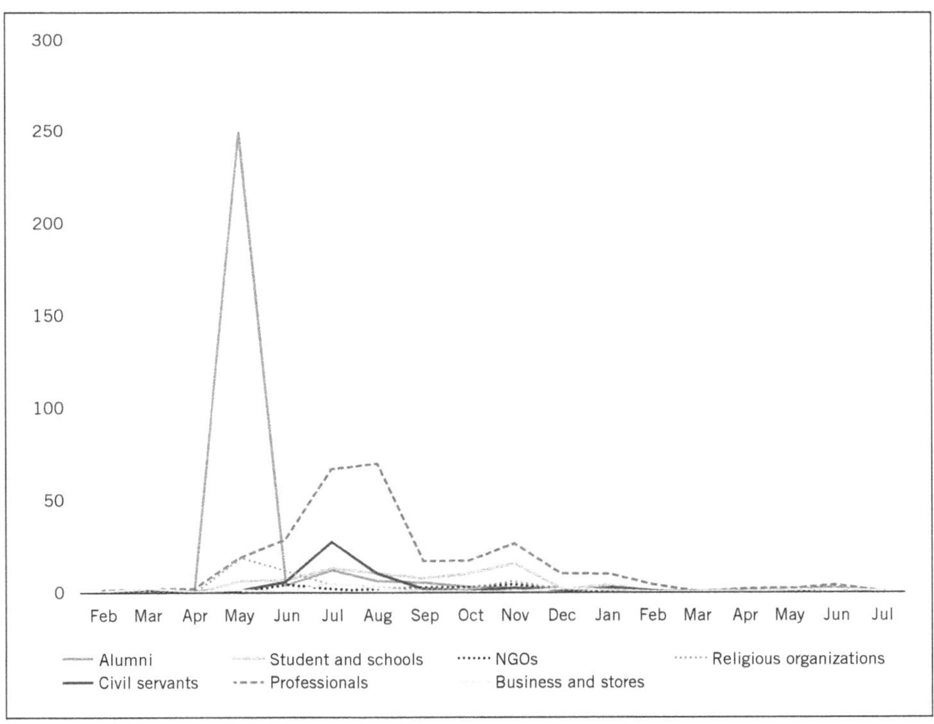

Figure 4.2 Initiators of group statements (by month). *Note: One statement is only attributable to one initiator category, and, in the case of joint statements, only the category of leading proposers is coded. NGOs here do not include conventional advocacy organizations like the CHRF and HKCTU.*

two distinctive activities. Typically, statements were drafted by a few individuals and then circulated in their communities for the purpose of collecting signatures. Endorsers only played a passive role, mostly via the internet connection. By contrast, group-initiated protests needed active participation among their members to be present physically.

In addition, the role of professionals, not including teachers and civil servants, is significant in that they seldom initiated protest actions but were actively involved in issuing group statements, accounting for 31% of the collected sample. Understandably, their professional organizations were a less suitable vehicle for protest mobilization, but when it came to the core concerns of their trade, these preexisting networks helped launch a more moderate form of participation.

As the movement evolved, the public became more or less used to some form of professional discourse in support of the movement demands, such as the legal arguments against the ELAB by barristers and solicitors, journalists' asserting freedom of the press, and medical workers' warning about the clinical consequences of the police's use of weapons. Nevertheless, some professionals' statements offered fresh insights into the intensifying contention. For example, Hong Kong's clinical psychologists urged the government to tolerate the sprouting Lennon Walls because free space for expression contributed to mental health.[8] A group of chemical engineers raised a red flag over the excessive use of tear gas, which caused immediate skin and respiratory harm as well as second-degree damage when it was decomposed into nitrogen oxides, carbon monoxide, hydrogen chloride, cyanide, and other chemical compounds. Their open letter ended with practical suggestions in the case of tear gas assault.[9]

In some cases, the process of collecting signatures incidentally activated a dormant interpersonal network that ended up facilitating protest mobilization. A feminist veteran I interviewed (who happened to graduate from St. Francis Xavier's College, the same middle school as Hong Kong's chief executive Carrie Lam) was involved in the statement campaign, which helped her reconnect with alumni who had left school more than forty years ago. During the demonstration on June 9, more than thirty statement signatories gathered under the alma mater's flag and sang the school song together. Expectedly, they took the opportunity to condemn that Carrie Lam deviated from the alma mater's teachings by railroading the ELAB.

While most of these promovement statements emanated from a preexisting group with clearly delineated professional, religious, academic, and other boundaries, there were some statements initiated by people whose group boundaries were blurry, weak, or nonexistent in the past. In Table 4.1, I list these "unconventional" groups who also publicized their statements in chronological order.

TABLE 4.1 THE FIRST APPEARANCE OF UNCONVENTIONAL GROUP STATEMENTS (BY WEEK)	
Week	**Groups**
7th week (April 1–7)	Overseas Hongkongers
15th week (May 27–June 2)	Parents, elders, neighborhood residents, sports lovers, housewives (*sinaai*), sexual minority, persons with disabilities, mainland migrants, and fans of Japanese animation, comics, and games (ACG)
17th week (June 10–16)	Civil servants
18th week (June 17–23)	Chatroom and page admins
20th week (July 1–7)	Storeowners
21st week (July 8–14)	Chinese human rights lawyers
22nd week (July 15–21)	Police family members
23rd week (July 22–28)	Football referees
24th week (July 29–August 4)	Middle class, YouTubers, public intellectuals
26th week (August 12–18)	Animal lovers
28th week (August 26–September 1)	Football fans
40th week (November 18–24)	Tiananmen incident escapees

A wide array of new identities and new groups surfaced as the protest movement unfolded. In some instances, the statements from these unusual groups reflected the extensive grievances caused by the ratcheted up police repression. Visually impaired Hongkongers issued a statement to protest an incident of a roadside police interrogation in which their white cane was erroneously identified as an assault weapon.[10] Similarly, animal rights activists found it unacceptable to deploy police dogs shortly after the release of tear gas.[11] More than two hundred police family members joined an open letter campaign pleading with government leaders to adopt political solutions to the ongoing conflict, rather than forcing police officers to follow "illogic orders" that aggravated the police-civilian relationship.[12] Aside from these group-specific complaints, these new actors also raised political concerns based on their particular situations. For instance, a group of mainland migrants claimed, "The life experience in the mainland let us know China's judiciary system completely follows the CCP's interests. . . . We cannot trust Chinese style rule of law." The statement urged the government to safeguard the defense of the two systems and encouraged mainland migrants to join the opposition movement.[13] Similarly, ACG fans cited a number of incidents in which their Chinese counterparts were persecuted and harassed to highlight the fact that the ELAB would have enabled the PRC government to pose a threat to Hong Kong–based illustrators, curators, publishers, and cosplayers, thereby constraining the freedom of artistic creation.[14]

In addition, some statements also aimed at redefining these groups' positions more broadly in society. Hong Kong's high-income professionals, often referred to as "middle class" in the local context, have traditionally assumed a bifurcated social image as they can be educated, enlightened, and cosmopolitan and, at the same time, self-regarding, materialistic, and conformist (So 1999). In the Hong Kong Middle Class General Strike Declaration, the drafters claimed they possess "assets, status, or knowledge" as well as "the ability to emigrate." The middle class intended to enjoy a "safe life and satisfaction from one's work" (*ongeoi lokjip/anju leye*), but, to pursue this personal goal, "democracy, freedom, and justice" must be its pillars.[15] This statement apparently attempted to remind these well-off middle-class professionals that their material comfort could be swiftly eroded.

In Hong Kong, housewives (*sinaai*) did not have a reputable image, as they were proverbially said to be small-minded, gossipy, and ignorant. In a statement that collected up to five thousand signatures, the initiator claimed housewives worked hard to take care of their families every day, but they were also solid members of society. Many mainland housewives could not visit their jailed husbands or properly bury their children who died in shoddy public construction, and they did not want to share the same fate. Therefore, for the sake of the next generation's future and their parents who fled the mainland, housewives should join the anti-ELAB campaign.[16] In fact, as a perfect illustration of the negative stereotypical view of Hong Kong's housewives, a female conservative lawmaker haughtily disparaged the campaign as unnecessary worries that their husbands who kept mainland mistresses would be extradited. The discursive mobilization of housewives bore resemblance to that of elders, sexual minorities, mainland migrants, and persons with disabilities as all of them attempted to shed preexisting stereotypes at the same time that they joined the campaign.

In short, the flurry of group statements is also best understood as performatives with two primary functions. First, they served to broaden the appeal of the anti-ELAB movement by activating those hitherto less active sectors. As a result, the Be Water Revolution appeared to be an inclusive and citywide campaign and its opponents were limited to a coterie of unreconstructed hard-liners. Second, drafting, signing, and circulating these statements also helped foster new groups, thus extending the mobilizing network for the movement. For those with stigmatized identities, it became a rare opportunity to establish a new social image. By joining the opposition movement, these groups symbolically secured a legitimate standing in the new community.

Geography of Protests

As prodemocracy Hongkongers were articulating an inclusive community through their verbal communications, their protest actions were also pregnant with symbolic meanings, alluding to their nascent community. As Jasper (1997: 183–84) has pointed out, protests are not only an instrumental action that aims at maximizing its political impacts but also expressive acts that consecrate certain values through ritualized performance. A protest is inspired by some moral vision and, at the same time, attempts to actualize it in reality. To dramatize the citywide unity in resistance, many actions were, in fact, carefully choreographed performances specifically designed to amplify their theatrical effects. The Hong Kong Way, a sixty-kilometer human chain rally on August 23 discussed in the Introduction, offers an illustrative case. As participants lined up and held hands in the designated routes and iconic spots, an insurgent community was born. Just as a pilgrim travels through religious sites for a passage toward holiness, the citywide human chain also carved out the geographic boundary of Hongkongers. The same goes with the neighborhood-based Lennon Walls discussed in Chapter 3. Precisely because of their ubiquitous and mundane presence, they became a sort of fixture in the urban landscape, highlighting the fact that resistance was embedded in many local communities.

The same logic applies to the frequently mentioned theme of simultaneous protests in eighteen administrative districts when protesters launched their actions. In the beginning, when participants attempted to frame their action as representative of all Hongkongers, they emphasized "Hong Kong Island, Kowloon, New Territories, and offshore islands," which also appeared in the housewives' statement title analyzed earlier. As protest mobilization intensified, the geographic imagination was also deepened to the extent that the call for "flowers to blossom in 18 districts" (*sapbaatkeoi hoifaa*/*shibaqu kaihua*) was often heard. In October 2019 alone, four waves of "no main stage" protest were launched with this ambitious call for action (October 4, 7, 13, and 18). Although the journalistic data remain incomplete without being able to verify whether these territory-wide actions really happened as claimed, the bold assertion—as well as the disruption it caused—lent credence to the powerful imagery of a citywide uprising.

The territorial trope was vital to the imagination of a newborn community. Most Hongkongers were mainland migrants or their descendants, and, as such, their claim to be a distinctive people could not take the ethnic-genealogical route but rather the civic-territorial one, according to Anthony Smith's (1991: 15) distinction. In terms of language and culture, it was virtually difficult to distinguish Hongkongers and Cantonese-speaking Chinese in neighboring Guangdong Province. Thus, all the narratives about the British legacy of rule of law and core values served to emphasize the distinctive features of being Hongkongers. Edward Leung, the localist leader, was born in the mainland, and he justified his advocacy for the city's independence on the grounds of civic nationalism. According to Leung, anyone who fully embraces the core values and sees the city as home can become a Hongkonger. It is in this context that the territorial display emerged as the leitmotif in the dramaturgy of protest, and the city's compact size and well-developed transportation made it easier for protesters to deploy this territorial strategy.

Lion Rock, the majestic mountain peak visible in many places in the Kowloon peninsula, has long been an iconic landscape representing the city. Due to a namesake television series that began to be broadcast in 1972, the mountain came to symbolize grassroots Hongkongers as well as their willingness to work hard amid material deprivation, giving rise to the popular notion of "the Lion Rock spirit." The subsequent rise of social protests gave a political twist to the cultural imagery of the landscape. During the Umbrella Movement of 2014, protesters scaled the peak and hung a giant banner, "I Want Genuine Suffrage"; since then, the mountain has become an indispensable backdrop for protest-making, conveying the collective will to resist. As such, the cultural meaning of that iconic peak morphed from economic endurance to political determination. The Be Water Revolution inherited this action repertoire and further elaborated its connotations. From May to August 2019, my dataset indicates that there were five incidents of protest banners hanging at the peak (May 12, June 6, June 16, June 23, and August 24), and the messages became angrier, evolving from "Opposing the Evil Law of Extradition to China" to "Black Police's Excessive Violence and a Murderous Regime." Typically, the government removed these protest banners within a few hours.

With the advent of the human chain rally on August 23, Lion Rock became a de rigueur site for protest gatherings. In the evening hours, hundreds of participants on the hill turned on their cell phone flashlights and other illuminating devices, and the mountaintop light could be seen from a distance—thus creating a photogenic spectacle for the international media. Protesters repeated the mountaintop human chain on the Mid-Autumn Festival evening (September 13), making use of the moon-watching custom in the hope that more citizens would notice their action. The next day, several progovernment mainland Chinese copycatted the tactics by displaying a People's Republic of China flat on Lion Rock, and protesters responded by hanging their protest banners in Fei Ngo Shan (Kowloon), Braemar Hill, and Victoria Peak (Hong Kong Island) (for locations see Figure 3.6).

With a sea elevation of 495 meters, Lion Rock is not easily accessible, as it takes a strenuous thirty-minute hike on a craggy footpath from the nearest trailhead. An evening walk can be perilous and fixing colossal banners on the peak requires rock climbing skills and experience. Protesters also had to be mindful of government patrols along the trail and needed to stealthily install their protest objects. Yet, these difficulties did not stop Hong Kong's protesters from using Lion Rock as their stage, even knowing their carefully prepared banners would be removed quickly. Among these trials, the greatest effort consisted of placing a statue of the recently created Lady Liberty Hong Kong, with a height of 4.5 meters and a weight of 80 kilograms, on the peak. On October 13, a team of twenty volunteers spent four hours scaling the mountain in pitch dark and assembling the artwork. Yet, within one day, the piece of artwork was trashed and broken into pieces. In addition to these protest actions, many promovement video materials used aerial photography on Lion Rock for its visual effects. For instance, in a five-minute video clip titled "DANZMOCRAZY,"[17] there is a concluding scene where a dozen dancers performed at daybreak on the panoramic mountaintop around a Lady Liberty Hong Kong statue. One can imagine the laborious preparation work behind the scenes.

The obsession with Lion Rock among Hong Kong's activists does not make tactical sense from an instrumental and utilitarian perspective, but it taps into a crucial aspect of nationalist imagination, that is, the need to historicize the natural scenery of their *patrie* (A. Smith 1991: 127). Lion Rock does not just represent Hong Kong; rather, it is Hong Kong in a metonymic sense. The turf war over the iconic mountaintop is, after all, a contention about the political meaning of the city. By layering the peak with movement messages, participants intended to reclaim their space and reassert the control over their own future.

A National Anthem

Another acoustic breakthrough further broadened the Be Water Revolution's territorial strategy. On August 31, a young composer named Thomas uploaded a newly created music video to YouTube that featured an orchestra and choir production of "Glory to Hong Kong" alongside video images of scenes from the movement.[18] The song became an instant success as many protesters quickly learned how to sing it, initiating a wave of sing-along rallies. My database indicates that there were only four protest events with singing in August, and the number sharply climbed to 96 and 53 in September and October, respectively.

The song's creation is a perfect demonstration of how collective improvisation works through peer production. Thomas spent two months writing the lyrics and composed the melody in private before sharing a prototype version on LIHKG on August 26. He received overwhelming approval and many suggestions. One of the key modifications was to insert "Revolution of Our Times" and "Liberate Hong Kong" into the lyrics. The absence of these defining protest slogans would have significantly dampened the song's appeal, and, fortunately, the timely intervention of anonymous netizens avoided the potential mistake. More than one hundred volunteers contributed to singing, instrument playing, audio mixing, and other tasks before its final release. While this is not the first time that Hong Kong's protesters created a song to represent their collective action, "Glory to Hong Kong" surpassed the previous creations in many ways. Thomas chose to compose his work in the style of a military march, rather than conventional Cantopop, and the solemn use of orchestra with heavy brass further added to its aural splendidness. The lyrics depicted a predawn and difficult battle scene for freedom (akin to the "Star-Spangled Banner") and extolled the valor and wisdom among the committed sons and daughters. The keyword "Glory" carried rich magisterial and religious connotations, which were absent in past protest songs, including "For Freedom" (1989) in the wake of the Tiananmen incident and "Holding High Our Umbrellas" (2014). By contrast, empowered by a newfound sense of community, "Glory to Hong Kong" superbly offered a dignified and stately imagery of the ongoing movement precisely because it started with a sense of collective pride and destiny, not from individuals' commitment and feelings. It is no surprise that the song immediately won the endearing moniker "Hong Kong's national anthem" for its grandeur.

The song's advent made sing-alongs a powerful medium to convey the movement message, as students sang "Glory to Hong Kong" in their school auditoriums, football fans in the stadium, and ferry passengers in the terminal concourse. A novel "no main stage" protest action was invented by netizens to make use of Hong Kong's ubiquitous and highly accessible shopping malls adjacent to metro stations. From early September 2019 onward, there were several evenings when shopping mall atriums throughout the city were flooded by hundreds of black-clad participants. At an appointed time, they began to sing "Glory to Hong Kong" in unison. In a second, commercial atriums were turned into an arena theater for people on different floors to sing together while facing each other. The panoramic spectacle was awe-inspiring, and the visual and audial display of solidarity was made greater as all on-site participants knew that other Hongkongers were doing the same thing in different shopping malls.

Benedict Anderson (1983: 24) points out a particular consciousness of time that is endemic to all nationalistic imaginaries. To form a community, people need to be imagined traveling through the same abstract and empty time together. And such temporal awareness that something is happening at the present is restricted to those people situated within a defined territory. Hongkongers who sang "Glory to Hong Kong" together were enacting what it meant to share the feeling of temporary simultaneity in a dramatic fashion. Thus, with the creative deployment of this powerful acoustic device, Hong Kong's mundane and commercial venues were transformed into holy sanctuaries that offered blessings to the birth of a young nation.

The creative outburst and dramatized collection in celebrating the new birth of Hongkongers' community is akin to the group dynamics that Émile Durkheim has pointed out in his analysis of primitive societies. Durkheim maintains that participating in religious rites reinforces members' solidarity and, during its emotional high tide, the so-called collective effervescence—an ecstatic and mystic feeling of unity—gives rise to artistic creativity. Speaking of how ritual participation contributes to solidarity, he explains:

> For a society to become conscious of itself and maintain at the necessary degree of intensity the sentiments which it thus attains, it must assemble and concentrate itself. Now this concentration brings about an exaltation of the mental life which takes form in a group of ideal concentrations where is portrayed the new life thus awakened. (Durkheim 1915: 470)

Following this insight, the collective performative to bring into life the idea of a Hongkonger community is more powerful and more persuasive than mere dissemination of ideas. The great upheaval of the Be Water Revolution made possible this dramaturgic enactment, enabling this community to come alive and to be experienced as a living reality, albeit only momentarily.

Visualizing the Revolution

Visual images were another front of the Be Water Revolution, where activists produced posters, illustrations, cartoons, photos, and other graphic materials to publicize the movement demands. These visual materials were first digitally created and circulated, and some were later printed and either distributed as flyers or pasted on numerous Lennon Walls. These graphic designs can be analyzed in many ways. They were in part the idealized self-projections among movement participants, attempting to win the support from outsiders. In this sense, they were "propagandistic" for the movement's purpose. Since no individual or organization was authorized to speak officially for this improvised movement, they helped by directing attention to the ongoing development, highlighting incidents of police brutality, responding to the officials' claims, broadcasting an upcoming rally, and so on. Facing the government's intransigence, protesters also needed a common outlet to express their frustrations. In short, these visual materials were a set of highly heterogeneous sediments randomly deposited by a powerful flood, leaving many telltale clues to a bygone upheaval.

At its height, a private chat group composed of more than two hundred graphic designers was working at full capacity around the clock.[19] Although

AI-generated drawing was still not readily available for lay users in 2019–2020, the then available programs and apps for computer-aided design as well as free online image archives eased the participation of nonspecialists in creating these visual materials. This aesthetic explosion brought about worldwide attention, and, by comparison, the government and its conservative allies could only come up with unimaginative responses. The government's abject failure on the aesthetic front showcases the power of collective improvisation over its better-resource-endowed foe. Due to their artistic values, from September 2019 to June 2021, there were eight exhibitions on the movement's visual creations in Hong Kong, four in Taiwan, and six elsewhere (M. Chang 2023: 192–93). Zines (*siuzi/xiaozhi*), the small-circulated and self-published "magazines," have been the ideal publication outlet for amateur creators who intend to contribute their efforts. The explosion of zine production was also a noticeable phenomenon, leading to exhibitions of these movement-themed works in many countries. In a way, these visual works amounted to an artistic arsenal of seemingly unlimited supply. A Lennon Wall volunteer spoke of rich diversities that she was able to tap into online:

> We need to target different audiences. For instance, teenagers are more interested in the love theme, especially the picture of young couples holding hands together during the protest. Frontline militants are attracted to the Righteous Mountain because he assaulted police to save other people. Some people want to read more words, and special infographics for seniors are needed.

In Cantonese and Mandarin, these visual materials were often called "propaganda" (*mansyun/wenxuan*); however, its English equivalent was inevitably confused with the Nazi and Communist practice of camouflaging informational warfare as news making. To avoid this misleading connotation, this book avoids using that loaded term and interchangeably refers to these awareness-raising efforts in Hong Kong as visual, communicative, or graphic materials or works.

For analytical purposes, I downloaded the shared images on a Telegram public channel, "Anti-extradition to China Communicative Materials Valley" (*faansungzung mansyun guk/fansongzhan gu*) (available at https://t.me/hkstandstrong_promo), a popular hub for sharing promovement visual materials. This channel relied on anonymous contributions and its admin did not explain the selection and screening policy. Similar to the making of protest events, the logic of collective improvisation was at play in the generation of visual content. Numerous and largely unknown participants designed and drew these materials based on their own decisions, thus reflecting a wide array of styles and aesthetic tastes. Except for a few autographed cases, most objects were deliberately anonymous, and there was no way to identify the authorship. While there were other digital outlets, this Telegram channel was the most popularly used one for sharing and circulating promovement graphic images, with 63,743 followers as of April 20, 2023. Although the collected samples are neither complete nor exhaustive, they still can lay claim to being a representative and meaningful subset. My research team collected all the posted images from June 13, 2019, to June 30, 2020, and the sample number is 49,157, with a daily average of 128 images. A team of research assistants manually coded all these materials according to a set of determined rules.

In terms of purposes, 27% of these collected visual works were devoted to criticizing movement opponents by blaming or satirizing them, be they officials, police, progovernment business, or others. Clearly, the prolonged movement had to engage in a constant verbal war with the authorities, debunking their lies, retorting their claims, and deflecting criticism. There were 25% each for announcements or calls to action (e.g., "See you at August 18 Rally in Victoria Park") and values advocacy (democracy, solidarity, etc.). And 8% of the sample served the purpose of explaining and guiding the protest actions.

How these designers portrayed the protest movement provided another insightful clue. There were 12,288 pieces, or 22%, that contained protester images. Excluding those whose intended meanings were vague or uncertain (3,078), 6,846 of them presented peaceful protesters (71%), whereas 1,889 (20%) and 785 (8%) showed disruptive and violent ones, respectively. In the event database, peaceful, disruptive, and violent protests accounted for 65%, 28%, and 6%, respectively (see Chapter 3). While the numerical ranking remains the same, creators of these communicative materials overrepresented the peaceful protests and understated the disruptive and violent ones. Probably out of the intention to win broader sympathy and support, there was clearly a tactic of euphemism, as the more militant and threatening actions were deemphasized for the sake of impression management. In the few cases where violence was graphically presented, designers took care to downplay the use of force. For instance, a half-lion and half-bird creature was used for vigilante violence against proregime mobsters because the Cantonese expression (*siliu* or *siniu*) also suggested the nonexistent species. Instead of throwing a petrol bomb (often referred to as "fire magic" [*fo mo*/*huo mo*]), the hurler in the picture was often holding an umbrella, a bouquet of flowers, or the characters of "Liberate Hong Kong." There were instances in which illustrators attempted to plead for these acts by adding explanations such as "the police's selective enforcement is the cause." Violence was seldom glorified per se. These communicative works were more about what the Be Water Revolution would like to be seen as, rather than what it really was, in other words, an idealized self-portrayal.

Surprisingly, only around one-fifth of these graphics conveyed emotions (8,537 cases). In those materials that revealed emotions, anger (40%) was the most common one, such as those that vowed "never to forget, never to forgive" incidents of police atrocity. Sadness (26%) came in second place, often expressing sorrow for something that had been irretrievably lost, like the expression "Hong Kong is dead." Standing together with a huge crowd of like-minded citizens brought about a shared sense of elation, and such joy (17%) made up the third most frequently seen emotional expression. Fear (14%), such as the apprehension that the city would become another Xinjiang, was the fourth type of emotion. Interestingly, guilt (1%), which motivated movement participation and donations, particularly among overseas Hongkongers, the established middle class, and senior citizens, was rather infrequent. This emotion was clearly not the top priority of concern among creators of these informational materials. The prevalence of anger is largely in sync with the emotional outrage discussed in the Introduction, namely, Hongkongers took to the streets mainly because they were indignant about the government's coercive promotion of an unpopular extradition bill as well as the excessively repressive measures. In addition, grief over the deceased and the injured was another motivation that triggered their protest actions.

Cross-tabulating emotional expressions and protester images generated the following results: sadness and joy shared more affinity with peaceful protests, whereas anger was more correlated with disruptive and violent protests. Among the pieces with peaceful protester images, 384 (39%) were associated with sadness and 210 (21%) with joy, and the corresponding figures for those with images of disruptive and violent protesters were 143 (31%) and 38 (8%). By contrast, only 220 (22%) peaceful protester images presented anger, and the equivalent was 179 (39%) among disruptive and violent protesters. The differential results of emotional responses should not be difficult to understand. Sadness, in the form of grieving and mourning, and joy, such as the empowering feelings of being in solidarity with others, were more likely to come from peaceful actions. Anger projected negative feelings toward opponents and, thus, encouraged more militant actions to take place.

Visual Creation in the Protest Cycle

While humanities and arts researchers tend to examine the intrinsic meanings of these visual works, often focusing on some better-known masterpieces (e.g., see M. Chang 2023), social scientists are more interested in their external functions and roles in the mobilization cycle. Set against the backdrop of the evolving Be Water Revolution, these artistic works by professionals and amateurs represented an intervention into the ongoing contention. As such, the way in which they affected the movement changed according to the context.

Table 4.2 presents the production of these visual materials in the weekly ebb and flow of protest events. In general, the number of these artistic works reflected the intensity of street mobilization, with a significant and positive correlation at 0.6235 throughout the entire period. In other words, more street protests stimulated more visual production, and, reciprocally, more communicative materials encouraged popular participation. Noticeably, the strength of the association between street protests and artistic creation was strongest during the most intensive period between the 38th week and the 49th week, or from two University Battles in mid-November to the onset of the COVID-19 pandemic in late January 2020. Afterward, the association was considerably weakened and no longer statistically significant. Clearly, in the declining phase of the movement, the tempo of visual production began to deviate from that of protest making, suggesting that more artistic intervention was unable to revive protest participation. As discussed in Chapter 3, an improvised movement was also liable to exhaustion and fatigue with the accumulating numbers of arrestees. By contrast, producing informational materials with one's own digital device and uploading them to a social media hub was not a risk-taking act. In fact, committed creators were likely to devote more time to this endeavor precisely because they knew the street protests were on the wane and intended to use their artistic outputs as a means to reverse the movement's decline.

The creation of these visual materials also followed a rise-and-fall pattern. Although a collectively improvised movement was able to draw strength from many unknown and dispersed contributors, such a decentralized pattern of mobilization still remained a finite source whose supply was likely to diminish over a sustained period of intensive deployment. During the

TABLE 4.2 CORRELATION COEFFICIENTS OF VISUAL MATERIALS, PROTESTER IMAGES, AND PROTEST EVENTS (BY WEEK)

	All weeks	16th to 37th weeks	38th to 49th weeks	50th to 71st weeks
Visual and materials and Protest events	0.6235*	0.5663*	0.8909*	0.2197
Peaceful protester images and Protest events	0.3003*	0.3919	−0.1066	−0.0249
Disruptive and violent protester images and Protest events	0.5820*	0.5488*	0.8679*	0.1930

Note: (1) The protest event database started on the week of February 18, 2019, but the Telegram channel began its operation on June 13, or the 16th week according to the former's calendar. (2) $^{*}p = .05$.

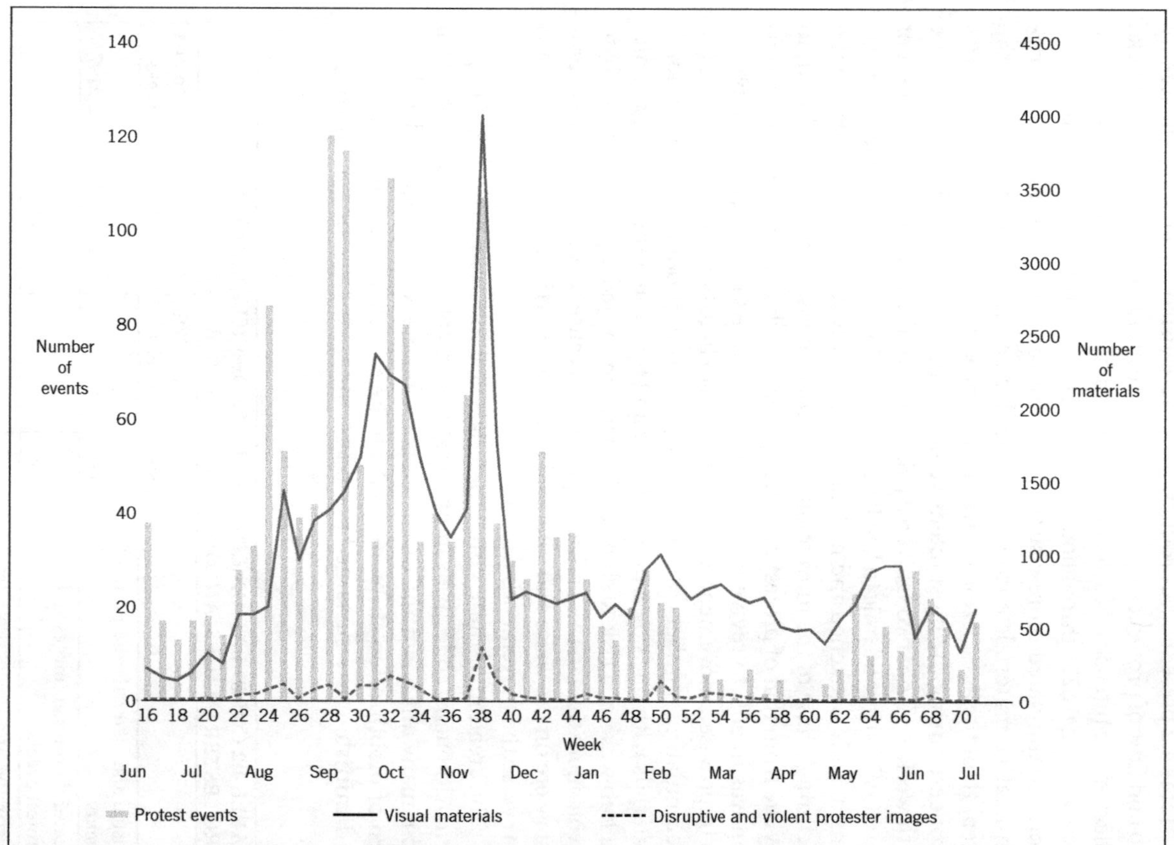

Figure 4.3 Visual materials, protester images, and protest events (by week).

movement, there were three peaks of visual artwork production, which all corresponded to the heightened conflicts (see Figure 4.3). The first peak with 1,435 pieces in the 25th week (August 12–18) happened in the wake of the general strike on August 5. The second peak with 2,225 pieces in the 32nd week (September 30–October 6) coincided with the police shooting of a teenage student with live ammunition on October 1. The last one with 3,995 pieces took place with the onset of two University Battles in the 38th week (November 11–17).

Another interesting finding relates to the image of the protester. Although peaceful protester images (6,884) vastly outnumbered those of disruptive and violent protesters (2,674), the latter were more closely associated with the protest-making rhythm. Table 4.2 indicates that the correlation coefficients with weekly protest events were stronger for disruptive and violent protester images (0.5820) than those with peaceful ones (0.3003). As indicated in the preceding section, visual artists tended to downplay militant actions to gain outsider sympathy, and, here, the stronger association reflected the urgently felt need to justify these unconventional tactics as the conflict intensified.

The New Community and Its Discontents

Despite the remarkable display of creativity, it must be acknowledged that a minority of visual materials bordered on discrimination or hate speech. Within our sample, 112 pieces exhibited misogyny (depicting Carrie Lam and police officers' wives in a pornographic manner), while 381 ostensibly dehumanized opponents of the movement. Needless to say, such problematic content has undermined the movement by offering fodder for its detractors. These instances were an unavoidable consequence of a collectively improvised visual arts archive, reliant on a broad and voluntary pool of contributors.

Moreover, as prodemocracy Hongkongers were solidified into a nationalistic community, liberal-leaning Chinese mainland migrants who initially supported the anti-ELAB protest felt marginalized and eventually chose to stay silent. Some of them still harbored a strong Chinese identity and resented the increasingly vocal proindependence sentiments, while there were others whose lack of Cantonese fluency resulted in unpleasant experiences of discrimination. A mainland migrant who participated in the drafting of the earlier-mentioned anti-ELAB statement became disenchanted as the situation unfolded:

> I am actually not moved by the song "Glory to Hong Kong." My feeling is like I just escaped a national anthem, why should I embrace

> another one? Is it really important to be patriotic? But we know these feelings are best left unsaid. . . . My experience as a new migrant in Hong Kong is very dissonant, and it has become very difficult for Hongkongers and mainlanders to communicate with each other. The movement resulted in an atmosphere that does not tolerate free discussion, and it is becoming like what the CCP is doing in the mainland.

Similarly, while the imagined community of *sauzuk* could be very inclusive, mainland Chinese in the city were not seen as part of it. Hostilities toward mainland students were documented, and even those who were privately sympathetic to the movement felt excluded (Ling 2020; Matthews 2020). While some commentators saw these unfortunate incidents as evidence of xenophobic nativism, what they often neglect was the fact that the anti-ELAB protests were fundamentally a resistance against China's political and judicial colonization (Katy Chan 2021). Moreover, while there were mainland migrants who sympathized and even took part in the protest, many of them explicitly endorsed the ELAB by joining the progovernment rallies or even assaulting protesters, even though their own civil liberties would be jeopardized.

While a rising nationalistic tide during the Be Water Revolution emerged as a strong impetus to cement Hongkongers' unity, mainland migrants who used to support the movement out of liberal convictions felt alienated and marginalized in the process. The difficulties to enlist the support of mainland migrants in the city as well as PRC citizens in the mainland limited the appeal of Hong Kong's Be Water Revolution. During the 2014 Umbrella Movement, Hongkongers' protest was able to elicit solidarity responses from mainland dissidents who were willing to take their personal risk to endorse the city's prodemocracy struggle. But such support was conspicuously absent in 2019. Beijing's mouthpiece fully exploited this vulnerability by portraying Hongkongers' protests as fueled by an "anti-mainlander mentality" in order to stir up domestic "patriotic" sentiment. Consequently, the city's fearless pursuit for freedom inadvertently turned into a cautionary tale about democracy, if not a justification of its autocracy, for the mainland audience.

Conclusion

Hon Lai Chu, a Hong Kong literary writer, observed:

> People always said this was a rootless city in the past. In this summer, the city finally took root, developing out of many intertwined wounds, and the root has become our common identity. (Hon 2022: 342)

The preceding chapter examined the Be Water Revolution as a series of street rallies and demonstrations, whereas this chapter looked at what happened inside participants' minds and the realm of verbalized and visualized expressions. There was a dialectical relationship between people's outward actions and their internal consciousness. Protests happened when they shared the firm determination to promote a desired change, and yet, their acting together was likely to bring about a chemical reaction that in turn affected their own ideas. Visceral experiences of suffering and grieving became intensively transformative as they redefined community membership. The Be Water Revolution began as an anti-ELAB resistance to preserve the city's rule of law, but the government's intransigence and repression triggered a great awakening as to what it meant to be Hongkongers. In the pitched battles in the street and over the numerous declarations, statements, symbolized actions, and graphic creations, a political community was born and asserted its newly acquired agency.

This chapter has surveyed the plethora of discursive, dramaturgic, musical, and graphic interventions. Similar to street protests, the outburst of these creative productions followed the pattern of collective improvisation, heavily relying on anonymous crowdsourcing and mixed use of online and offline connections. The joint result of these large-scale peer productions in the realm of consciousness was no less spectacular than a demonstration of two million participants or a sixty-kilometer human chain. Prodemocracy Hongkongers were united by brotherly and sisterly *sauzuk* connections that were fortified by the shared experiences of suffering. New group identities emerged, intending to carve out their space in the new community. A commercial city now had its sacred site (Lion Rock) and even an underground national anthem.

It is true that the many forms of activism this chapter analyzed were symbolic, rhetorical, and discursive, existing only in the sphere of communication and imagination. But they should not be seen merely as an auxiliary to or a secondary reflection of physical protests: they were performative in the sense of inventing and using ideas in order to change the world. Once they were successfully performed, they were embodied and became part of reality. As such, they had abiding power even when street actions died down in the NSL-ruled Hong Kong. In fact, the first protester convicted by the NSL was a motorcyclist who carried a "Liberate Hong Kong, Revolution of Our Time" flag on July 1, 2020. The defendant was given a previously unthinkable heavy sentence of nine years for his "act to incite others to secession" and "acts of terrorism."[20] A protest slogan that only became popular and well accepted in 2019 was later officially deemed secessionist and an act of "terrorism"—revealing how explosive these ideas were to the regime. Similarly, in June 2023, the SAR government filed a legal request for the court to ban the playing of "Glory to Hong Kong" on all digital platforms, which also testified to the staying power of these movement-inspired creations. Apparently, free thought has the magic power to outlast physical actions, even though it appears immaterial, free floating, and detached from reality. The following two chapters further examine how these unfulfilled ideas and the promise of a new community continue to inspire activists abroad and at home.

5

Global Fronts

From a British colony to a Chinese SAR, Hong Kong has always been "an interface" between China and the rest of the world (Duara 2016).* Since its retrocession in 1997, the PRC accepted the modus vivendi of "high-degree autonomy" for the city because it needed an economic conduit for Western capital, goods, and technology (Hung 2022a). However, when Beijing's rulers became emboldened enough to embark on a revisionist agenda of the international order, the hitherto tolerance of the city's civil liberty and political freedom came under pressure. Since the announcement of ELAB in February 2019, officials or representatives of the United States, the United Kingdom, the European Union, Canada, and Taiwan had expressed their grave concerns. Prior to the eruption of the Be Water Revolution in June, prodemocratic politicians visited Taiwan and the United States to publicize their opposition.

The Taiwanese government was quick to respond to the escalation of the ELAB dispute as the legal revision allegedly sought to address an unsolved murder in Taiwan, and the amendment speciously claimed the self-governing democratic island Taiwan was part of the PRC's territory. Taiwan's pres-

* Portions of this chapter previously appeared as Ming-sho Ho, "Hongkongers' International Front: Diaspora Activism during and after the 2019 Anti-Extradition Protest," *Journal of Contemporary Asia* 54 (2): 238–59. Available at https://doi.org/10.1080/00472336.2023.2168208, © 2023 Journal of Contemporary Asia, Reproduced by permission of Taylor & Francis Group, tandfonline.com.

ident Tsai Ing-wen expressed support for the opposition movement in her social media posts. On June 17, 2019, Taiwan's lawmakers announced an official statement condemning the Hong Kong government's crackdown and urged the withdrawal of the ELAB. While Taiwan was the closest international stakeholder in Hong Kong's ELAB controversy, other countries were also involved because of their economic and political stakes in the city. This chapter examines the transboundary operations of the Be Water Revolution, including the city-based diplomacy, diaspora activism, and the offshore responses to the waves of exiles and migration.

Social movements have been known to habitually traverse national boundaries since their advent in modernity. The British and American abolitionists were among the first pioneers that "invented social movements" as a modern form of contentious politics with their efforts to end the transatlantic slave trade in the late eighteenth century (Tilly 2004: 32–33). Leveraging international pressure to advance a domestic reform agenda has long been a common practice among movement advocates (Keck and Sikkink 1998). Globalization and regional integration created various supranational arenas where activists could make their voices heard (Marks and McAdam 1999; J. Smith 2008). Furthermore, diaspora communities, the overseas compatriots that retained the allegiance to their places of origin, have played a multifaceted and significant role, especially when these migrants were able to enjoy personal safety and political freedom (Koinova and Karabegović 2020; Moss 2022). Due to repression in the PRC, the overseas Chinese dissident community has historically been a thorn in Beijing's side. The Hong Kong–educated Sun Yat-sen famously claimed overseas Chinese were "the mother" of the Republican Revolution that overthrew the last imperial dynasty in 1911. This pattern continued after the communist revolution in 1949, as evidenced in the cases of the overseas Taiwan independence movement (Fleischauer 2016), post-Tiananmen dissidents (He 2014), and Falun Gong members (Junker 2019).

Here, Hong Kong's role as a global hub populated by well-connected citizens sheds light on the extent that a social movement thoroughly utilized its international linkages. Moreover, diaspora mobilization is predicated on the existence of a native identity; yet, in this case, the emotional attachment to the home city and the political assertion of its unique identity were mostly forged during the Be Water Revolution (see Chapter 4). Despite its recent vintage, such ideational forces released a powerful torrent that continued to vibrate even after the forced ceasing of street protests in the home city. This chapter examines a host of consequential acts of cross-border improvisation, which can be divided into (1) a city-based diplomacy to oppose the ELAB, (2) diaspora mobilization on the part of overseas compatriots, and (3) the post-NSL diaspora activism continuing the city's prodemocracy campaign.

Advocating on a Global Stage

Edged between contending powers, Hong Kong's leaders have long known the city's political and economic interests rested upon a delicate international balance of forces. During the Sino-British negotiation in 1982–1984, a group of native leaders shuttled between Beijing and London to represent the citizens' voices, and yet their embryonic efforts at city-based diplomacy failed to bear fruit as Hongkongers were ultimately excluded from the negotiation table over their own future (S. Chung 2001: 62–79). In the 1990s, the city's nascent prodemocracy movement continued the effort of international advocacy in the hope that Beijing would duly respect the promise of high-degree autonomy. Martin Lee, the widely acknowledged father of Hong Kong democracy, was a frequent visitor to Washington, DC, where he developed personal ties with American politicians. Lee praised the 1992 United States–Hong Kong Policy Act that defined the city as a separate territory from mainland China in terms of immigration, commerce, and other issues. Following the dominant thought at the time that economic liberalization brought about political democratization or the doctrine of "constructive engagement" (Hung 2022b: 22), Lee urged the United States to delink human rights concerns from trade with China, contributing to the historical decision of the Clinton administration to permanently grant most-favorable-nation status to the PRC in 1994.

In the first few days of the Umbrella Movement in 2014, student leaders decided to adopt a self-limiting strategy by rejecting the widely circulated moniker "Umbrella Revolution" to avoid association with the worldwide "color revolutions" that Beijing found unpalatable (M. Ho 2019: 133). In line with such tactical moderation, the Umbrella leadership initially did not engage with foreign media to avoid giving credence to Beijing's hackneyed accusations of "black hands" and "foreign interference" (Law 2021: 118–19). They also chose not to eagerly solicit international support, even though the image of polite and civilized protests garnered overwhelmingly positive coverage in Western media. Nevertheless, in its wake, the younger generation of Hong Kong's prodemocracy movement, such as Joshua Wong, was able to establish an Asia-wide transnational network, connecting young activists in Taiwan, Thailand, Japan, Malaysia, and beyond (M. Ho 2019: 204; Phattharathanasut 2024; Wasserstrom 2023), planting the seeds for the #MilkTeaAlliance.

Understanding that the city's prodemocracy force has long operated its overseas campaign, it was during the Be Water Revolution that the so-called international front (*gwokzaisin/guojixian*) entered popular discourse, reflecting a widespread understanding among participants that they needed to enlist more global support in their fight against the ELAB. A survey in August 2019 indicated nearly 70% of Hongkongers believed that the international community's response could force the SAR government to concede to the movement demands (F. Lee 2023: 237). As Hongkongers improvised their international campaigns, their demands became more radical and participants more diversified. In tandem with the drive to improvise collectively, nonelites now joined the diplomatic efforts on the world's stage.

"If We Burn, You Burn with Us"

The catchy line from the Hollywood movie *The Hunger Games* has a pithy Cantonese equivalent *laam caau* (mutual destruction), a poker lingo meaning the assured mutual loss. In the wake of the Umbrella Movement, the localist camp circulated the idea of "scorched earth policy" (*ziutouleon/jiaotulun*), advocating for more drastic measures to resist Beijing's encroachment on the city. They contended that the PRC's reliance on Hong Kong as an economic intermediary to the world was its fatal weakness and, as such, the threat to the city's financial viability could be utilized against the PRC's growing interference. Departing from Martin Lee's thinking in the 1990s, they grew disenchanted with the presumed liberalizing effect of international trade. They contended that should the United States annul the Hong Kong Policy Act, Chinese companies would forfeit a conduit to purchase high-tech products from the West, and the Chinese currency (*renminbi*) would no longer have an offshore clearinghouse since it was not freely convertible.

In early June 2019, Finn Lau, then a twenty-six-year-old surveyor, used the internet ID "I want *laam caau*" to pitch the idea that ELAB opponents should write letters to American, British, and Canadian governments to demand the cancellation of SAR officials' foreign passports. The suggestion went viral, and *laam caau* became a widely used vocabulary during the Be Water Revolution. Lau later explained his inspiration from witnessing the storm stirred up by a Boston-based student article, "I Am from Hong Kong, Not China," published in May 2019, which was vehemently denounced by PRC overseas students. The lesson Lau learned was that the international front had a "low participation threshold" and did not necessarily require political celebrities with the caliber of Martin Lee and Joshua Wong (DB Channel 2022: 53–54). With the emergence of the *laam caau* narrative, the immediate psychological effect was that protesters were no longer willing to accept the previous self-imposed moderation, and, instead, they deliberately disregarded Beijing's dislike for "foreign intervention" by actively soliciting Western governments for proactive actions against the city's political leaders.

The G20 Osaka Summit on June 28–29, 2019, provided a ready international stage for Hongkongers to broadcast their opposition to the ELAB. A few days earlier, a post was made by the user "Campbell Macaroni" to a crowdfunding project to place advertisements in major international news outlets. Originally, the anonymous team aimed to raise HK$3 million (US$382,657), but within just eleven hours they received HK$6.73 million (US$858,427) in donations. On the next day, they installed full-page advertisements in ten leading newspapers, including the *New York Times*, *Washington Post*, *Financial Times*, and so on (22 Hongkongers 2019: 113–14). The person who created the "Campbell Macaroni" account was Anna Kwok, then a twenty-two-year-old student in New York. As she revealed later, the whole team amounted to around two hundred participants spread across different time zones. Tasks such as accounting, contracting, graphic design, writing, and so on, were entrusted to people who had never met in person before. As such, many participants thought Kwok was a male, and she was referred to as "Campbell Brother" for a long time.[1]

Both Finn Lau and Anna Kwok remained anonymously active on the international front for a while until their true identities were revealed, involuntarily or willingly. Lau was a political novice. When he made the first foray, "He had no network, resources, history of political organizing, or social circle" (Mahtani and McLaughlin 2023: 183). By contrast, Kwok has been actively engaged since her middle school student years. Nevertheless, both initiated their efforts without working with preexisting organizations, and their teams were assembled via personal networks, involving online and offline communications. Such peer production appeared ideally suited for transnational collaboration, because participants were scattered in different countries, and they could contribute their local knowledge to the team effort.

Another interviewee Gina was involved in a different international front project, and her experience revealed how transborder improvisation worked. Gina had been working as a newspaper journalist in Hong Kong and later joined the staff of an opposition lawmaker. She went to London for her graduate study one year before the Be Water Revolution erupted. Shocked by the June 12 crackdown, a group of Hong Kong's animators immediately created a short video clip to publicize the movement's major demands. To seize the opportunity of the G20 Summit, Gina was given the task of translating and dubbing the video into different languages. Her offshore location allowed her to recruit different language speakers for this project, especially from her fellow graduate students. In the end, there were twenty-four language versions for the animation, including Filipino and Indonesian (for migrant workers in Hong Kong) and Urdu (for Southeast Asian Hongkongers). In addition, she also volunteered as the admin for the YouTube channel that hosted this video content because she appeared less exposed to risks than those Hong Kong–based creators.[2] Gina's previous experience made her a trustworthy partner for those politically engaged animation artists, and her London base allowed her to broaden the international audience safely. In short, improvising for the international front also involved making innovative use of interpersonal ties as well as building new working relationships.

Protest-Making for a Distant Audience

A protest action typically proceeds with the domestic targets and audiences in mind; Hong Kong's Be Water Revolution followed the same logic, as the majority of protest targets were first the SAR government, politicians, and police officers and later progovernment businesses. Yet, in line with the *laam caau* philosophy that sought to evoke responses from foreign governments, fifteen rallies and demonstrations emerged from June 2019 to January 2020 that were specifically orchestrated with an international audience in mind. Characteristically, all these protest events were peaceful, tactically designed as a charm offensive to woo international observers. The dense presence of foreign diplomatic corps in Hong Kong provided a ready-to-use backdrop for these actions. On June 26, around fifteen hundred demonstrators joined a marathon petition at nineteen foreign consulates in response to an initiative from a Telegram group. The action was part of the international campaign that aimed to use the occasion of the G20 Summit. Subsequently, there were four protest events held in the British consulate and one each in the American and Indonesian consulates. Indonesia was not a typical "Western" country that Hongkongers would appeal to. It was related to a police shooting incident that led to loss of vision in one eye of an Indonesian reporter on September 29. Since her legal actions were repeatedly stonewalled by the SAR government, migrant worker organizations in Hong Kong lodged a protest to demand a response from her home government.

The largest event, "Thanksgiving Day Rally," took place on November 28, which purportedly attracted an attendance of one hundred thousand people. The gathering was designed to express gratitude for the recent passage of the Hong Kong Human Rights and Democracy Act (authorizing the sanctions against human rights violators) and the PROTECT Hong Kong Act (banning the export of lethal weapons to Hong Kong). The event began with one-minute of silent mourning for the deceased, which was then followed by the singing of the American national anthem as participants turned on their cell phone flashlights. Such a symbolic gesture was clearly choreographed for the consumption of an American audience, with the expected angry reaction from PRC officials. In addition to these events that specifically addressed distant audiences, there were forty-five reported activities of carrying foreign country national flags or playing their national anthems in the 1,770 protest events of the same time span. In addition to the Union Jack and Stars and Stripes, protesters also brought the flags of the Republic of China (Taiwan) on the national day (October 10) and those of Catalonia, since its pro-independence activists also paralyzed the airport, claiming the inspiration from Hong Kong.

Among the fifteen internationally facing events, five were initiated by ad hoc and anonymous online teams, or in the "no main stage" manner, while the rest were sponsored by preexisting political, student, and professional organizations. Among the organizational sponsors, the CHRF launched a rally on June 26 that attracted more than ten thousand participants. The Hong Kong Higher Institutions International Affairs Delegation (HKIAD), a new outfit of students formed in July, also played a significant role. HKIAD represented a creative response from student activists who found themselves no longer able to enjoy the spotlight as they used to during the Umbrella Movement. While many university students actively joined the ranks of frontline militants, first-aiders, and scouts, they did not present a collective voice (M. Ho and Wan 2023). An interviewed university student association leader acknowledged their diminished role in Hong Kong's political movement, but he insisted that students still had some influence, especially in communicating localist ideas and persuading moderate supporters to tolerate militant actions. There was an organizational vacuum for student activists, too. The post-Umbrella HKFS suffered from a walkout wave and found it difficult to represent the city's students, even though the organization still possessed considerable assets. As such, twelve university student associations jointly formed the HKIAD, while, at the same time, HKFS contributed its financial resources from behind.

In many aspects, HKIAD turned out to be a successful intervention by students to avert their marginalization in a movement that seemed to proceed without a figurehead leadership. HKIAD sponsored two major events, the aforementioned Thanksgiving Day Rally and another one on August 16 (estimated to have attracted sixty thousand participants), which were the largest among these internationally facing events. Externally, HKIAD also spearheaded the efforts to represent the city on the world stage, as its delegates traveled to Australia, Germany, Taiwan, and the United Kingdom within the first few months of its establishment. HKIAD's global visibility reached an apex during the U.S. congressional hearing on September 17, as the student representative Sunny Cheung joined hands with Joshua Wong, Denise Ho (an activist pop singer), and Sharon Hom (a New York–based legal expert) as the testimony witnesses.

The successful reinventing of student activism, and their forays into global diplomacy, indicates that preexisting organizations were not completely obsolete or paralyzed in a decentralized movement. Their reputation, personal connections, economic assets, and other resources still mattered, and if rightly retrofitted to meet the emerging circumstances, they were capable of garnering international attention in the way that anonymous and online collaboration was unable to. The same logic applies to celebrity leaders like Joshua Wong. Although start-up efforts led by Finn Lau and Anna Kwok accelerated tactical innovation by moving beyond the conventional thinking that typically constrained preexisting organizations and leaders, their global operations largely remained anonymous, and the lack of name recognition and social legitimacy limited the scope of their actions.

Prior to his anticipated imprisonment in November 2020, Joshua Wong posted a summary report of his recent activities on his Facebook account, which included fourteen op-ed contributions in the international media, such as *Financial Times* and *Washington Post*, thirteen lectures in Cambridge, Oxford, and other international locations, and visits to twenty countries for movement advocacy. In addition, he also voiced his support for prodemocracy protests in Belarus and Thailand as well as Taiwan's bid for the World Health Organization membership. Wong wrote letters to companies like Apple and Sony to warn against their technological products being used for political repression.[3]

Undoubtedly, Joshua Wong has become Hong Kong's de facto ambassador-at-large for its antiauthoritarian struggle and his formidable global presence could in no way be outsourced or delegated to other leaders of lower stature, let alone anonymous online teams. As one of Wong's closest allies observed, foreign parliamentarians loved to meet him and shared their meeting photos on social media. "If they knew Joshua was not coming, they just sent staff to see us."

Agnes Chow was Joshua Wong's ally and played a particularly important role in the campaign in Japan, as her language fluency and passion for the ACG culture attracted many supporters in the country. During the Be Water Revolution, Agnes Chow used her YouTube channel with three hundred thousand followers to broadcast the movement message.[4] As such, after she was arrested for the second time in August 2020, Japanese netizens launched a #FreeAgnes campaign and politicians expressed the concern for her safety.

Recognizing that the Be Water Revolution would not provide a main stage for him, Joshua Wong willingly gave up the impossible role of leading the protest crowd. By launching his globe-trotting mission, he not only found an irreplaceable niche position for himself but also created more arenas where Hong Kong's prodemocracy activists could gain additional international spotlight. Similarly, Agnes Chow spoke louder than any officials from Hong Kong in Japan. As indicated by the case of HKIAD, movement organizations and leaders were able to improvise successfully as long as they could nimbly adjust and respond to the ever-changing movement dynamics.

Hong Kong's Diaspora Communities

In addition to home-based actors, Hong Kong's far-flung overseas communities[5] were an integral part in the making of the international front. Postwar Hong Kong was a city of immigrants escaping the political turmoil in the mainland, and the city also generated its own waves of emigrants. In particular, the 1989 Tiananmen Massacre sent a shudder down the spine of the city residents, fearing that communist tanks would one day roll into their city. Middle-class Hongkongers emigrated to Canada, Australia, the United States, and other countries in droves, and it was estimated that nearly eight hundred thousand had left by 1997. After obtaining foreign citizenship, around five hundred thousand migrants returned to their home city (Sussman 2010: 6).

The influx of Hong Kong's migrants changed the composition of overseas ethnic Chinese communities. Although many Chinatowns in Western cities were established by Cantonese-speaking pioneers (Sinn 2014), the newcomer Hongkongers were largely middle class with better English fluency and more cosmopolitan values than previous Chinese migrants (Mitchell 1999). These Hongkongers continued to identify themselves as Chinese, and yet, there existed a distinctive, albeit unarticulated feeling of their "Hong Kong identity" (B. Wong 1994: 249). The Tiananmen incident also gave birth to a number of Hongkongers-only migrant associations. Since the candlelight vigil commemoration had become an iconic annual ritual in the city, its overseas migrants continued this political tradition, thus planting a demarcation line between Hongkongers and the mainland Chinese. As a consequence, the Alliance of Hong Kong Chinese in America, with chapters in California, New York, Chicago, Los Angeles, and Washington, DC, emerged across the United States (Lary and Luk 1994: 155).

With the fading of the Tiananmen memory and the attraction of growing business opportunities in China, many of these Hongkonger immigrant associations ceased to be active. By the time of Hong Kong's Umbrella Movement in 2014, many overseas Hongkongers found it necessary to set up new organizations, such as NY4HK (New York), the Hong Kong Overseas Alliance (London), and the Alliance of Hongkongers in Japan Tokyo Branch. But again, as Hong Kong's subsequent prodemocracy movement was sluggish, these organizations—many of which only existed online—ceased to be active.

Some interviewees said that Hongkonger migrants tended to "shun in-group association" as they intended to assimilate into their host societies. In English-speaking countries, university-educated Hongkongers found it easier to blend into the mainstream culture because they could continue their professional jobs, whereas in Taiwan, Mandarin fluency was not a challenge for younger Hongkongers who grew up in the posthandover years and were more exposed to Mandarin in education and entertainment. It was the eruption of the Be Water Revolution that spurred the formation of new overseas immigrant associations and galvanized those who were previously apathetic about politics. In some cities, there were no preexisting Hongkonger associations, and new organizations emerged, sometimes after a haphazardly organized protest rally. In Paris, a housewife from Hong Kong created a Facebook event page for a rally, and the announcement was circulated in online chat groups and Facebook fan pages in early June 2019. Unexpectedly, the event attracted more than one hundred participants who were previously unknown to each other. After the rally, around fifty Hongkongers decided to gather in a nearby café, thus laying the foundation of En Solidarité avec Hongkong.

Taiwan had adopted preferential treatment for Hong Kong immigrants and students. Since Taiwan's government applied the same policy to students from both Hong Kong and Macao, these students tended to join the same university-based associations. However, Macanese students were more politically conservative, meaning that the preexisting student clubs failed to become vehicles for protest mobilization. Thus, Hong Kong students in Taiwan chose to announce on social media that they would stage their first protest in early June 2019, rather than through university-based organizations. As the event gathered hundreds of youthful participants the students soon established a new organization later called Hong Kong Outlanders. The fact that existing overseas Hong Kong student associations failed to be the launchpad for the international front was not limited to Taiwan only. A Melbourne-based student noticed that many Hongkongers in Australia migrated at an early age, so they did not share the feeling of belonging. Hence, many Australian student associations with the name of Hong Kong declined to join the petition (To Freedom Committee 2020: 292–96). Another student I interviewed in the United States also noticed that his university's Hong Kong student association needed to fundraise from its established alumni who were generally more conservative. As such, it was difficult to mobilize such apolitical organizations for the movement's purpose.

In some cities, the protest movement literally generated communities of Hongkongers that did not exist before. In Zurich, a Swiss supporter observed:

> Unlike Taiwanese, Vietnamese, or Chinese, Hongkongers just worked here, or they got married and raised kids without mutual interaction. They came to know each other at this photo exhibition [about the anti-ELAB movement in September 2019]. They were conversing in Cantonese, which was probably the first time they ever did that in

> Switzerland. They later organized a WhatsApp chat group and held a gathering and a hiking activity. Our photography exhibition curating team did not expect this, and neither did Hongkongers.

An Oslo-based participant mentioned a similar experience. To hold a solidarity rally, he began to search for local Hongkongers on Facebook and was surprised to find many compatriots in Norway.

In short, the emergence of a separate Hongkonger identity and their immigrant organizations were punctuated by political incidents in their home city. Like the 1989 Tiananmen incident and the 2014 Umbrella Movement, the 2019 anti-ELAB movement stimulated a new wave of activities among overseas Hongkongers. This had two notable features. First, while newer organizations emerged in large metropolitan areas where there had been a long presence of migrants from Hong Kong, the wave of organizing also swept through smaller cities like Brisbane and Adelaide, in Australia, and unexpected places like Texas in the United States, the Netherlands, and Poland. Second, a more prominent Hong Kong identity surged along with an aspiration for self-determination and political separation from the PRC. Gone was the post-Tiananmen era when overseas Hongkongers campaigned as good faith patriots for China's democratization; now, among the newer generation of diaspora activists, the desire for political independence was prevalent. A study of Hongkonger Americans found that Cantonese fluency and the frequency of homeward communication are not correlated with protest participation, but the salience of Hong Kong identity turned out to be a significant factor (Shum 2023).

No International Main Stage

On the home front, the Be Water Revolution proceeded as a decentralized movement, and diaspora activisms appeared to replicate the same pattern, as their cross-border and local connections were mostly ad hoc and loose, at times laden with tensions. In 2019, three synchronized global rallies emerged that connected Hong Kong with twenty-two cities (June 12), thirty-six cities (August 17–18), and sixty-five cities (September 29). There were also three waves of crowdfunding campaigns to place advertisements in international newspapers on June 28 (the G20 Summit), August 19, and October 1. These actions did not emanate from a centralized leadership, but were coordinated by anonymous online teams, such as Stand with Hong Kong, Hong Kong Liberty (of Finn Lau), and G20 Team (of Anna Kwok). Overseas Hongkongers were closely observing the unfolding of events in Hong Kong and responded with in situ improvisation. As an Amsterdam-based activist explained:

> Groups in Europe are spontaneously formed. We watched what other places were doing because we did not have organizing experience. We know of their existence and sometimes contact them. I know who is in charge in Germany, France, and Northern Europe, but most of the activities are launched on our own initiative.

In several cities, more than one organization formed, each with its own preferred style of action. When holding a joint rally or demonstration, frictions emerged over any number of things: the choice of sites, slogans ("Hong Kong Independence" too radical for the moderates), and songs ("Under the Lion Rock" too old-fashioned for the younger generation) and whether to allow speakers to wear face masks to hide their identities (a major concern for students, but not for permanent residents or naturalized immigrants). These disagreements then resulted in splits or separate actions. In addition to these tactical disputes, some disputes involved deeper ideological contrasts. For instance, Lausan was a U.S.-based organization, originally from New York City, which self-consciously pursued "decolonial leftist politics" (Liu et al. 2022), whereas NY4HK managed to stay in the political mainstream by carefully maintaining a bipartisan stance. At a protest rally at the city's PRC consulate, a Lausan organizer spoke about solidarity with Black Lives Matter (BLM) and invited Filipinos to share their story of resistance to their authoritarian president Rodrigo Duterte. Immediately afterward, she received a barrage of criticisms from NY4HK supporters, which she describes this way:

> Why were there so many solidarity speakers? Why weren't there more Hongkongers taking the podium? Why did you not invite Taiwanese and Tibetans? Why did I talk about BLM on the stage? . . . Lausan is the only Hong Kong organization expressly supporting BLM, unfortunately so till now. People are still angry about Lausan's activities with BLM.

While Lausan activists were dedicating their efforts to coalition building with progressive forces, other participants deemed these gestures an unnecessary distraction, if not a dangerous flirtation with an extreme fringe that could jeopardize the public image of their movement. This incident indicates that an emerging Hong Kong identity connected global diaspora communities, yet this was not enough to prevent occasional tactical disputes.

The polycentric nature of diaspora activism means that overseas activists had to improvise with their own wit. With their eyes glued to their home city's ongoing street protests, they constantly adjusted their roles. As street protests grew more intense and protective equipment for demonstrators became scarce in Honk Kong, it was the diaspora communities that became a source of supplies. In Taiwan, where scooters have long been a popular vehicle for transportation, collecting motorcycle helmets and shipping them to Hong Kong–based protesters appeared to be an obvious choice. Both in Taipei and Kaohsiung, such donation drives emerged, and the number of collected helmets far exceeded the original expectation of organizers.

Some overseas Hongkongers chose to fly back to join street demonstrations. One interviewed Hongkonger marriage migrant in Taiwan went back for weekend protests continuously for two months. During the 2019 summer vacation, many overseas students returned and gained firsthand experience with the ongoing protest. Perhaps the high tide of overseas Hongkongers' proactive actions culminated in a proposed global rally to cast votes in the Legislative Council election originally scheduled for September 2020. The campaign aimed to replicate the prodemocracy camp's landslide victory in the district council election of November 2019. The planners had recruited more than two thousand participants in the United States and Canada and began to negotiate charter flights that included a layover in Taiwan. However, as the Hong Kong government postponed the election by citing COVID-19 as an excuse, this plan was aborted.

With the increasing arrests, the number of protesters fleeing prosecution increased. Taiwan played a crucial role in the escape route for those endangered activists. The Taipei–Hong Kong route had high traffic, and the journey was less than two hours. Hongkongers could enter Taiwan with a tourist visa easily available through online application. As such, Taiwan often became the first stop for Hong Kong's political refugees before embarking on their further journeys. The Taiwan Hong Kong Association was legally registered in 2020 to provide assistance to those who chose to settle in Taiwan. Similarly, Haven Assistance (with participation from activists in Taiwan, the United Kingdom, the United States, and Germany), Hongkongers in Britain, Hongkonger in Deutschland e.V. (Germany), and Walk with Hong Kong (San Francisco) were all recent creations that sought to serve newly arrived Hongkongers.

Young escapees from Hong Kong needed all kinds of assistance. Some arrived with physical wounds and psychological trauma, and some had already become estranged from their families during the protests. Finding accommodation, applying for residence permits, resuming studies, or getting new jobs required financial resources and assistance. Many already-settled Hong Kong migrants and volunteers provided this assistance. As for middle-aged migrants with families, an effort to build community ties with the "yellow economic circle" emerged in Taiwan and other countries. These attempts replicated the economic campaign to patronize promovement stores in Hong Kong. While the campaign participants in Hong Kong aimed at creating a self-sustaining prodemocracy ecology of small businesses, overseas counterparts were more geared toward strengthening ties among Hong Kong's diaspora communities. With this goal in mind, a Chicago-based activist created an online global directory that listed all kinds of business venues operated by Hongkongers in six countries.[6]

Knowing that Hong Kong's political future is inseparably bound to what happens in China, overseas campaigners engaged in a plethora of activities to counter the PRC's authoritarian expansion. With Hong Kong's protest losing the mass media's attention, campaigners had to find new issues to engage with. Since the presence of a coercive Beijing was ubiquitously felt, overseas Hongkonger activists could easily pick an issue from their surroundings. For instance, a Germany-based campaigner eagerly joined a municipal movement against the Chinese purchase of a nearby castle. Some Hongkonger Bostonians took part in a weekly vigil against a Confucius Institute at a suburban university, considering the PRC-funded language teaching institution as part of a pernicious influence campaign. They also joined the monthly Outreach for Taiwan activity at Harvard Square to show their solidarity with the threatened island democracy. London's D4HK participants joined the campaign to pressure the U.K. government to reject the use of Huawei communication equipment and to raise public awareness of privacy concerns with Chinese-made platforms such as Zoom, WeChat, and TikTok. In Australia, Canberra Hong Kong Concern activists joined a Uighur-led campaign to boycott the Beijing 2022 Winter Olympics. Many Taipei-based Hongkongers were active in the local #MilkTeaAlliance, in collaboration with Thai and Burmese activists. Furthermore, in several Taipei-based solidarity events with Ukrainians after the Russian invasion in February 2022, the Black Bauhinia flag, which symbolized Hongkongers' resistance, was constantly seen.

Finally, a self-conscious effort emerged to strengthen overseas communities. In the 2020 U.S. Census, campaigners encouraged writing in "Hongkonger" in the category of ethnicity, rather than choosing the existing option "Chinese." A similar campaign followed for the 2021 Australian Census, where, in addition to ethnic labels, Australian Hongkongers were asked to write in their home city and choose Cantonese as the frequently used language. As a result, Cantonese emerged as the fourth most used language in Australia.

In short, Hong Kong's overseas activists proceeded in step with the evolution of the domestic front. As street protests as well as political freedom were stamped out in the home city, overseas campaigners transitioned from proactive to supportive roles. From the original concern over Hong Kong's deteriorating civil liberties, these activists broadened their horizons to include China sanctions and branched out to a wide array of issue campaigns that confronted China's global projection of sharp power.

The Specter of a Global China

During the 2014 Umbrella Movement, the Chinese government was on the defensive as Hongkongers' peaceful protest had won the global sympathy. Five years later, the PRC was able to turn the table by mounting an offensive campaign to smear and intimidate Hongkonger campaigners with its honed-in skills in disinformation warfare. In particular, as the Be Water Revolution proceeded with some violent acts, it provided a useful talking point for the PRC propaganda machine to portray the movement as "lawless" and "terroristic." In the West, Chinese-language newspapers often printed pro-PRC advertisements endorsed by overseas Chinese associations.

The greatest threat to Hong Kong's diaspora activists emanated from pro-PRC Chinese hostility. Around the globe, solidarity rallies and demonstrations by Hongkongers met with countermobilization by the Chinese who shouted patriotic slogans, sang the PRC national anthem, and sometimes destroyed Hongkongers' placards and posters or forcefully silenced speakers. Occasionally, physical confrontations and brawls ensued. Even academic forums held in universities saw the swarming of so-called Little Pink students who made ultranationalistic remarks to disrupt the events and discredit the solidarity events. Many of the Hongkonger interviewees firmly believed that Chinese embassies and consulates were masterminding from behind as a part of the PRC's global strategy to counter Hong Kong's antiauthoritarian struggle.[7] In a gathering in New York City in August 2019, one Hongkonger activist described their cautious preparation:

> Our event was to be held in Confucius Plaza of Chinatown, and we knew Chinese would be there. We had people who joined their WeChat group to monitor the discussion. The night before, someone said he would bring a gun and kill Hong Kong independence activists. We immediately reported the case to the New York Police Department.

On these occasions, Hongkongers were typically outnumbered by pro-PRC Chinese. They generally applied for permission for outdoor events in advance and relied on the police's on-site management to keep Chinese hecklers at a distance. Rowdy provocations from pro-PRC Chinese caused personal safety concerns for some participants, with the organizers of a gathering in Helsinki hiring private security guards for additional protection. While these hostile measures from pro-PRC Chinese intimidated some potential participants into not taking part, they tended to backfire by bringing more publicity to Hong Kong's movement, which was exactly what overseas campaigners hoped to achieve. Speaking of a violent episode at the University of

Queensland in July 2019, where pro-PRC Chinese physically assaulted Hongkonger protesters, a Brisbane-based activist said:

> The incident was widely known. It was reported in the national TV news and helped more Australians to know the Hong Kong issue. Frankly, we should thank these Chinese nationalists as they helped us to receive media attention. Most Australian citizens would ask themselves why such an incident happened in their land. Aren't we still a democratic country?

A Vancouver-based activist shared a similar view. According to him, these disruptive behaviors ended up being counterproductive because they violated Canada's core values such as freedom of speech. He stated: "Little Pinks' actions actually alarmed Canadians, reminding them the Hong Kong problem is right there, beside them."

Far from a passive victim of pro-PRC violence, Hongkonger activists were sometimes able to deploy their creative responses. For instance, Montreal-based Hongkongers signed up for the city's pride parade in August 2019, and yet, prior to the event, the host abruptly canceled their registration citing a vague security concern. They believed the Chinese consulate was pulling the string from behind. They decided to hold a parallel event to advocate for Hong Kong's democratization as well as LGBTQ+ rights on the same day. As they emphasized, "the opposition to bullying" was the shared demand of both Hongkongers and sexual minorities. This episode was reported in the national news media; if they had been able to join the pride parade as originally planned, their voices would probably not have reached a nationwide audience in Canada.[8]

Nevertheless, the fear of being personally harassed lingered. Some PRC supporters took photographs of Hongkonger demonstrators and uploaded these images to chat groups seeking identifying information. Some members of the Hongkonger opposition made it a routine to practice the art of evading stalkers. One of my interviewees in a Taipei café insisted on relocating to another place midway through our conversation because she suspected eavesdropping from a guest at the neighboring table. Some interviewees said they always changed clothes after a rally or avoided returning home directly, taking extra train stops and then circling back. Their leaders were disproportionately targeted. An Ottawa-based campaigner shared her experience:

> Two days after the launching ceremony of our organization, I received a blackmail threat in a phone call in the hotel where I stayed but which was not booked under my name. On WeChat, people doxed me [pub-

> licly providing personally identifiable information], shared my personal photo, and called me a traitor to the Chinese race. I often received intimidating messages, and I thought it was possible that my phone had been tapped. Our website has been attacked many times. I reported these incidents to the police, and they registered the case without really being helpful.

The PRC's overseas influence campaign capabilities evolved to the extent that it was able to mobilize not only its own migrants but also overseas supporters of ethnic Chinese origin. For instance, Chinese Malaysians, who made up roughly one-quarter of Malaysia's population, were overwhelmingly pro-Beijing and thus held a dim view of Hong Kong's protest movement. In a silent rally for Hongkongers in Kuala Lumpur in July 2019, participants encountered not only a police blockade but also condemnation from the local Chinese association. In Taiwan, where polls indicated strong support for the Hongkongers' campaign with a solid two-thirds majority, violence against noticeable advocates for the Hong Kong cause took place anyway. On September 29, Denise Ho was personally assaulted by pro-China mobsters in Taipei when she joined a local demonstration. Lam Wing-Kee, the operator of Causeway Bay Bookstore, who was abducted for interrogation in the mainland for seven months, decided to restart his bookselling business in Taiwan in 2020. Yet, right before the relaunch of Causeway Bay Bookstore in Taipei, he was assaulted with red paint thrown all over his body. Similarly, a Taipei restaurant that aimed to provide employment opportunities for Hong Kong protesters was vandalized in the same year. Although all those perpetrators were brought to justice, these incidents demonstrated the reach of the PRC's coercive power.

Hong Kong's overseas campaigners appealed to the universal values of judicial independence, civil liberties, and political freedom, and yet, they faced the most resourceful dictatorship that the world has ever witnessed. In a way, their struggles epitomized the contemporary geopolitical conflict between an enfeebled political liberalism and a growing authoritarianism that cynically resorted to brute force and blind jingoism without moral scruples.

Embedding Hongkongers' Campaign Locally

Overseas Hongkongers were not temporary sojourners or rootless exiles; many of them were settled migrants, already obtaining permanent residence or citizenship. They knew that Hong Kong's overseas campaign must be aligned with the national goals of their host countries in order to be sustainable. There was a risk of isolation if the Hong Kong issue failed to connect with mainstream opinions. As a Toronto-based activist commented:

> If our situation were similar to Syrians and Palestinians in Canada, who have troubles with their homelands, people might sympathize with their plight, but still think it is their problem after all. . . . We need to localize the Hong Kong issue so that it becomes a major concern for Canadians.

A Washington, DC–based advocate put it bluntly, "My job is to frame the issue of the Hong Kong movement from the perspective of US political interests." The same hard-nosed realism was shared by an Ottawa-based activist who argued it was vital to craft a Canadian version of the Five Demands rather than repeating the same claims of Hong Kong's anti-ELAB protesters:

> We need to be connected with mainstream Canadian society. The CCP's totalitarian control does not end at Hong Kong. In fact, Hong Kong is just the beginning, and we can also feel it here in Canada. Canadians are going to ask us why we should be concerned with Hong Kong. Our explanation is that our Hong Kong experiences of being controlled by CCP are equally vital for Canadians. . . . The point is not just what Canada can do for Hong Kong, but also what Hong Kong can do for Canada.

In this vein, overseas Hongkongers sought to speak from the standpoint of their host countries, rather than as fleeing refugees. A Melbourne activist emphasized:

> We use the identity of Hong Kong Australians, not Hongkongers. We do not speak from Hong Kong's perspective, but rather from Australian interests. It is simply useless if we just start from a moral high ground. Otherwise, we will constantly face the question why Australia should help Hong Kong.

Concomitantly, there were efforts to promote a positive public image of overseas Hongkongers in the host countries. In Britain, Hongkongers donated money to hospitals for the battle against COVID-19. As one participant put it: "We need the UK government to stand with Hong Kong for democracy, but when it comes to the pandemic, we also claim to have stood with the UK." Similarly, Hongkonger communities in America launched a fundraising campaign to distribute face masks in several cities. The campaign Hongkonger4US aimed at "expressing gratitude for the American support for Hong Kong." A Hongkonger leader in Taiwan also emphasized:

> Many of us want to become new Taiwanese citizens. Citizens need to have a national identity by safeguarding Taiwan's national security and always prioritizing Taiwan's interests. We need to have this understanding in order to be good Taiwanese and good citizens.

Yet, the ideal of a locally embedded movement is not easy to realize. Table 5.1 looks at whether the overseas protest events had local collaborators. With the noticeable exception of Taiwan, rallies and demonstrations in the United States, the United Kingdom, Canada, and Australia were mostly Hongkongers-only affairs, with the occasional participation from Tibetans, Uighurs, and Taiwanese.

Clearly, with the exception of Taipei, Hongkongers in other international cities found few joiners. The situation in Taiwan requires some explanation, as it highlights the conditions by which the Hong Kong issue can be successfully localized. The PRC has stated that it intends to annex Taiwan and considers the self-governing island a "renegade province." Since the PRC apparently wanted the Hong Kong "model" to be something of a road map to the island's future, the Taiwanese were naturally concerned about events in Hong Kong (Li and Fung 2022). As such, Taiwan was both a site for Hongkongers' international front and also where Taiwanese proactively joined the resistance against the ELAB. As Table 5.1 indicates, collaborative protests outnumbered Hongkongers-only protests in Taipei. As the popular slogan "Today Hong Kong, Tomorrow Taiwan" indicates, it was precisely the existential threat from the PRC that encouraged Taiwanese to support the Hongkongers' campaign, and the absence of such menace elsewhere explained why Hongkongers found it difficult to find local partners.

Outside Taiwan, there remained inherent difficulties in deepening the connection of Hong Kong's movement in host societies, including that Western democracies have been beset with problems of political polarization and

TABLE 5.1 PROTEST EVENTS WITH AND WITHOUT LOCAL COLLABORATORS IN SIX CITIES, JUNE 2019–JANUARY 2020

	Taipei	Sydney	Toronto	London	New York	Los Angeles
Only Hongkongers	12	14	25	38	20	20
With local collaborators	33	0	1	3	4	1
Total	45	14	26	41	24	21

Notes: (1) Protest event data in Taipei are from Taiwanese journalistic sources, see Appendix 1. (2) For cities in the United States, the United Kingdom, Canada, and Australia, local newspapers cannot be used because overseas Hongkongers' activities were infrequently reported in the mainstream media. Instead, the author examined the Facebook pages of the most representative organizations, NY4HK (New York), D4HK (London), Canada–Hong Kong Link (Toronto), NSW Hongkongers (Sydney), and Hong Kong Forum (Los Angeles), and coded their posts regarding events in their cities.

the rise of anti-immigrant populism and right-wing extremism. In the United Kingdom, political polarization meant that whenever Hongkongers invited the rightist MP of the Conservative Party Iain Duncan Smith to take the podium, Labour MPs would refrain from joining the event. The protesters' appeal to the U.S. intervention, and their deliberate use of some "infelicitous" slogans, such as "President Trump, please liberate Hong Kong" (A. Tang 2022), led many liberals to question whether the Hongkongers' campaign was genuinely prodemocracy or not. Since Hong Kong's protesters often carried American flags, one interviewee felt that many left-leaning European academics held a dim view of the movement. According to another interviewee, some doctrinaire leftists—colloquially known as "tankies"—literally believed Hong Kong's prodemocracy movement was a sham creation of American imperialism, with the CIA manipulating from behind the scenes, unwillingly replicating the exact narrative that the PRC promoted in its propaganda.

On the other hand, Hong Kong's antiauthoritarian struggles should have shared the affinity with progressives and liberals who embraced human rights, but, instead, it found strong responses from the right-wing camp for anti-communist, anti-foreigner, and other reasons. In Japan, if a solidarity rally were framed as a protest against the PRC, it would have attracted the uninvited participation of Japan's right-wing ultranationalists, whose radical anti-China slogans often worried Hongkonger event planners. A rally in Warsaw in December 2021 attracted a bewildering array of participants including antiwar pacifists, Solidarność supporters, anti-communists, and libertarians who thought Hong Kong was a free market paragon that was being destroyed by Chinese communists. A participant commented: "It's like capitalists and communists joined together. Socialists supported Hong Kong because of democracy, but libertarians for freedom."

In the United States, when Hongkonger activists protested against police violence, they sometimes encountered gun rights enthusiasts who eagerly suggested they should arm themselves. American anti-immigrant activists were also interested in broadcasting the message that a free and prosperous city declined due to "uncontrolled waves of immigrants." Hongkongers I interviewed had a deeply felt ambivalence toward the #StopAsianHate campaign in 2021. On the one hand, they found themselves equally vulnerable to the surge of racist violence, but, on the other hand, knowing that some far-left organizations and nationalist Chinese had hijacked the movement to demand "stop bashing China," they were fearful that their participation would lend credence to such an interpretation. "It's like you cannot criticize the Israeli government. Because if you do so, you must be an anti-Semite," as one interviewee put it. In this way, Hongkonger campaigners sometimes ended up in an embarrassing situation of alienating potential allies and attracting strange bedfellows.

Trump's tough-sounding rhetoric against China attracted many Hongkongers who historically leaned toward Democrats (Chong 2020). Yet, there were still many liberal Hongkongers who could not accept Trump's racist and sexist politics. The Biden-Trump election of 2020 was extremely divisive among overseas Hongkongers.[9] Prior to the election, Trump's Hong Kong fans circulated conspiracy theories that Joe Biden would kowtow to China by selling out Hong Kong if elected, which invited angry refutations from Biden supporters. The fracas became so nasty that many Hongkonger chat groups became dysfunctional and were eventually abandoned. The tragic death of George Floyd in May 2020 and the subsequent wave of BLM protests deepened the existing rift. While Lausan activists maintained that Hongkongers should join the campaign against "racial capitalism" because they were also fighting against police brutality back home, such a gesture of solidarity enraged pro-Trump Hongkongers who largely saw BLM as a gimmick by Democrats. To add insult to injury, on January 6, 2021, as Trump supporters stormed Capitol Hill to stop the congressional confirmation of the presidential election result, there was a Black Bauhinia Flag flying at the scene. It was difficult to ascertain whether Hongkongers actually joined the riot, but the damage was done. Many U.S.-based Hongkonger associations swiftly condemned the incident of the Capitol riot and distanced themselves from the mysterious presence of the protest flag, thus further infuriating Trump's Hong Kong supporters.

In short, in their efforts to embed the cause for Hong Kong's democracy, overseas activists navigated an increasingly treacherous terrain, caught by the opposing forces and divisions that have plagued democracies in recent years. Nevertheless, it remained a remarkable accomplishment. Hong Kong's prodemocracy movement was able to gain the support of bipartisan politicians in several countries including the United States, the United Kingdom, Australia, and Taiwan. While Hong Kong's campaigners certainly deserve credit, one cannot overlook the rapid change in global perceptions of China, from the growing trade war to conflicts over South China Sea, Xinjiang, Taiwan, the pandemic, the Russian War in Ukraine, and beyond. With the advent of the so-called New Cold War, the exacerbation of global geopolitical conflicts incidentally made it easier for Hongkongers' worldwide advocacy efforts to reach more broadly.

A City-Based Diplomacy

From the onset of the ELAB dispute, many actors, recognized or anonymous, home based or abroad, improvised as they saw fit to enlist international support. And the cumulative results were a city-based global diplomacy to champion Hongkongers' political rights, when the SAR government slavishly toed the line dictated by Beijing. As has been pointed out (Fong 2021a: 1074), Hongkongers' democratic values made them more resonant among the Global North. Among the receptive Western countries and Taiwan, these movement advocates were received more or less as the de facto ambassadors for the city, gaining personal access to government officials in the host countries. Taiwan's Presidential Office secretary-general received Hongkonger petitioners on June 13, 2019, and the aforementioned U.S. congressional hearing on September 17 was probably the most-watched event globally. In many countries, Hong Kong's diaspora activists have established working relationships of various kinds with parliamentarians and officials. For instance, when the SAR government announced a wanted list of six overseas activists as fugitives allegedly violating the NSL, on July 31, 2020, Ray Wong, a former localist leader who later obtained German political asylum, immediately contacted his host government official. Within a few hours, Germany's foreign ministry announced the decision to suspend the extradition agreement with Hong Kong. These attempts, individualized or organized, sought to represent the city on a global stage, asserted the agency of Hongkongers, and challenged the PRC claim that Hong Kong had become a Chinese city.

For diaspora activists, policy advocacy in the host countries remained a central task ever since the ELAB was first proposed, and it became even more important as the NSL regime put an end to free political expression in Hong Kong. As the expansive and vaguely worded law criminalized acts of "collusion with a foreign country or with external elements (read: Taiwan)," Hong Kong–based activists ceased to be involved in global diplomacy, and this unfinished work was effectively delegated to those Hongkongers who were permanently based abroad and faced no immediate personal risk. As the city was coerced into silence, its offshore activists had to apply the playbook of the wartime Free France, Palestine Liberation Organization, Central Tibetan Administration, and other exile organizations to represent the genuine voices in an enemy-occupied territory.

In many countries, overseas Hongkongers have established their representative organizations to champion their demands. Hong Kong Democracy Council (established in September 2019), We the Hongkongers (March 2020), Campaign for Hong Kong (formerly Project Hong Kong, November 2021), and Committee for Free Hong Kong (November 2022) were organizations permanently based in Washington, DC. In the United Kingdom, Hong Kong Watch (2017), Stand with Hong Kong (June 2019), and Hongkongers in Britain (July 2020) were among the prominent representatives. In Taiwan, Hong Kong Outlanders (July 2019) and Taiwan Hong Kong Association (January 2021) played a similar role in representing diaspora communities. Other countries witnessed similar efforts of policy advocacy in a less professionalized manner. In addition, with growing repression in the city, there emerged a wave of offshoring of Hong Kong's civil society organizations in order to continue their campaigns when it was no longer tolerated at home, including Hong Kong Democratic Alliance of Overseas Postgraduate Students (September 2019), Hong Kong Labour Rights Monitor (July 2022), the 29 Principles (August 2022) (an organization of legal specialists and its name referred to a 1990 United Nations document on lawyers), and Hong Kong Media Overseas (November 2022). All these attempts represented the concerted efforts to transplant Hong Kong's professional activisms abroad on the part of early stage scholars, labor activists, lawyers, and media professionals.

Here, the decentralized nature of diaspora activisms showed its strength as well as weakness. The absence of a coordinating center made possible the free improvisation among scattered actors who intimately knew their local terrain. Yet, when it came to policy advocacy, there was a need to coordinate the efforts so as to present a singular voice to host countries. Confusion was bound to occur as different groups proceeded on their courses without mutual communication. In the United States, the legislation for Hong Kong refugees (the Hong Kong People's Freedom and Choice Act of 2020) eventually failed, partly because different groups were contacting lawmakers with their own versions—an inevitable weakness for an improvised movement. Similarly, some London-based group hired commercial lobbyists to advance their cause, and such a decision invited intense criticisms from other Hong Kong diaspora organizations because it was no less than "outsourcing the movement" and "buying influence."

These overseas advocacy efforts had two main focuses: sanctions and migrants-friendly policies. Inspired by the *laam caau* philosophy, they demanded sanctions be applied to officials who were responsible for human rights violations. In the United States, both Trump and Biden administrations applied sanctions to a number of PRC and Hong Kong officials who were banned from U.S.-bound travels and financial services. As a result, the SAR executive chief Carrie Lam once admitted that she had to stash a large sum of cash at home because her bank accounts became inoperative. In addition, the Hong Kong Autonomy Act (July 2020) revoked the special treatment of Hong Kong as the territory could no longer import American-made sensitive technologies. Yet, so far, the United States was the only country that adopted these punitive measures; in spite of the best efforts on the part of overseas Hongkongers, other countries (e.g., Australia and the United Kingdom) appeared reluctant to antagonize Beijing on behalf of Hongkongers.

British Hong Kong has been a shelter for revolutionaries such as Sun Yatsen, Ho Chi Minh, and Thomas Liao (a Taiwanese independence movement leader). Ironically, the city under Chinese rule began to generate its own overseas exiles and refugees. Prior to the Be Water Revolution, there had been dissidents who successfully obtained political asylum abroad. As protesters were leaving Hong Kong to escape indictment and imprisonment, diaspora activists lobbied their host governments for more lifeboat schemes. Immediately after the NSL became effective, the Taiwanese government launched a humanitarian assistance program by establishing a new office and providing case-based consultation, monetary support, and other services for endangered Hongkongers. While COVID-19 restrictions suspended the tourist visa application, a special arrangement had been made for them to board a plane and enter Taiwan without valid travel documents. In 2020, Australia, Canada, the United States, and the United Kingdom announced various plans to facilitate staying longer or entering the job market for migrants. In particular, the United Kingdom's 2020 decision to grant the right of abode and a path to citizenship to holders of the British National (Overseas) (BNO) passport, a U.K.-issued travel document for Hongkongers born before 1997, and the 2022 announcement to broaden the BNO eligibility by including the descendants born to its holders after 1997 were hailed as milestone achievements.

Clearly, Hong Kong's overseas activists were riding on a wave of international sympathy. The British enfranchisement of BNO passport holders was estimated to open a path for three million Hongkongers to become citizens, and yet, in the prevalent post-Brexit climate of skepticism over migrants, there appeared to be little opposition. The same overwhelming support for Hongkongers and their political struggles also existed in the United States. A DC-based advocate proudly claimed:

> We are fiercely bipartisan. . . . If you go to Capitol Hill and meet a member of Congress, you'll find Hong Kong is almost the one unanimously bipartisan issue. We have survived polarization.

While Australians and Canadians were eyeing the influx of young talent to make up for their labor shortage, and the British discussion revolved around how Hongkongers' wealth would stimulate post-Brexit economic growth, Taiwan's government actually adopted more stringent requirements for investment migration from Hong Kong. A vetting procedure for national security has been imposed for those applicants who were born in mainland China or used to work in governmental institutions and Chinese-invested enterprises. Apparently out of concern not to provoke the PRC, Taiwan's government rejected suggestions to offer political asylum or a shorter path to citizenship to protesters who had fled. In 2022, a government proposal to lower the naturalization threshold for Hongkonger students was unexpectedly opposed by the ruling-party lawmakers, citing the fear of PRC infiltration. As such, a number of frustrated Hongkongers in Taiwan opted to leave for Australia, Canada, and the United Kingdom, as they offered an easier route to citizenship.

The Taiwanese eagerly supported the Be Water Revolution during its heyday in 2019, and Hong Kong's political crisis helped the independence-leaning Democratic Progressive Party win a landslide reelection in January 2020 (M. Ho 2021). Why did this apparent mass enthusiasm quickly evaporate and, in its place, skepticism over Hongkongers emerge? A poll survey in 2021 indicates profound ambivalence among the Taiwanese. While 29% of respondents agreed that Taiwan had a responsibility to help Hong Kong, another 33% disagreed. There were 36% in favor of more Hongkongers being able to settle in Taiwan and 23% in opposition (Nachman et al. 2021). The shift in public opinion and political attitudes in Taiwan demonstrates that exposure to geopolitical tensions is likely to affect the recipient country's attitude toward Hong Kong refugees. Standing on the front line of the emerging U.S.-China rivalry and a potential PRC invasion, the Taiwanese appeared more risk averse, fearing that their solidarity gestures with Hong Kong might incur the ire of a humiliated Beijing.

A New Migrant Wave

Aside from those Hongkongers who needed to flee abroad for their own safety, the imposition of the NSL and subsequent repressive measures resulted in the loss of confidence in the city's political future, stimulating a new wave of migration (Li and Liao 2023). As of mid-2022, there had been a net outbound migration of more than forty thousand people since the NSL, and the city has been losing its population consecutively for three years.[10] An acute shortage of human resources emerged in health care, education, social welfare, and other professions. A study found the intention to migrate was particularly strong among those who embraced their Hong Kong identity and those who perceived the recent political changes negatively (S. Wong et al. 2023). It was not a surprise that these disappointed Be Water Revolution supporters chose to exit. However, even among progovernment or apolitical Hongkongers, emigration became an increasingly popular option because of newly imposed constraints on freedom of movement and monetary flow. In November 2020, the SAR government ordered a freeze on the bank accounts of Ted Hui, a former opposition lawmaker who fled abroad, and his family members. The abrupt act of confiscating personal savings sent a shock wave to many risk-conscious middle class with means. In addition, starting in August 2021, SAR immigration officials were authorized to prevent anyone from leaving Hong Kong without a court order. Therefore, while conservative and affluent Hongkongers might be satisfied with the cessation of protest activism, they also had legitimate reasons to worry about their personal and financial safety.

Compared to the previous post-Tiananmen migration wave, the recent exodus of Hongkongers was also triggered by a profound political crisis, but there remained several outstanding differences. First, the recently departed were more likely to decide in a hurry because of the rapid deterioration of human rights, political freedom, and financial security in Hong Kong, whereas their predecessors had several years of preparation and planning before the 1997 transition. Second, while the previous wave of migration was motivated by a pervasive sense of uncertainty, recent migrants took it to heart that the worst was yet to come under the current political climate. As such, their migration was more likely to be long term or permanent, with little possibility of a future return. Last, the migrants of the 1990s mostly utilized the channels of investment migration to the West, which was exclusively limited to people with financial assets. As Australia, Canada, Taiwan, and the United Kingdom unveiled their lifeboat schemes, many young and less established Hongkongers were able to embark on their life journey abroad.

Facing a sudden surge of refugees and migrants, Hong Kong's overseas activists scrambled to meet the new challenge. While middle-class Hongkongers typically relied on commercial consultancies to deal with migration applications, more attention of overseas activists was devoted to the aftercare of young escapees, who were not financially secure and often arrived with physical and mental trauma. In such a case, diaspora communities often needed local partners for collaboration. For instance, Chi Nan Presbyterian Church in Taipei, located a stone's throw from the city's main station, was often the first stop of fleeing protesters. Reverend Chun Sen Huang, who had developed an underground logistic network with fellow Christians in Hong Kong, often received these unannounced visitors with their luggage in tow.[11] In addition to regular gatherings at the church, he also provided referrals to medical and psychiatric services for those in need.

While financial assistance to these new arrivals was undoubtedly important and many diaspora organizations were busy collecting resources for this purpose, there were needs that money could not buy. For instance, a Taiwan-based group was formed to address the specific needs of middle school student escapees. They provided free tutoring in math and Mandarin and arranged board game activities so that young Hongkongers could meet their Taiwanese peers. Another organization targeted more established migrants, and its activities included Hong Kong–style street fairs, forums on migration, house purchases, and entrepreneurship, and local in-depth tourism. Its leadership firmly believed that Hongkonger migrants should know their new home better. Their tours included visits to rural farms and indigenous communities in the mountain—an immersive education for Hong Kong's urbanites.

Whether they targeted teenagers or adults, community building was among the top priorities for these diaspora organizations. Annual protest gatherings in early June (in commemoration of the Be Water Revolution's beginning) and the screening of films like *Revolution of Our Times* helped sustain the collective memory and unite like-minded overseas compatriots. However, over time, many organizations gravitated toward more reliance on a "softer" approach by holding events on "less heavy" topics, like Hong Kong's food, entrepreneurship, and real estate. Lunar New Year and the Mid-Autumn Festival were occasions for Hongkongers with family to celebrate together. Holding cheerleading parties for Hong Kong athletes in the 2021 Tokyo Olympics was also another popular get-together. A New York–based activist even proposed a nationwide mah-jongg tournament for Hongkongers.

The transition from the political to the everyday appeared inevitable as a consequence of the movement's decline and waning enthusiasm. As a Seattle-based activist explained, "People grow wary of political topics. Many are frustrated because of the lack of movement progress." In fact, such a sense of powerlessness was pervasive among overseas Hongkongers. Some diaspora organizations reported a decline in their event attendance and diminishing donations. Understanding that the return to normalcy was unavoidable, diaspora activists also responded by perpetuating their presence abroad. Aside from institutionalizing their political representatives in capital cities, resourceful Hongkongers also contributed to the founding of Hong Kong Studies centers or programs in American, British, Canadian, and Taiwanese universities and research institutions. At the same time, there were efforts to preserve and archive the records and files of disbanded NGOs and student organizations that were smuggled out of the city. In addition, some participants worked to expand the library collection of Hong Kong–related books, particularly since the SAR government had carried out a massive cleansing of political books from the city's public libraries. Academic activities and library collection might not attract mass attention, but they help preserve a distinctive collective memory and secure an independent research field that could not be assimilated into China Studies.

After the NSL crackdown, Hong Kong's overseas communities became the only actor capable of launching oppositional collective actions and thereby continued the unfinished mission of the Be Water Revolution. Many of my overseas interviewees knew that it would be a prolonged campaign for the city's democracy, and some were keenly aware of personal danger if they returned to the city. As such, they preferred to identify themselves not as transient sojourners in foreign lands but as settled migrants. Understandably, such a framing was difficult for young escapees because they were forced to undergo drastic changes in their life course that were not of their own volition. My informants reported cases of mental issues, idleness, alcoholism, and other maladjustments among these young exiles.[12]

Reluctant or not, the new arrivals enlarged the size of the existing overseas Hongkonger communities. But how about the future vision of these diaspora communities? Reflecting the diversity of Hong Kong's migrants, different visions arose. At one extreme was the widely circulated proposal to create an international charter city. Inspired by the American economist Paul Romer's idea to lease a piece of land from a developing country to practice a new political and economic system, a team of real estate developers, professionals, and academics launched the project to build a new Hong Kong. Hong Kong 2.0 would preserve the existing institutions and thus a welcoming home for migrants. Its proponents even contacted the Irish government to discuss such a plan, though without making much progress.[13]

The international charter city idea apparently aimed at re-creating the experience of a British colony, except that Hongkongers would become the ruler. As such, this experimental idea smacked of old-school colonialism. Few self-respecting nations could seriously consider this proposal. While this novel idea reflected a certain way of thinking on the part of affluent Hongkongers who thought their political troubles had an economic solution, its main attraction was that Hongkongers could leave their city without having to abandon the ways of living they were used to. Since the New Hong Kong would adopt the same institutions and rules, migrants were more likely to find an authentic home.

Contrary to such thinking, many of my interviewees emphasized the need to be a part of the host countries. Typically, they negatively referred to Hong Kong's new immigrants and post-1997 mainland migrants as the latter were said to "live off the city and did not speak Cantonese." As such, these activists tried to assimilate into the host societies and, at the same time, retained their Hong Kong identity. In Taiwan, these migrants were especially sensitive to the stereotypical views of Hongkongers, such as having a sense of superiority for being able to speak more fluent English. One interviewee recounted a restaurant episode:

> There were many such Hong Kong migrants in Tamsui [a suburb of Taipei] and they always thought they were better than others. Once I had a meal there and overheard a Hongkonger who kept bad-mouthing Taiwan. He said Taiwan was backward and his daughter would go to the US in the future. I felt so angry that I scolded him in Cantonese, "You have been in Taiwan for thirty years, and you cannot even speak proper Mandarin!" I left immediately after saying these words.

Apparently, my informant's sudden outburst at his fellow compatriot originated from his moral expectation of being good migrants who should learn to adapt to their host societies rather than the other way around.

Conclusion

Rey Chow, a Hong Kong–born literary scholar based in North America, first applied the term *diaspora* to Hongkonger's colonial experience. Chow (1995) contended that an in-betweenness consciousness and the necessity of having to constantly negotiate with Chinese and Western powers were the defining features of being a Hongkonger. Different from other colonies originating from imperialistic aggression, Hong Kong was largely started as a city of voluntary migrants. As such, Hongkongers could not resort to a prior native culture to assert their autonomy. Chow also rejected the narrative of official PRC nationalism, which maintained Hongkongers were Chinese by blood, and the PRC's anti-imperialist language is inherently problematic because it serves to buttress the repression of the Chinese people. Instead, Chow noticed a diasporic consciousness permeating the films, popular songs, and poetry of the 1990s, which attempted to assert a distinctive voice for the city. The fashionable nostalgic themes represented a collective attempt to narrate Hongkongers' stories on their own terms. As such, Hongkongers' Chineseness was highly selective and noticeably different from that in the mainland.

With the benefit of hindsight, Chow's theorization of Hongkonger consciousness as diasporic was startlingly prescient and ahead of the time. Her diagnosis correctly saw the PRC as a potentially colonizing force and identified the budding of a nascent Hong Kong identity prior to the 1997 handover. Yet, there remained a conspicuous enigma: if the British colonial existence was diasporic, where was the homeland for Hongkongers? It could not be China since most Hongkongers had called the city home and few of them eagerly anticipated the transition to PRC rule. If the homeland was the city itself, how could people lead a diasporic existence in their own land? In Chow's idiosyncratic usage, the diaspora referred to the contradictory experience of simultaneously belonging to and being different from the Chinese.

What was enigmatic in the 1990s became a nightmarish reality during the Be Water Revolution, as Hongkongers were literally recolonized by their fatherland, with the alarming encroachment of the PRC judiciary system and security apparatus. To resist the political displacement in their homeland, activists in Hong Kong and abroad launched a series of internationally facing protests and global diplomacy. For the first time, overseas Hongkongers identified themselves as a diaspora community and their collective actions, political or not, accentuated the fact that Hong Kong was their shared land of origin.

This chapter has analyzed how multiple acts of improvisation, anonymous or recognizable, online or offline, place-based or border-crossing, made possible the international front of the Be Water Revolution, thus successfully triggering responses from other countries. Nevertheless, improvisation was not a panacea to overseas campaigning; peer-produced strategic responses could exacerbate the existing divides in ideologies and worldviews due to the lack of a coordination core. While more broadly based participation and more flattened decision-making processes made it possible to tap into broader contributions, it also planted seeds of internal discord, as witnessed by the fracas between Hong Kong's Trump supporters and Trump haters before and after the 2020 election. In short, improvising for the international front was innovative, effective, and divisive.

6

Postmobilization Activism

The national security regime's sweeping dragnet compelled numerous protesters to flee the city. Even those who were not immediately imperiled foresaw a bleak horizon and thought migration was the best choice for them and their family. Yet, amid the exodus, not all prodemocracy Hongkongers embraced departure. For some, departing during tumultuous times seemed ethically questionable. Instead, conscientious stayers found a purpose in their decision to stand firm. An art teacher I interviewed said:

> Many protesters have not completed their legal procedures, and some are still waiting for trial, which I expect will result in prison sentences. You can imagine the shock after they finish the jail term only to find that all of us have left. For me, as long as I am not caught and my risk is not that high, I have no reason for leaving, and we should not do that.

In line with this thinking, leaving is synonymous with abandoning one's moral responsibilities toward those who have paid a personal price for safeguarding the city's political freedom. Another middle-class professional in the construction industry shared a similar thought:

> Seeing my beloved place become this way, I really have complex feelings. When I saw the film *Ten Years*, I wondered whether Hongkongers would really die for political causes, and now it happened. I feel so

> sad that Hong Kong entered this stage. On the other hand, I am also glad that many friends are supporting the movement with the same conviction and willingness to contribute their efforts for democracy. I have talked with my wife and we have decided to stay and to witness the subsequent developments of our city.

Kiwi Chow, the director of the awarded film *Revolution of Our Times*, was among the stayers, even though many of his friends were worried about his safety. Citing his Christian belief to follow Jesus's example by "walking with those who suffered," Chow said:

> Many people tried to persuade me to leave, and these concerns make me reflect a lot. I want to set a good example for my family, especially for my kids. What I want to achieve is not happiness, but justice. (Cheung 2022: 196)

Whether out of moral obligation or religious belief, those who remain in Hong Kong can engage in a range of in situ movement-related activities that are denied to overseas activists, even though they have to constantly look over their shoulders in a growingly repressive environment. This chapter examines a plethora of home-based or home-oriented activism that emerged when street protests and other public expressions of dissent were suppressed by the pandemic and the NSL. I identify activities, such as alternative media, community newspapers, independent bookstores, and support for defendants and prison inmates, as "postmobilization activism" because these activities were designed to address those unfulfilled needs when the protests came to an abrupt end. I employ this term specifically to address the critique that contemporary contentious politics research adopts a "movement-centric perspective" (McAdam and Boudet 2012: 2) and is narrowly synonymous with "mobilization studies" (Walder 2009: 397–400). By extending the observation to the long aftermath of an intensive spell of protest actions, we can better understand how committed activists continued to pursue their goals by other means.

Conceptually, postmobilization activism is different from two commonly seen alternatives: everyday resistance and abeyance. As expounded by Scott (1985, 1990), everyday resistance encompasses a series of locally embedded tactics for survival. In extreme domination, the subordinate can only practice the so-called "hidden transcript" to minimize the intrusion of the officially sanctioned definition of reality—the "public transcript"—with the resigned understanding that it is nearly impossible to reverse the power imbalance. Everyday resistance comprises a vast concealed realm of foot-dragging, soldiering, evasion, cheating, pilfering, and so on, which all aim at minimizing the subordinates' loss. For instance, the NSL brought about a major revamp in education to the extent that schoolchildren were periodically required to sing the PRC national anthem and attend the flag-raising ceremony. Liberal studies in middle school were abruptly removed from the curriculum, and Hong Kong history was now rewritten with materials in line with official Chinese nationalism. To counter such overt brainwashing, some parents who remained in Hong Kong began to teach their children to manifest outward conformity in school while counterbalancing this at home with lessons on critical thinking and universal values (Lui 2023a). At the same time, schoolteachers who were obliged to instruct national security education deployed a rich repertoire of passive resistance to frustrate the intended pedagogical results (Lui 2023b).

On the other hand, Taylor (1989) introduces the idea of abeyance to make sense of how American feminists managed to survive the conservatism in the 1950s by withdrawing to a closely knit and exclusive group. Abeyance essentially means a pattern of holding people together, and it aims at preserving interpersonal ties by disengaging from the public. The term is widely used to understand a wide range of responses of movement activists in mitigating hostile environments (Holland and Cable 2002; Sawyers and Meyer 1999). As discussed in Chapter 1, I found the application of abeyance structure to post-Umbrella activisms (2015–2019) largely misplaced because they were more proactive than inward-looking and defensive. In view of the repressiveness of the NSL regime, abeyance appeared to be a more suitable description in this context. Compared to what happened in the wake of the Umbrella Movement, NSL-era Hong Kong witnessed a much wider legal and police dragnet (not just targeting movement leaders): a determined effort to cleanse the independent media and judiciary, the restriction of political opposition, and the eradication of civil society organizations, which made retreating to a secluded circle a more sensible choice.

However, postmobilization activisms analyzed later differ from everyday resistance and abeyance in that they largely operate in the public arena by cautiously observing the NSL-related rules, rather than confining their activities in the private sphere only. In addition to preserving the old ties, they also intend to construct new ones. They aim at more than mere self-preservation but attempt to solve the emerging problems and issues left behind by a forcibly silenced movement. Last, although not adopting an overtly confrontational gesture, postmobilization activism continues to uphold a set of values that are frowned on by the NSL regime.

"Blending Protest into Life"

As mentioned in Chapter 3, the protest dynamics of the Be Water Revolution peaked during the two University Battles in November 2019; with the number of arrests increasing, it became difficult to mount large-scale and challenging actions. As rally and demonstration participation became riskier, the idea of "blending protests into life" (*kongzang jungjap sangwut/kangzheng rongru shenghuo*) began to be circulated widely, indicating that activists were keenly aware of the need to find alternative arenas to continue the movement momentum. Initially, the idea of a yellow economic circle—an embryonic idea to build a self-sustaining solidarity economy and, at the same time, to boycott progovernment conglomerates—gained the most attention (D. Chan 2022). By patronizing yellow stores, everyday consumption now became a conscientious act of political insubordination. And yet, the search for alternative routes of protest activism did not stop at mundane shopping but overflowed to other issues and avenues.

The COVID-19 pandemic, first publicly manifested in the Wuhan Lockdown on January 23, 2020, became a double-edged sword for Hong Kong's protesters. On the one hand, with their painful lesson in the 2003 SARS incident, Hongkongers intimately knew the health dangers of coronaviruses originating from the mainland; thus, many appeared less willing to join crowd gatherings out of fear of human-to-human transmission. The SAR government imposed social gathering bans in March, which made it easier for police to disperse and to fine participants. The emergency measure provided a convenient excuse to prohibit the annual June Fourth commemorative rally for the Tiananmen incident—a political ritual that prodemocracy Hongkongers had sustained for thirty years.

On the other hand, the inept responses of the SAR government, especially its reluctance to close the border with the mainland and the insufficient provisioning of protective equipment for frontline health care workers, fanned public outrage. In the journalistic database, 64 COVID-19-related protest events erupted between the first day of the Wuhan Lockdown and early March 2020, which made up more than half of the 114 events within the span of seven weeks. Protesters demanded the immediate closure of the border with China and opposed the building of quarantine camps and the designation of COVID-19 clinics in their neighborhoods. As Hong Kong faced an acute shortage of face masks, prodemocracy politicians scrambled to distribute them from their overseas procurement. Among these COVID-19-related protests, the most well-attended was the five-day strike launched by nine thousand public hospital workers who demanded the border closure and adequate supply of protective equipment. Although this unprecedented action restricted public access to health care, it enjoyed wide popular support and ended with the government's partial concessions (Li and Ng 2021). Clearly, protesters attempted to make political use of the pandemic to continue their activism with the goal of further delegitimizing the SAR government (Whitworth and Li 2023). In the wake of the NSL being imposed on Hong Kong—which basically outlawed any street action—regime opponents still agitated for resistance against the government's antiepidemic measures, such as boycotting Chinese-made vaccines, mass testing, and a mobile vaccine pass app. Since the SAR government–promoted app (called LeaveHomeSafe) was suspected of poor privacy protection, anonymous IT engineers produced various similar-looking apps (generally referred to as ReturnHomeSafe) for free download for concerned users who were reluctant to share their personal data with the government—another indicative case of anonymously improvised resistance.

Organizing new labor unions turned out to be another unexpected terrain to continue the movement's momentum. In the early days of the Be Water Revolution, the CHRF called for a general strike in early June, which was later hastily canceled. As organizational leaders balked at this radical proposal, online activists initiated several waves of strikes, including the August 5 general strike, which purportedly attracted nearly three hundred thousand participants. Our journalistic database indicated twenty-two incidents of strike (or taking leave from work collectively) from June to December 2019. With so many workers deciding to contribute their effort to the antiauthoritarian struggle, the moment became ripe for a unionizing campaign, especially when Hong Kong used to have a rather low threshold for officially registered unions, requiring only seven persons to be founding members. Aside from deepening the movement participation within each profession, campaigners for new labor unions also targeted the three labor legislative seats, which hitherto had been monopolized by pro-Beijing unions. Since each registered labor union had one vote in electing these functional representatives, the union organizers thought they could harness the protest wave to outnumber the conservative camp (A. Chan 2020).

HK on Strike, an online group formed in November 2019, spearheaded the new organizing drive. On the New Year's Day demonstration, more than forty newly formed unions set up roadside booths to recruit new members. The aforementioned five-day strike by health care workers was launched by one of these new outfits (Hospital Authority Employees Alliance), whose membership grew from three hundred in December 2019 to ten thousand in January 2020, representing around one-fifth of the city's health care workers (Tsui and Chan 2021). On the eve of the NSL implementation, HK on Strike held a general strike vote to oppose the draconian law in June, which failed to pass the validation threshold. Under the NSL, many union leaders were dismissed and arrested, and their new unions ceased to be active.

In short, the yellow economic circle, lodging COVID-19-related protests, and organizing labor unions represented innovative attempts to continue the movement drive when the Be Water Revolution was visibly depleted. Ultimately, however, all these improvised strategies were no longer applicable after the NSL became effective on June 30, 2020.

The Aborted Electoral Route to Power

Worldwide large-scale protests brought about drastic impacts on electoral politics, even though elected politicians and political parties were usually not the initiators. In the wake of the 2011 antiausterity protests in southern Europe, start-up political parties like Spain's Podemos and Greece's Syriza rose on the wave of popular discontent. With the banner of democratic socialism, Syriza was catapulted into the governing position of the debt-torn country in 2015–2019. The Occupy Wall Street movement bequeathed a long-lasting legacy in the American politics. The insurgent campaign of Bernie Sanders in the Democratic Party primary in 2015–2016 and the election of self-avowedly democratic socialists into the Congress in 2018 were its clear consequences. In Taiwan, the 2014 Sunflower movement contributed to the peaceful power turnover in 2016 and the emergence of movement-oriented political parties (M. Ho and Huang 2017; Nachman 2018). Perhaps the most dramatic impact takes place in Chile. The 2011 student protests against neoliberal education reforms gave rise to a new generation of activists-turned-politicians, and the widespread protests over the government's economic mismanagement in 2019 further fueled the voter discontent. The result was that Chileans elected Gabriel Boric as their president in 2021. Bori hailed from the student movement in 2011 and was the youngest president in the country (aged thirty-six) ever.

Great social protests unleashed the power of popular mobilization and thus delegitimized the governing incumbents. Furthermore, they inspired and encouraged protest participants to take up the challenge of electoral politics, and they provided fresh and attractive alternatives to existing politicians. The same radical transformation of the political landscape also happened in Hong Kong. The Umbrella Movement of 2014 generated a new corps of localist insurgents in the 2015 district council election and the 2016 legislative election. In November 2019, riding on the massive wave of the Be Water Revolution, the prodemocratic camp won in a landslide by obtaining 389 (out of 452) district councillor seats and control of 17 (out of 18) district councils. Although district councils were by design a consultative body with few decision-making powers, they represented a strategically important site for directing the movement's momentum through institutional channels, especially when many of the newly elected councillors were veterans from the Umbrella Movement or deeply involved in the Be Water Revolution.

Each district councillor was entitled to a monthly subsidy of HK$44,000 (US$5,618), which could be spent on renting an office, hiring assistants, and other duty-related purposes. Many of the newly elected district councillors hired ex-protesters who were freshly released from jail or had lost their jobs. Also, when protesters were detained in the police station, local district councillors were allowed to visit them before their lawyers arrived. Furthermore, each district council could decide on the use of a yearly grant from the SAR government, which amounted to around HK$25 million (US$3.2 million). In the past, these grants were lavished on a number of useless construction projects, or what Hongkongers contemptuously called "white elephants." Under the control of the prodemocracy camp, district councils stopped reimbursing these wasteful projects and, instead, redirected the money to sponsor gay pride parades and other grassroots activities.

Many of the new district councillors originally intended to implement the demands of the Be Water Revolution; in particular, they planned to investigate the police's illegitimate use of force. Some district councils invited ranking police officers to their meetings, but, when councillors raised sharp questions, police delegates simply left in protest, claiming law enforcement was not a local issue. Facing these bottom-up offensives, the SAR government responded by curtailing the grant and not sending officials to sit in the district council meetings. As an interviewed councillor in the Eastern District revealed:

> They use a lot of administrative excuses to prevent our actions. . . . Now they only allow us to deal with livelihood-related issues, and political issues are not permitted to be discussed in district council meetings. Our requests for government data are rejected. Our district council can thus only make some symbolic gestures, such as holding a press conference or releasing a statement.

Clearly, the dogged resistance on the part of the SAR government frustrated these locally initiated democratic reforms, prompting some district councillors to adopt a more confrontational posture. In August 2020, Central and Western District councillors decided to hold an emergency outdoor meeting to oppose the installation of a COVID-19 analysis facility. The decision was to circumvent the social gathering ban, which the government arbitrarily used to forestall protests. While they claimed the district council had the authority to convene a meeting in any place, police officers simply disregarded these legal niceties and proceeded to disrupt the district council meeting and filed criminal charges against five councillors. An involved district councillor defiantly claimed, "We are going to fight the lawsuit, and we are going to take our district council to the streets!"

While the authorities deliberately stonewalled these requests, more threatening to them was the fact that district councillors were able to select 117 seats in the chief executive election committee (1,200 seats in total). The prodemocracy camp's supermajority was expected to corner all seats, and since it had already taken more than 300 seats in the previous round, Hong Kong's political opposition was poised to become a significant player in the upcoming election originally scheduled for March 2022.

Following the district council election, the legislative election originally scheduled for September 2020 would be the next battleground. Elated by the previous victory, the prodemocracy opposition was expecting a surge of voter support to obtain the majority of legislative council seats (the so-called 35+ plan). The indefatigable prodemocracy strategist Benny Tai proposed that the opposition-controlled legislature reject the budgetary plan so as to create a political crisis in the SAR government. He further envisioned that Beijing would have to impose direct rule over Hong Kong, which would lead to renewed protests, bloody repression, and, finally, the West's economic and political sanctions against China. While not every opposition activist endorsed Tai's Ten-Steps-*Laam-Caau* plan and it attracted savage criticisms from Beijing's mouthpieces as expected, the proposal indicated that Hong Kong's prodemocracy camp was sanguine about their seat growth. Such optimism was reflected in the unprecedented primary held in July 2020, in which established opposition parties, localists, and new activists of the Be Water Revolution agreed to join to maximize their seats. More than six hundred thousand voters turned out to cast their vote, and, unsurprisingly, many new faces edged out prodemocracy veterans.

The development unnerved Beijing because the opposition had a considerable chance of success in a deliberately unfair and unrepresentative electoral system for the first time. To stave off the imminent threat, the SAR government quickly postponed the legislative election for one year in the name of the pandemic. The NSL also hastened the political repression, as the authorities removed the elected lawmakers and arrested the participants in the prodemocracy and Benny Tai and his associates (see later). In hindsight, the sudden imposition of the NSL regime certainly precluded the opposition's electoral route to power. Beijing's decisions resulted in the endgame of Hong Kong's semiautonomy at the cost of breaking an international promise and thus compromising its global credibility.

Not Yet a Prostrate Society

Reflecting on the disastrous social engineering projects of the twentieth century, such as Soviet Russia's collectivization and the forcible settlement of nomadic people in Tanzania, James Scott (1998: 98) maintains that a "prostrate society" was one of the preconditions that enabled state rulers to impose their utopian scheme unhindered. The NSL was ostensibly promulgated to "perfect" the OCTS design, but the real effect was to bring about a sanitized Hong Kong where dissident voices were no longer tolerated. In fact, such a scenario has long been advocated by some Beijing policymakers in the notion of so-called second retrocession, meaning that the first one in the form of the sovereignty transfer in 1997 was only the initial step to eventual assimilation into the PRC's system. For these hard-liners, the eruption of a citywide uprising in 2019 was no less than a perfect storm to expedite their agenda.

Under the draconian NSL rule, Hong Kong was becoming a police state, effectively undermining civil liberties and political freedoms (Davies 2024; Fong 2021b; V. Hui 2021). Major changes include the following:

1. **Political opposition purged:** in November 2020, all prodemocracy legislative council members resigned in protest against Beijing's decision to disqualify four lawmakers who were suspected of advocating for Hong Kong's independence. As Beijing reduced directly elected seats from forty (out of the total seventy seats) to twenty (out of the total ninety seats), practically no politicians from the prodemocracy camp joined the 2021 legislative election. As a result, the prodemocracy force was entirely absent in Hong Kong's representative institutions for the first time since their advent in the 1980s. More importantly, the authorities claimed that the July 2020 primary election among the prodemocratic camp was an act of NSL-defined subversion and arrested forty-seven participants, including prodemocracy veterans and younger generation leaders (the so-called case of forty-seven). As for the 389 prodemocracy district councillors who were newly elected in November 2019, the SAR government no longer tolerated their presence. They were openly warned that any violation of the NSL would bring about not only a prison sentence but also the retroactive return of received salaries and subsidies—a convenient way to bankrupt young activists. By the summer of 2021, more than half of the district councillors "voluntarily" gave up their position. Hence, Hong Kong's opposition collapsed, with its leaders either languishing in jail or fleeing in exile.
2. **Civil society uprooted:** some avowedly proindependence organizations had already announced their disbandment and suspended their social media pages prior to the NSL. In the summer of 2021, the SAR government pressured many veteran prodemocracy NGOs to surrender their financial records or face the NSL criminal charge of collusion with foreign forces. As such, the CHRF, HKCTU, Alliance in Support of Patriotic Democratic Movements of China,

Professional Teachers' Union, and more than forty other NGOs chose to dissolve themselves.[1] The victims also included student associations of the University of Hong Kong and the Chinese University of Hong Kong, which had been the vanguard of the territory's student movements. In short, Hong Kong's civil society organizations that had undergirded the city's prodemocracy movement underwent a swift spell of mass extinction.

3. **Press freedom stamped out:** while British Hong Kong was able to enjoy an enviable degree of press freedom that allowed dissident voices in Taiwan and the mainland to be heard, PRC rule over the city witnessed its slow but steady erosion. Yet, the preceding development paled in comparison with the determined effort to wipe out independent and critical media. The city's most popular newspaper, *Apple Daily*, published its last issue on June 24, 2021, as its bank account was frozen and its founder, Jimmy Lai, was taken into custody. After a reshuffle in the top management in March 2021, the public broadcaster, Radio Television Hong Kong (modeled after the BBC and widely acclaimed for its journalistic independence) experienced a massive exodus of its staff. More egregiously, the SAR government revived a criminal charge of spreading seditious intention dating back to 1938 and weaponized it against critical journalist reports. By the end of 2022, twelve media outlets were closed, and fourteen people were indicted for their media roles. (International Federation of Journalists 2022)

The manner in which Beijing and its collaborators in the SAR government forcefully transformed Hong Kong into a submissive city demonstrated their long-standing perception of the Be Water Revolution as an organization-based and leadership-centered protest. This assumption led to the implementation of NSL criminal charges against well-known political figures and the establishment of formal organizations and traditional media outlets, with the belief that, once their ringleaders were neutralized, their followers would automatically cease their activities. However, as previously discussed, this top-down perspective does not align with the decentralized nature of the Be Water Revolution. During intense periods of protest mobilization, preexisting leaders and organizations still hold significance, and the movement is not entirely flattened to the point where everyone is equally important. Leaders and organizations continue to serve essential functions that cannot be outsourced to anonymous online teams. The loss of these leaders and organizations constituted irreparable damage to the Hongkongers' movement. However, due to the movement dynamics being driven by numerous acts of improvisation from diverse and distributed participants, many of whom have managed to survive the regime's manhunt unscathed, they have been able to initiate new forms of activism. These new initiatives may not adopt an openly oppositional stance, but they contribute to sustaining communities that share the same prodemocracy conviction and work to alleviate the suffering caused by regime suppression.

The following sections explore four variants of postmobilization activism: alternative media, community newspapers, independent bookstores, and legal and prison support. The emergence of these improvised activities indicates that Hong Kong, despite the imposition of the NSL, is far from being prostrate and powerless.

Alternative Media

The supply-side explanation for the emergence of alternative media has to do with the forced closing of Hong Kong's prodemocracy media and the mass emigration of laid off journalists, who found their personal safety endangered at home and needed new ways to make a living after settling down abroad. Being a self-conscious contingent in the city's growing diaspora community, in October 2022, these former reporters and editors organized a U.K.-based Association of Overseas Hong Kong Media Professionals to facilitate their adaptation in the host countries (International Federation of Journalists 2023). These professional migrants often took a personal stake in safeguarding the city's press freedom because of their direct experiences in the Be Water Revolution, as reporters and photographers on the front line also became the target of the police's use of force. With the connivance of the SAR government, police assaulted, arrested, and obstructed media staff at the scenes of conflict. For their own safety, the journalists I interviewed revealed that they began to wear military-grade helmets, bulletproof vests, and other protective gear—standard equipment for war correspondents. In police press conferences, media representatives broke with their professional norms and lodged protests against police brutality. In 2019, three incidents of journalist-initiated rallies and demonstrations erupted (July 14, July 23, and September 18). Understandably, these media practitioners intended to contribute to the anti-autocratization campaign with their professional capabilities, while, at the same time, they faced the challenge of financially securing their livelihoods after relocating overseas. As such, launching alternative media for a Hong Kong audience became a popular strategy among these exiled professionals. A personal episode suffices here to demonstrate the commitment of these exiled professionals. The author once met a young journalist who decided to tattoo her right arm with the Chinese characters meaning

"Better to Roar and Die" (*ning ming ji sei/ning ming er si*), shortly after the *Apple Daily* was forced to close. She later single-handedly founded an independent media.

From the demand side, Hongkongers have long been used to a vibrant media ecology in which journalism of all stripes, highbrow and vulgar, prodemocracy and pro-Beijing, jostled for attention. As the NSL swiftly resulted in a monochrome mediascape, there emerged a large market of unsatisfied news consumers. In the last few months of *Apple Daily*, prodemocracy Hongkongers sought to express their solidarity with the prosecuted media outlet by newspaper bulk buying for free distribution, installing advertisements, and purchasing the stock of its parent company. These acts of voluntary contribution suggested that new media might be able to survive if they could find a way to tap into these prodemocracy constituencies. When *Apple Daily* was coerced into closing, it maintained a list of over seven hundred thousand paying subscribers.[2] Moreover, with overseas communities continuously growing in numbers, there emerged new information needs for these migrant Hongkongers who were more interested in immigration issues and diaspora activism—topics that the remaining home-based media tended to avoid because the SAR government frowned on the outward flow of the moneyed middle class. With such a targeted audience in mind, the London-based Green Bean Media declared the following mission statement on its website:

> A platform to continue recording Hongkongers' stories. In the era of forced silence and diaspora, many Hongkongers left without abandoning the city. This platform will let everyone plant seeds in the new soil and grow, and we aim to keep amplifying our voice.[3]

Such a mission statement aptly outlines the guiding philosophy for these emergent alternative media, which intend to continue their advocacy for the city's democracy and, at the same time, establish themselves financially in a new environment. From January 2020 to April 2023, eighteen alternative media outlets emerged, and Table 6.1 summarizes their details.

This table indicates that the rise of these alternative media peaked in 2021, clearly as an emergency response to the demise of home-based media outlets. As one former *Apple Daily* reporter noted, the newspaper used to be the "main stage," and now many had to struggle on their own. These new outfits had to pull themselves up by their bootstraps. As indicated, as many as ten of these outlets adopted paid membership so that only subscribers could access the full content. As for those who did not use a paywall, they resorted to keeping the operation afloat by securing funds from donations, crowdfunding, and other sources. To reduce the outlay, many of these media relied heavily on freelancing. As a U.K.-based media staff revealed:

TABLE 6.1 HONG KONG'S ALTERNATIVE MEDIA, 2020–2023	
Number	18
Using paid membership	10
Starting year	
2020	1
2021	9
2022	5
2023	3
Facebook followers	
Average	58,499
Maximum	322,516
Instagram followers	
Average	56,105
Maximum	313,389
YouTube subscribers	
Average	115,931
Maximum	604,000

Note: (1) The information here excludes the so-called we media, which are operated by one or a few individuals, or those whom Hongkongers call "key opinion leaders" who typically share their video content via YouTube. All of them were online media. Sources are from the International Federation of Journalists (2022) and other journalistic reports. (2) Since these media seldom revealed the number of paid members, the online platform followers represented an approximate estimate of their circulation. (3) All the online data were accessed on May 29, 2023. (4) One of the listed media has ceased its operation.

> We cannot afford to hire a full-time journalist. We do the shooting for internet media during our lunch break or in the evening. We often have meetings at night. For instance, during the funeral of Queen Elizabeth II [in September 2022], our freelancer took a ride to the funeral site during his lunch break. After finishing shooting and interviewing, he went back to his regular work.

While some alternative media targeted a niche audience interested in sports and entertainment news, most of them originally focused on political reporting on irregularities in SAR officials and diaspora activism, which were absent from media based in Hong Kong. However, they were careful not to incur political trouble, especially when one media (DB Channel) was accused of "spreading seditious ideologies" even after it had disbanded itself.[4] For safety reasons some media deliberately chose not to show the author's information in articles they published. At the same time, some of these outlets eventually abandoned political journalism to avoid legal entanglements. In short, political or not, these nascent media outlets served to sustain a Hongkonger community spanning across the national boundaries. In this sense, alternative media also make up part of the far-flung global fronts.

Community Newspapers

While alternative media were primarily based abroad and operated digitally, community newspapers were squarely rooted at home and relied on traditional print materials to sustain Hong Kong's prodemocracy community. The idea that the city's democratization should begin in one's neighborhood and its newspaper dated back to the British era. The so-called Community Charter movement initiated after the conclusion of the Umbrella Movement, which inspired many neighborhood-based post-Umbrella organizations and attempts in this direction. These activities were rooted in the conviction that one should expand and multiply the zones of engagement beyond street protests and elections. By reconnecting with community residents on everyday issues, the prodemocracy movement could harness new sources of support from mundane place-making activities (Huang 2018). Following this strategy, a Hong Kong digital media organization launched a crowdfunding project to train and finance community activists to publish their community newspapers in January 2018, with the explicit goal to foster a new generation of grassroots politicians who could outvote progovernment incumbents.

After the eruption of the Be Water Revolution, the spread of protest activities to unconventional areas of bedroom neighborhoods was another triggering factor. As many resident activists came to know each other and joined the protests that highlighted local grievances, launching a community newspaper was a natural option for continuing place-based activism. For instance, a community paper based in the northwestern part of the New Territories originated from a local concern group that focused on the district council election, whereas another from the southeastern New Territories was initiated by local Lennon Wall activists. Significantly, among the twenty-one community newspapers that emerged in 2019–2021, only two were geographically located in conventional protest districts (see Table 6.2). The shift away from the preexisting hot zones of contention reflected the participants' intention to reconnect with their communities on everyday topics. Also, indicative of the attempt to reach out to a broader constituency, they emphasized paper publication so that elder citizens who were not accustomed to digital media could have an enjoyable reading experience. Among the surveyed community newspapers, only one existed exclusively online while two did not even bother to set up a social media page.

Initially, some community newspapers tended to print stories on local police violence, yellow stores, and protest activities and worked closely with prodemocracy district councillors. After the NSL, political content began to fade and seemingly neutral stories about local history, fauna and flora, and daily life began to fill the pages. Community newspapers were not just communicative media; participants used the platform to engage in a number of local activities, such as distributing face masks and food, helping with elderly care, and joint purchases of local agricultural products. Some also encouraged local residents to contribute articles to collect more grassroots voices.

Launching a community newspaper is not technically sophisticated, and, in fact, two media platforms were operated by middle school students. Typically, a small group of volunteers self-financed and chipped in to write, edit, print, and distribute their newspaper. These participants mostly had regular jobs, and their engagement was avocational and voluntary. Their publication frequency varied widely. Some disappeared after publishing the first issue, and some managed to continuously churn out issues, up to seventeen issues of their paper at least. Community newspapers were subject to the liability of newness and eleven out of twenty-one have ceased operation. For those that survived, several have turned to donations, crowdfunding, or sales to remain in business. There were also indicators that the community newspaper movement had passed its prime. The peak of initiating new ones came in 2020 and then declined; there appears to be no new entrants in the field since 2022 (see Table 6.2). However, community newspapers were by nature experimental, and the operation would continue as long as participants were willing and able. This exemplified one essential characteristic of peer production in collective improvisation: as failures had become cheap and bearable, people were more willing to undertake new initiatives. In this sense, those community newspapers that stopped publication after a brief period were not "dead" as activists could easily revive them or launch other community-based projects.

As for the ten community newspapers that remained active as of June 2023, although they assumed a nonconfrontational attitude by avoiding

TABLE 6.2 HONG KONG'S COMMUNITY NEWSPAPERS, 2019–2023

Number	21
Ceased operation	11
Starting year	
2019	4
2020	13
2021	4
Location	
Conventional protest areas	2
Emerging protest areas	19

Note: (1) Sources are from various journalistic reports and social media pages. (2) Among the eleven community newspapers that ceased publication, two continue to manage their social media pages. (3) Following the definition provided in Chapter 3, conventional protest areas encompass Central and Western District, Wan Chai District, and Yau Tsim Mong District, and the remaining fifteen administrative districts as the emerging area. (4) Data on social media followers were retrieved on June 10, 2023.

political topics, they represented an improvised way to retain the collaborative networks among core activists when street protests were no longer allowed. The pro-Beijing forces certainly kept tabs on their publication for any content that they did not like. One of the discontinued community newspapers used to be criticized by Beijing's mouthpiece for accepting donations from prodemocracy district councillors. A community paper participant revealed in an interview:

> The values behind the anti-ELAB movement are liberty and democracy. What community newspapers say is that residents have the right to participate in their communities and the value of autonomy. These two activities join hands in the emphasis of being open and progressive. When we know more about our communities, we will have a stronger sense of belonging and more feelings of being connected with Hong Kong. It is about local attachment and identity.

Clearly, these community participants saw the strategic values of this seemingly harmless attention to local cultures and identities. As the NSL hastened the political integration of Hong Kong into the mainland and the monumental project of Guangdong–Hong Kong–Macao Greater Bay Area threatened to remove its borders with neighboring Chinese cities, the tenacious attachment to these local distinctive features amounted to acts of silent resistance to coerced assimilation. In the face of this attempted erasure of Hongkongers' distinctive collective memory and identity, local resistance matters. As long as these communities continue to cherish their own local culture, Hong Kong will never be reduced to a mere Chinese mainland city.

Independent Bookstores

Across the globe, operating independent bookstores has been a common practice for activists committed to socialist, feminist, environmentalist, and other causes; their stores have always been not just a retail outlet but rather a gathering place for like-minded people. Yet, in the current context of Hong Kong, they have taken on a different political meaning. For a long time, a Chinese state-owned enterprise, Sino United Publishing, has virtually monopolized distribution channels in the city to prevent critical books from finding their way to the shelves. Under the NSL, the SAR government launched a campaign to remove books on the Tiananmen incident and other materials written by the city's dissidents from the public libraries, thereby sanitizing the city residents' reading lists to Beijing's liking. As such, before PRC-style censorship was imposed in Hong Kong, selling books that the government frowned on constituted a defiant act.

Similar to community newspapers, independent bookstores emerged as a way to sustain the connection among prodemocracy Hongkongers amid political repression. According to journalistic sources, from 2019 onward, there were twenty-one independent bookstores with a pronounced promovement tendency that emerged in the city (see Table 6.3). Since bookstores were less connected to neighborhoods, they were more likely to be located in the urban centers of Central and Western District, Wan Chai District, and Yau Tsim Mong District than community newspapers as this table indicates. As physical bookstores required advance payment in terms of rent and interior furnishings, their proprietors needed more financial resources for such ventures. Ironically, this higher threshold resulted in a higher survival rate for bookstores, as evidenced in the lower number of those that have ceased operation in comparison with community newspapers (see Tables 6.2 and 6.3). Bookstores began as commercial ventures, which easily blended into the yellow economic circle project and thus enjoyed the patronage of prodemocracy consumers; by contrast, community newspapers often began with free distribution and then solicited donations or resorted to sales for follow-up operation.

There are several ways that bookstores have continued the unfulfilled mission of Hong Kong's political movement. Many storeowners meticulously curated their book selections with a particular focus on titles related to politics, philosophy, and history. Hong Kong's Be Water Revolution has generated a prodigious production of journalistic reports, photography albums, commentaries, and literary works, which were staple items in these outlets. In addition, books on worldwide resistance movements were also a favorite

TABLE 6.3 HONG KONG'S INDEPENDENT BOOKSTORES, 2019–2023

Number	21
Ceased operation	5
Starting year	
2019	1
2020	6
2021	10
2022	4
Location	
Conventional protest areas	6
Emerging protest areas	15

Note: (1) The table here counts only those bookstores with a physical presence, excluding online sellers. Sources are from various journalistic reports and social media pages. (2) Among those ceasing to operate, three were from an experimental project of social enterprise that planned to open and manage new bookstores for six months. (3) Data on social media followers were retrieved on June 9, 2023.

choice as they provided alternative and inspiring perspectives and lessons relevant to the core concerns among prodemocracy readers. Some bookstores have dedicated exhibition corners to showcase books that have been removed from public libraries or whose authors have been imprisoned, serving as a testament to their commitment to free expression. Simultaneously, certain stores specialize in self-help books, aiming to assist readers in navigating their traumatic experiences. As one interviewed storeowner proudly declared, "My book selection constitutes my position statement." In addition to food for thought, craftworks or artworks with prodemocracy messages were often sold within the premises. Locally made food or other agricultural products were also on sale as they symbolized an alternative to made-in-China mass production. One bookstore owner defiantly stated on their website, "When reading becomes an act of resistance, bookstores will be the basis of revolution."[5]

These bookstores not only served as retail spaces but also functioned as intimate venues for lectures, forums, and various interactive activities. Some of these events were dedicated to explicitly political themes, featuring the works of renowned figures like Vaclav Havel, Nelson Mandela, and local dissidents. Additionally, these bookstores provided a platform for the screening of films that were prohibited from commercial theaters, ensuring that these films reached their intended audience. Certain bookstores organized letter-writing events aimed at sending messages of support to the imprisoned protesters. In addition to these political initiatives, these establishments also endeavored to cater to a broader clientele by hosting artistic workshops on leatherwork, floral art, painting, and more. They offered lessons in transcendental meditation, music therapy, and other healing activities, fostering a holistic and well-rounded experience for visitors. Implicitly or explicitly, the purpose of these bookstores extended beyond mere commercial transactions; their ultimate goal was to cultivate and sustain a prodemocracy community through the medium of bookselling.

Responding to the pervasive mood of depression, some bookstores aimed at creating a therapeutic space. These bookstores endeavored to establish a sanctuary for weary souls. Mindful of the emotional needs of their fellow travelers, storeowners carefully crafted an atmosphere of tranquility and seclusion, providing visitors with a stress-free environment to peruse the displayed books without feeling any obligation to make a purchase. They often used the expression "surrounding an oven for the warmth" (*wailou ceoinyun/weilu qunuan*) to emphasize that these bookstores served a particular set of clients. For instance, Have a Nice Stay—whose Cantonese pronunciation also meant "stay and write" (*lauhaa syuse*)—was a joint effort launched by five former journalists from prodemocracy media outlets. While their sudden unemployment due to the government crackdown forced them to find alternative sources of income, they also intended their bookselling venue to be a gathering ground for their colleagues in the same trade. A place for reunion was meant for those who stayed so that "they knew they were not alone."[6]

Widely seen as an extension of the yellow economic circle, these independent bookstores sometimes received unusual attention from the authorities as expected. One bookstore was once fined for selling alcoholic drinks without a license.[7] There were also unexpected inspections for fire safety, labor insurance, and other reasons, especially when there emerged complaints from citizens and the authorities were obliged to act, which amounted to a soft form of regime repression. There are some bookstores that decided to suspend their operation due to these constant official harassments. However, bookstore owners certainly knew the risks that they were exposed to and thus took efforts to minimize the danger. For instance, they were closely observing the book titles sold in other stores so that they would not incidentally cross the invisible red line. As for in-store events, since they required prior registration and proceeded in a closed-door manner, it was easier to prevent the intrusion of troublemakers. In short, independent bookstores have emerged as one of the few places where frustrated citizens could meet and interact with each other.

Court and Prison Support Actions

As the number of arrestees surged, Hong Kong's activists responded by directing attention to those who faced legal troubles. Aside from providing legal aid in the form of lawyer consulting and defense, they launched a series of support actions for those who were undergoing criminal prosecution as well as those serving prison sentences. On October 9, 2019, when Edward Leung appeared in court for his appeal amid the high tide of the Be Water Revolution, more than one thousand supporters gathered in support. They attended the court hearing and gathered to see him off when his prison bus left, chanting movement slogans and waving the protest flags. In December of that year, a letter-writing campaign came into being that encouraged supporters to write Christmas cards to those who were in pretrial detention centers or in prisons. Our journalistic database reported nineteen incidents of the so-called "write with you" from December 2019 to July 2020. Following the decrease in street protests, court and prison support actions emerged as one of the few ways participants could sustain their commitment to the movement. These actions gained increased significance due to the NSL's sweeping targeting of opponents. Demonstrating solidarity with those political prisoners served as both a defiant gesture and a symbol of solidarity with those in distress.

Court actions generally involved mobilizing people to observe court proceedings—referred to as "court observers" (*pongtingsi/pangtingshi*)—and another form consisted in sending off the defendants when they were about to leave the court. "Vehicle chasers" (*zeoicesi/zhuicheshi*), as they came to be known, usually surrounded the prison bus and shouted prisoner names and slogans. The purpose of these acts was to express camaraderie with these imprisoned protesters so that they knew they were not alone or forgotten. Famous arrestees, such as the case of forty-seven persons, usually attracted a large number of court observers and vehicle chasers. But, for those who were less known, there were several online groups that regularly reported the court schedule and encouraged supporters to join.[8] They explicitly aimed to call attention more evenly so that no imprisoned protesters were neglected.

There were several things that observers could do in the court. First, the mere act of being present for unknown defendants was a bold statement of support. Some enthusiastic observers clapped their hands or cheered when the defendants were allowed to make their statements, which was often disrupted and warned by judges. If the court granted bail, defendants often received food or gifts from these observers before leaving for home. A significant number of these participants were senior laypeople who knew little about legal procedures—giving rise to a phenomenon called "housewives going to court" (*sinaai tengsam*). Second, there were online channels that live broadcast the court trial with subtitles, which required the participation of committed volunteers to fulfill the designated task. At least two alternative media were specially devoted to reporting those legal cases that involved protesters.[9] These numerous acts of recording coalesced into a massive online catalog called the Hong Kong Compendium Project (available at https://hkcompendium.org/), which provides easily searchable functions. In some cases, court participation incidentally helped foster connection among those who suffered the same grief. Hong Kong's common law system practiced a particular coroner court in which the cause of unnatural deaths was adjudicated by judges. During the nearly two-month coroner court case on Chow Tsz Lok that ended in January 2021, many witnesses responded to his father's plea for more evidence and offered their testimonies. Thus, the legal procedure incidentally became a meeting place of mourning with surviving family members, first-aiders, and neighborhood residents.[10]

By comparison, prison support involved more diversified actions including interactions with prisoners and their family members, both directly and indirectly. A social worker who was detained before receiving bail described the situation behind bars:

> Protesters in prison need me to see them. They need petition letters for their legal cases. They want some legal professionals to look into their backgrounds and prove that they can rehabilitate themselves after being released. Keeping correspondence with them is very helpful, which is also my current job. In jail, they do not know what is hap-

pening on the outside, and they might think they are forgotten. Writing letters is therefore a form of encouragement.

Prison visits were another way of keeping contact with imprisoned protesters, especially for those who were already estranged from their family members. Shortly after taking office, many of the 389 prodemocracy district councillors formed a coordination platform to evenly distribute the task of prison visits. According to an interviewed source, each district councillor was responsible for three inmates whom they saw regularly. However, the COVID-19 pandemic brought about a tightening of prison visit regulations, making it difficult for opposition politicians to intervene.

In addition to letter writing and in-person visiting, inmates also needed money for cigarettes and palatable food as well as other material resources, such as donated books. As a result, many organizations were set up to fulfill these needs. They collected donations and forwarded them to those jailed protesters in need. Their assistance was not only limited to inmates but also extended to their family members who needed to cope with the consequences of economic deprivation and social stigmatization. Some inmates also needed these supportive networks to find jobs after their release from jail.

Some prison support organizations adopted a more institutionalized approach. Wall-Fare was founded by an opposition lawmaker Shiu Ka-chun who was jailed for five months for his participation in the Umbrella Movement (Shiu 2022). Wall-Fare was formally registered in December 2020 and maintained a staff of eight people. Wall-Fare became anathema to the authorities because of its constant petitions for prisoner rights. For instance, it launched a signature-collection petition to improve the situation of overheated jail cells during the summer. Under government pressure, Wall-Fare was forced to disband itself in 2021. Other participants pursued a semiunderground strategy to continue their prison assistance. An interviewed activist revealed that he made use of a preexisting registered charity group for fundraising from carefully screened supporters; the collected money was used to assist families with economic hardships and to facilitate in-prison study. He was careful that all the financial records were duly approved by professional accountants so that the authorities could not accuse him of money laundering.

Some organizations focused on recruiting pen pals for inmates. An interviewed activist revealed that her organization was in contact with around 180 jailed protesters, and each of them needed to be matched with eight letter-writing volunteers to maintain a steady stream of correspondence. There were explicit and implicit rules regarding letters in and out of prison, which she and her partners learned from experience. For instance, they needed to remind writers not to use English or mention political slogans in the letters, in case they were confiscated by prison authorities. Prisoners' right to receive letters was often not duly honored as promised by law, as the authorities often intercepted the correspondence without notice. As such, letter writers learned the trick of beginning their incoming message always by mentioning the previous ones so to alert their recipients. Support groups also helped resend outgoing postal mail from prison to save postage cost for inmates. In cases when receivers did not have a usable home address, the organization became a de facto mail relay center. Without soliciting outside donations, she and her colleagues processed up to one thousand letters per month on their own.

Compared to the three other forms of postmobilization activism, court and prison support action constituted the most oppositional one because it directly confronted the state's lawfare against movement participants. Rejecting the official definition of criminals, court and prison activists insisted on greeting them as comrades. As such, they bore the brunt of government reprisal. Court observers were warned, forced to reveal personal information to the police, and arrested for their overtly excited responses. In October 2022, for example, two court observers were found guilty of spreading "seditious words."[11] If their actions attracted public attention, prison support groups encountered a barrage of criticism from officials and pro-Beijing politicians. Aside from Wall-Fare, another organization known as Swallow Life was targeted by the authorities, which claimed their letters to inmates were tendentious and smacked of incitement. Consequently, Swallow Life opted for a digital death by not updating its social media account. Clearly, the SAR government was able to suppress and harass these court and prison support actions if they proceeded in a high-profile manner; but for those organizations that avoided publicized fundraising or advocacy for prisoner rights, they were more or less able to operate without interference.

Conclusion: The Art of Surviving the Repression

Students of contentious politics are interested in the questions regarding movement resilience, especially how activists continue their commitment after constraints from the government are suddenly imposed (Chenoweth and Stephan 2011: 57). Existing research indicates that methods of dispersion, such as adopting networked rather than hierarchical organizations, are among the typical strategies to survive a state crackdown (Nepstad 2015: 95; Schock 2005: 50). In the case of Hong Kong, six months of intensive mobilization resulted in escalating numbers of arrests and the movement's rank and file were depleted. The year 2020 brought about twin external shocks—COVID-19 and the NSL—that made street protests extremely difficult and risky. Within one year of the NSL's implementation, the city was deprived of its opposition politicians, independent media, student associations, and civil society organizations. Braving unexpected adversity, prodemocracy Hongkongers invented new forms of activism, and, even though this new activism was in no way able to stop the city's ongoing autocratization, it mitigated against acute damage wrought by a vengeful state apparatus and helped preserve the strength of like-minded citizens who chose to stay. In this sense, the protest actions of the Be Water Revolution have ceased to exist, but the movement has continued unabated as it flowed into more dispersed and less obtrusive channels.

It is always difficult to stave off movement decline under repression. Continuing in defiant gestures risks exposing more activists to state reprisal without securing movement gains, and taking shelter in dormancy appears safer but inadvertently ends up endorsing the regime's claim to have reestablished "order." Dissident Hongkongers certainly knew the dilemma between "preserving the momentum" and "demonstrating the will" (Pu 2020). However, between these two contrasting choices, Hongkongers who participated in postmobilization activism practiced the art of gray-zone tactics.

This chapter examined alternative media, community newspapers, independent bookstores, and court and prison support actions as cases of postmobilization activism. I chose not to apply the existing conceptual tools such as abeyance structure and everyday resistance because these newly invented forms of activism were not a tactical withdrawal into a small coterie of activists or a disengagement from the public sphere. On the contrary, as alternative media reached out to unknown readers, community newspapers to residents, and independent bookstores to customers and prison support groups cultivated epistolary correspondence between inmates and supporters, new interpersonal ties emerged and were fortified by a shared prodemocracy identity. Moreover, in light of the fact that Beijing has embarked on a hegemonic project of reengineering Hong Kong into a submissive Chinese city by cleansing its colonial heritage and memory, this activism explicitly upheld the values of press freedom (alternative media and independent bookstores), local identity (community newspapers), and solidarity (court and prison support actions), thus mounting assiduous resistance against the regime project. This activism came about as a consequence of creative improvisation among experienced participants, as reporters of closed media outlets reapplied their journalistic skills elsewhere and ex-prisoners launched prison support actions.

Their activism fulfilled two functions as the city descended into the NSL-induced political degradation. First, they were restorative in the sense of compensating for the loss. Alternative media continued independent journalism after the forcible closure of prodemocracy media, while independent bookstores provided the access to dissident writings when they were taken off the shelf in Hong Kong's public libraries. Second, they were also remedial for the frustrated movement supporters, as evidenced in those bookstores that meticulously set up a therapeutic corner for readers and the prison support groups that strived to keep inmates connected with the outside world. True, these actions were not proactive in the sense of openly opposing the top-down autocratization of the city, but they were at least capable of slowing down the process by creating more hurdles to the regime's political project.

Finally, postmobilization activism faced the daunting challenge of sustainability, especially when mass enthusiasm waned. One solution consisted of transforming the effort into a for-profit undertaking so that commerce and commitment would be nicely wedded together. In this regard, alternative media that operated on a subscription model and independent bookstores that enjoyed steady revenue were more likely to survive by successfully carving an economic niche for themselves, whereas community newspapers experienced a tough transition from their nonprofit origins. Court and prison support actions essentially relied on mass sympathy in soliciting donations and recruiting people to write letters; these ideational resources were difficult to replenish once popular attention declined.

There are rich implications of how these forms of postmobilization activism sustained themselves via market means. Students of contentious politics generally see the emergence of corporate social responsibility, stockholder activism, and socially responsible investment as a result of movement activists' application of market-conforming tactics (King and Pearce 2010; Soule 2009). For moneywise Hongkongers, sponsoring a movement by becoming a follower of the city's political and opinion leaders who operated a paid-for-view account on Patreon (a U.S.-based membership platform) was a common phenomenon. Against this background, it is easier to understand why new media and independent bookstores are more likely to stay because of their for-profit business models, at least compared to community newspapers and legal support groups, which typically rely on a charity model. Since the PRC renounced its socialist past and needed Hong Kong as an offshore financial clearinghouse, the city's vibrant market economy continued to provide resources to dissentient activities in a way that Beijing rulers were forced to tolerate. The observation here should not be read as an uncritical endorsement of neoliberalism, which sees individual economic freedom as a cornerstone for political liberty. However, once they faced relentless political repression, economic freedom was among the remaining means with which they could improvise their dissident activities.

Conclusion

Without a figurehead leadership nor a coordinating center, prodemocracy Hongkongers reinvented the way of making protests beyond the imagination of their opponents, international observers, and even the protesters themselves. The Be Water Revolution unleashed a torrent of participation, far surpassing the scale and militancy of the 2014 Umbrella Movement. Hongkongers were no longer satisfied with a peaceful occupy protest but engaged in disruptive (general strike and road barricade) and violent acts (storefront vandalism and throwing petrol bombs). From February 2019 to June 2020, 1,770 protest events took place: they included three large-scale demonstrations with over one million participants as well as numerous flash mob style sing-alongs in the shopping malls. Protest shock waves spread out from the city center to bedroom and overseas diaspora communities. To prevent the extradition to the mainland court, Hongkongers' protests were strategic because they forced the SAR government and Beijing to pay a higher price for their intended legal overhaul; at the same time, their actions were also highly symbolic and dramaturgic as they were carefully choreographed to demonstrate the agency of a newborn political community. The movement drew its strength from myriad preexisting networks and groups that made possible a plethora of militant and logistic collaborations, spanning across the online/offline, personal/organizational, and at-home/abroad divides. At the same time, the movement itself was also spawning new groups, stimulating housewives, elders, mainland migrants, animal lovers, disabled persons, and other categories of people to assume their political agency. In so doing, the anti-government protest assumed a territory-wide and inclusive profile, and, at the same time, these groups struggled to counter their stigmatization and carved out a new space in this newborn community.

Émile Durkheim (1915) discovered the mythic experience of collective effervescence as the fountainhead of artistic creations that celebrated the power of a united community in Australia's primitive tribes, and this insight is equally applicable to the twenty-first century financial hub of Hong Kong. The Be Water Revolution invented a new vocabulary (*sauzuk* and *laam caau*), fresh ideas (yellow economic circle), novel gestures (placing one's right hand over the right eye), and viral songs (an underground national anthem) that many Hongkongers recurrently and duly practiced as if they were part of a religious ritual. Untried and bold tactics (airport protests and human chains) became stunning realities that took the authorities by surprise, just as the emergence of numerous group statements and graphic materials demonstrate how a people could unleash their creative and innovative potential when each individual took seriously their collective membership. Even after the cessation of protest actions, Hongkongers continued to invent new forms of engagement that not only confronted the regime's political agenda but also recovered and remedied the loss and the injuries in the previous round of intensive activism.

To make sense of the scope and the intensity of Hong Kong's Be Water Revolution, this book adopts the perspective of actionist sociology. While social movement and contentious politics scholarship have generated a wealth of conceptual vocabulary to understand the rise and fall of protest activism, commonly used approaches like political opportunities, mobilizing structure, frame, brokerage, scale shift, and others help institutionalize and professionalize the research field by making it possible for practitioners to use the same set of conceptual tools to conduct comparative studies across the globe. However, most of these theoretical constructs are either static models or impersonal mechanisms that fail to capture the fluid and fuzzy situation that confronts citizens when they are about to make a strategic decision. True, actors at any given time do not enjoy unlimited freedom as their range of choices is necessarily proscribed by external circumstances as well as by their personal biography and cultural preferences. What is at their disposal are usually their interpersonal connections, control over material resources, professional competence and skills, experiences and reflections on previous activism, and their embodied judgment of what is appropriate in their context. Out of this complex matrix, protest actions are planned and performed. The process of selecting a protest strategy is emphatically more complicated than a cost-and-benefit analysis in rational choice theory assumes, simply because cost and benefit are not the only two considerations.

Protest, at its core, is an activity intended to make a change, and, as such, it requires individuals to depart from their habituated obedience. To be able to mount an effective challenge to the authorities, protests must be unconventional; that is, they need to depart from the routinized and expectable displays of dissent. As Jasper (2006: xiv) points out, "As long as you and your opponent have similar expectations about 'normal' moves, or even the 'best' moves, you have to break the rules to surprise them." In this light, the discussion of "social movement society," or the institutionalization of protests in democratic countries (Goldstone 2004; M. Ho and Ting 2023; Meyer and Tarrow 1998; Rucht and Neidhardt 2002; Soule and Earl 2006), points to the ambivalent results of the liberal tolerance of dissident activities. By accepting social movements as a normal exercise of the freedom of speech and accommodating street protests within the existing legal framework, democratic incumbents also made them conventional and routine, and perhaps harmless and useless as a result. Similar to Speakers' Corner in London's Hyde Park, Lafayette Square near the White House, and the Legislative Yuan's sidewalks in Taipei, there exist continuous protest activities that only a handful of passersby would notice. Deprived of elements of surprise and uncertainties, protests become self-defeating ritualism at best, rather than a vehicle for change.

Fundamental to the discussion of an actionist sociology of strategic choice is the notion of human agency. As Giddens (1984: 9) points out, agency always implies that "individuals could, at any phase in a given sequence of conduct, have acted differently." While his structuration theory is primarily geared toward an understanding of "social practices ordered across space and time" (2), a study of social movements from the actionist perspective is at its best when applied to making sense of those eventful and transformative, albeit infrequent, protest activisms that turn the pages of history. In other words, while an agentic account of these exceptional social movements might not be the only legitimate narrative, it remains the best perspective to illuminate how participants choose to make history in their own ways.

The Be Water Revolution happens to belong to this rare subset of history-making protests. What happened during 2019–2020 in Hong Kong was a string of unanticipated incidents that eventually led to an unexpected denouement of the hasted demise of the city's promised high degree of autonomy, earlier than its promised expiration year of 2047. When the SAR government first introduced the Extradition Law Amendment Bill (ELAB) in February 2019, the embattled prodemocratic forces were still recuperating from the depressing long shadow of the failed Umbrella Movement and appeared too weak to put up a spirited fight. When millions took to the streets peacefully in early June, they did not anticipate an armed-to-the-teeth regime that freely used tear gas, rubber bullets, and lawfare to suppress dissidents. Yet, over the long sweltering summer that year, the authorities failed to tame the proverbially law-abiding Hongkongers with gangster violence, live ammunition, and emergency decrees. Even Beijing was taken aback by the ferocious and tenacious resistance of Hongkongers, so it decided to get its hands dirty by unilaterally imposing the NSL in Hong Kong, thus worsening China's relationship with the West. Since Beijing has used Hong Kong as a demonstration site for the OCTS, which was the original formula to impose on Taiwan, Taiwanese had paid close attention to the Hong Kong's crisis. A poll survey documents how Taiwanese perception about China changed rapidly: in 2017, 68% of Taiwanese were confident about China's future development, and the figure dropped to 40% in 2020, fewer than those who were not confident for the first time (48%) (C. Chen and Zheng 2022: 258). Both in Taiwan and Hong Kong, the PRC's attempts to assert its authoritarian control backfired, as more and more Taiwanese and Hongkongers decided to embrace their distinctive non-Chinese identities because of their belief in democratic values (Chong and Pan 2022). Finally, even under the draconian NSL regulation and the global manhunt, Hongkongers, at home and abroad, were still campaigning for their freedom and resisting political assimilation. The series of unintended consequences would not be understandable if we took out the element of agency and activists' own choice. To paraphrase Karl Marx, "Hongkongers make their own history, but they do not make it as they please."

From Beijing's perspective, this meandering trajectory is perhaps an unnecessary detour toward the eventual assimilation to the political regime in the PRC. True, the ELAB was in the end aborted, but the NSL caused more damage to the city's judicial independence. Following the thinking of Beijing hard-liners, recalcitrant Hongkongers paid a dear price for their insubordination, which turned out to be futile and counterproductive. Perhaps, they should have the stoic wisdom to accept the inevitable fate considering that PRC's global strength was gaining by the day? Some Beijing policymakers had long seen Hong Kong as "a spoiled child" who wantonly disavowed the beneficence of the fatherland for economic achievement (Carrico 2022: 120–21). In this paternalistic understanding, Hongkongers' agency and their pursuit for self-determination amounted to nothing but ingratitude and impiety, which should have been stamped out in the first place. Considering the viewpoint of Hongkongers, however, would the outcome have been more favorable if they had initially acquiesced obediently? This inquiry naturally centers around Hongkongers' own decision and whether they would like to assert their agency. If the ELAB had been approved without much resistance, it is a reasonable guess that Beijing and their SAR collaborators would have come forward with more revisions to further undermine the city's autonomy and quicken the pace of political assimilation. Some hawkish policymakers in China, who viewed the remaining British legacy in the city as an eyesore, or worse, a sign of national humiliation, had explicitly advocated for such a policy. Nevertheless, the decision made by prodemocracy Hongkongers has contradicted Beijing's wishful thinking and upended its strategic road map. From then on, Beijing has paid dearly for every step as it proceeds to stamp out any remaining freedom in Hong Kong; democratic countries in East Asia and the West are already forewarned by the Be Water Revolution and its long subsequent reverberations.

The actionist perspective adopted here does not claim that movement participants' capacity is unlimited—it is often constrained by their own material endowment, personal experience, ingrained disposition, cultural heritage, interpersonal connections, and other related factors. I have specifically chosen not to use structural metaphors (such as political opportunity)—as many researchers (including my own previous books) used to do—in order to highlight the *strategic choices* made by Hong Kong's participants, which I have argued are the fundamental catalyst of this transformative movement. Retrospectively, Hongkongers had alternative choices at many critical moments, including not to resist the ELAB when it was first proposed, not to escalate the confrontation when the SAR government made known its determination, not to take a militant turn when encountering gangster violence and police crackdown, and not to devise novel forms of activism under the NSL repression. At each juncture, Hongkongers could have easily taken the path of least resistance, but the fact that they chose to remain defiant against the odds resulted in the Be Water Revolution as we know it. To paraphrase the memorable words of the great labor historian E. P. Thompson (1980: 8), "Hongkongers did not rise like the sun at an appointed time. They were present at their own making." As such, an actionist sociology is the best analytical approach to shed light on the role of agency as well as the difference it makes.

Collective Improvisation: Strength and Limitations

The Be Water Revolution demonstrates the powerful agency of prodemocracy Hongkongers, and how this subjective force unfolded in the course of the movement needs explanation. This book finds that a recurrent process of collective improvisation—peer-produced strategic responses without prior planning—constitutes the microfoundation of this great movement. In lieu of centralized leadership, many participants joined the decision-making process, and they willingly took up the tasks that they were most capable of. The accumulated results of these innumerable acts of discussion and coordination are stunning spectacles such as the Hong Kong Way and the two University Battles, for which there is not a single identifiable initiator. In fact, it is doubtful whether any individuals or organizations could have such power of moral persuasion to mobilize participants on this massive scale for these endeavors. Pierre Bourdieu (1977: 72) describes how individual habitus brought about stable social order as follows: "Collectively orchestrated without being the product of the organizing action of a conductor." Despite the fact that Bourdieu is more concerned with the reproduction of existing structures, rather than their rupture, the imagery of a conductorless orchestra can also be applied to Hong Kong's decentralized campaign. Regarding this matter, the often repeated conspiracy theory in Beijing's narrative, suggesting that external powers (such as the United States and Taiwan) orchestrated the protest activism, seems even more absurd. If not a single resident of Hong Kong could take credit for initiating these actions, it raises questions about the potential involvement of foreigners.

The notion of collective improvisation seeks to move away from the sterile debate between leaderlessness and leaderfulness, as both perspectives suggest an overly simplified view. It is true that a great number of participants were deeply involved in the planning and executing of the protest actions, but that does not warrant a radical egalitarianism as if everyone's contribution were equally consequential. The belief that everyone counts is a useful stimulus for broadly based participation, but never a truthful account of reality. Having a personal stake in the ongoing campaign encourages participants to contribute their knowledge, expertise, resources, and effort so that the movement benefits from such wide-ranging peer production. Decentralization is at its best when it can enlist the contribution from widespread participants beyond a narrow circle, thus avoiding the trap of groupthink. Contribution is also by nature differential and remains unequal. Spatially distributed participants knew intimately how to connect their neighborhood issues with the anti-ELAB campaign, just as how diasporic Hongkonger activists were skillful in framing their homeland issue for the consumption of foreign audiences. The involvement of the community of illustrators, cartoonists, and visual designers further generated an aesthetic front line to engage with the authorities. All these forms of participation could not be accomplished if the movement were to proceed under a rigid command-and-control center.

As a central process of coordination, collective improvisation assumes a variety of forms. Anonymous netizens, friends, acquaintances with preexisting ties, and established leaders all responded in their own ways as the movement unfolded. Collective improvisation repurposed interpersonal connections, aggregated the supply of resources, and formed militant teammates who were willing to shoulder the risk together. The same dynamism produced numerous group statements, artistic works, and songs that bedazzled the observers. Newer forms of activism were invented in the course, both during the high tide of the protests and after their disappearance. In short, collective improvisation is creative, resourceful, and resilient.

Contrary to the writers of anarchism and technological optimism, social movements can proceed in a decentralized manner without being completely flattened to the extent that preexisting leaders or advocacy organizations are hopelessly obsolete. Amateurs like Anna Kwok and Finn Lau emerged as the nodal points for the city's global diplomacy because they were able to coordinate activisms across different time zones due to their international experiences. Yet, Joshua Wong became the de facto ambassador-at-large on the global stage because he had been the world-renowned face of Hong Kong's democracy that has befriended many foreign dignitaries on a personal basis—a pivotal position that could in no way be delegated to other people. In the same way, Shiu Ka-chun reflexively applied his personal experience of imprisonment to launch his prison-support activism. All these cases show that certain individuals continue to play an outsize role throughout the movement, and their contribution cannot be written off as a part of a faceless and nameless "multitude."

The same reasoning applies to those preexisting advocacy organizations that are proverbially criticized as ritualistic and unimaginative in Hong Kong's context. However, such criticisms fail to do justice to their contributions and thereby overestimate the role of individual protesters. The CHRF, which single-handedly initiated the anti-ELAB campaign, remained the most trustworthy civil organization that was able to stage a rally with over one million participants. Although HKCTU did not initiate the call for a general strike, its experienced labor activists played an important role in the strike rallies and the launching of new unions. HKFS had a diminished presence among Hong Kong's student movement following the disheartening failure of the Umbrella Movement, but it successfully reinvented itself in the form of HKIAD, which played a pivotal role in the city's global diplomacy.

As such, collective improvisation makes room for a more nuanced understanding, which acknowledges the inspiration and effort among many anonymous participants without unduly and prematurely relegating existing leaders and organizations to the dustbin of history. As the Be Water Revolution shows, a collectively improvised movement can be imaginative, versatile, militant, and numerous, thus creating the worst nightmare for government incumbents.

Nevertheless, while collective improvisation represents a more evolved model beyond conventional organization-led and leadership-centered movements, it is not all-purpose, and neither is it a panacea to solve the dilemmas inherent to all collective actions. I list the constraints discovered in the Hong Kong case here:

1. Collective improvisation is not an everyday phenomenon, as it happens infrequently and is only triggered under certain dramatic conditions. Hongkongers were cornered into a last-ditch defense of their proud legal legacy, which guaranteed personal liberty. A series

of suicide protests triggered a great emotional upheaval so as to motivate an unprecedented level of participation. In reality, most social movements simply do not reach such a level of mass alert and emotional intensity and, thus, are unable to tap into contributions beyond the narrow circle of those who are immediately involved.

2. Collective improvisation is not a permanently renewable source that can provide participation and ideas indefinitely. A ratcheted up crackdown decimated the available protesters and made militant actions more difficult and costly. Tactical innovation and spatial diffusion had their natural limits, and, beyond a certain threshold, it became more exponentially difficult to come up with new ideas for making protest. Even though its sources were dispersed, fatigue and depletion sets in eventually.
3. To err is human, and the same goes for collective improvisation, which was never failure proof. Quite the opposite, it was precisely because failure was not attributable to any individuals that collective improvisation could indulge in the wildest speculation of possible trajectories. A close examination reveals that many acts of collective improvisation were ineffective and futile, but these downsides were not widely publicized and largely harmless. Therefore, the so-called crowd wisdom is clearly overrated because people tend to disregard its failure, and such failure is also not accounted for.
4. Collective improvisation could leave a debilitating legacy of extreme fragmentation, especially when it required a coordinated voice in championing the city's demands on the global stage. The entrenched belief that one was always empowered to act as she or he saw fit unilaterally without the need for mutual negotiation could easily dilute the collective voices of Hongkongers, further contributing to the centrifugal tendency among diaspora activism.
5. Everything did not necessarily become more beautiful when the amount was plenty. While collective improvisation made it possible to tap into many underexplored sources and solicited contributions from those previously less involved, it also opened the floodgate to problematic ideas that no centralized screening procedure was able to prevent. As previously mentioned, some online visual materials explicitly used the themes of misogyny, dehumanization, and discrimination to make their points, which was perfectly expectable since such attitudes already existed prior to the onset of the protest.

In short, while collective improvisation can be a powerful weapon in enlisting broad participation and stimulating creative protests, its shortcomings cannot be simply ignored.

Improvising Contentious Politics Studies Collectively

How does collective improvisation fit into the already abundant conceptual vocabulary in contentious politics studies? As the research field becomes more mature and institutionalized, practitioners are fortunate to possess a wealth of analytical tools, and one hesitates to introduce a new one for fear that it might never gain traction. With the actionist assumptions in mind, I suggest the term is best used to shed light on the subjective and agent-based dimensions of many existing approaches, rather than an outright replacement for existing conceptual tools. Collective improvisation is a particular manifestation of agency flourishing only under unusual circumstances, which calls attention to the fact that history-making protests are usually unexpected precisely because participants choose to deviate from their routine responses. In a word, revolutions are made; they do not just happen.

In the existing studies, the emergence of social movements is often seen as a result of some favorable conditions, such as the availability of resources (Cress and Snow 1996; Edwards, McCarthy, and Mataic 2019; Zald and McCarthy 1987), the existence of networks (Useem 1980; Diani 2015; Diani and McAdam 2003), and the opening of political opportunities (Kitschelt 1986; McAdam 1982; Meyer 1990; Tarrow 1989). Yet, these external conditions exist only as a potentiality; without the active intervention of movement participants, they alone can never contribute to the genesis of social movements. The swift expansion of Hongkongers' capacity further shows that resources do not exist in a pregiven quantity, and neither are networks fixed in a preexisting configuration. Just as opportunities emerge only insofar as when the actors are capable of seizing them, resources and networks are always codetermined by their capacity.

Moreover, collective improvisation is capable of radically reconfiguring these conditions for movement mobilization by transforming obstacles into facilitators and thereby engendering an "unthinkable revolution" (Kurzman 2004). In Hong Kong's Be Water Revolution, the low likelihood of stopping the ELAB in the legislature (or "closed political opportunities") actually invited transgressive protest-making since opponents were keenly aware of the numerical disadvantage of opposition lawmakers. Precisely because protesters knew the ELAB would be passed in a legislative vote, they gathered to prevent the session from taking place. In hindsight, the legislature besiegement in early June 2019 turned out to be the opening salvo of a series of increasingly innovative and disruptive protests. The way in which Hongkongers appropriated their preexisting interpersonal ties for the movement, forged fresh connections during the intense conflict, and creatively used money and other materials further demonstrated that networks and resources do not exist in a fixed quantity, nor are they always ready at hand. An ex-ante description of "objective" situations prior to the rise of protest actions always remains static and incomplete because one can never fathom the source and the depth of movement agency. In other words, networks and resources are also codetermined by actors' capacity and, above all, commitment.

By contrast, collective improvisation shares more affinities with culturally sensitive concepts, including framing (Snow and Benford 1988; Snow et al. 1986), identity (Larana, Johnston, and Gusfield 1994; Melucci 1996; Stryker, Owens, and White 2000), and repertoire (Tilly 1978, 2008; Traugott 2010), because of the same constructionist perspective that recognizes social movements are largely of participants' own making. Nevertheless, the new concept can add fresh insights into existing approaches. The persuasive appeals of Five Demands, the *sauzuk* appellation, and the *laam caau* strategy have been the consistent driving forces in the whole episode, but these new ideas or "frames" could not be traced to a single proponent, which testifies to the power of anonymous peer production, which easily traverses the online/offline, professional/amateur, and national borders. Similarly, a strong identity empowers movement mobilization, which, in turn, encourages new identity formation and group making. The sudden proliferation of new social categories (housewives, ACG fans, and others) and the neighborhood-based protests accentuate the interactive and collaborative process of identity making. Both collective improvisation and repertoire pay attention to the dramaturgic dimension of social movements, whose claims need to be performed and ritualized in public. Still, repertoire, at least in the original Tillyan scheme, emphasizes the stability and finite set of choices for protesters at a given time, whereas collective improvisation is more interested in explaining the tactical innovation via decentralized peer production.

Finally, collective improvisation echoes the recent shift of research attention from opportunities to threats (Almeida 2003; Goldstone and Charles Tilly 2001; Maher 2010) and the growing attention to emotion in movement mobilization (Einwohner 2003; Goodwin, Jasper, and Polletta 2001; Peña, Meier, and Nah 2021). The Be Water Revolution was triggered by an alarming sense of "endgame" among prodemocracy Hongkongers, who chose to resort to previously unthinkable measures not because of the lower cost of action or the higher rate of success, but rather of the suddenly imposed cost of *in*action, which encouraged all kinds of experimental and bold actions because participants widely saw it as a last-ditch effort. And such decisions were made in a high-pressure crucible of anger, guilt, and pride, which was quite unusual in an ubercapitalist city that used to take pride in expediting commercial transactions and supporting a moderate and polite prodemocracy opposition. These emotional responses were present as Hongkongers came to experience the tumultuous unfolding of events involving suicides, suspicious deaths, and police violence together. Hongkongers' collective improvisation also indicated that emotionally charged responses do not stand in the way of rationally strategizing. As shown in Chapter 3, their reactions to a series of unexpected shifts were largely measured and appropriate, carefully balancing the contradictory imperatives in pressuring the government with disruption and securing the popular support. To use the terminology of Jasper (2018), while most prodemocracy Hongkongers experienced the outrageous incidents with "reflex emotions" like anger and disgust or "urges" that needed immediate bodily releases individually, these were those emotional outcomes that could be regretted later. Through the process of peer production, or the widespread online and offline discussions, these strong feelings translated into a more durable "moral emotion" that was more compatible with planning and executing responses rationally. In short, feeling is not antithetical to thinking, and, at every critical juncture, Hongkongers made the appropriate strategic choice that nicely agreed with the emotional state of that moment.

Like other fields of social science research, social movement students are usually avid observers of the latest developments pioneered by bold and imaginative practitioners in the field. They broke ground for a new direction and created a wave of protests that aimed to change the world as we knew it. As the preceding analysis has argued, collective improvisation will probably remain one of the central features of protest-making in the years to come since the world has witnessed the waning of mass membership organizations, the rise of digital media, and the quest for personal authenticity in participation.

Beyond Hong Kong

From a historical perspective, the evolution of Hong Kong's political movement has been a progressive unraveling of leadership toward the point of complete self-annihilation. Professional politicians rose to prominence in the 1990s and became the leading voices of the city's prodemocracy camp. Ten years later, the Democratic Party–led opposition gave way to a boisterous collection of smaller parties commonly identified as "pan-democrats." Seeing little prospect of politician-led democratization, the OCLP emerged as a civil disobedience movement proposed by civil society leaders (two university professors and one pastor) in 2013. However, when the Umbrella Movement broke out the following year, it was the students who came to the fore, and yet they proved ill-prepared for coordinating such a massive movement.

The disappointing end of the Umbrella Movement left an enduring distaste for any form of leadership. As such, when Hongkongers rose up in opposition in mid-2019, their resounding rejection of leadership was, in fact, the accumulated result of what happened during the preceding two decades. But is this trend of movement leadership dissolution a universal process?

Certainly, there are contextual factors that contributed to the gradual hollowing out of leadership in Hong Kong. The post-1997 change in the electoral system favored smaller parties at the expense of the once-hegemonic Democratic Party. Frustrated political reform gave rise to firebrand insurgents who were no longer satisfied with the gentlemanly moderation of opposition lawmakers. The involvement of civil society activists took the debate out of political institutions and into the streets and public square. Acknowledging that there were specific factors about Hong Kong that expedited the centrifugal process, one cannot fail to notice that such decentralized protests have assumed greater prominence on a global scale. Although the label "leaderless" is often incorrect and easily misleading by overlooking the reliance on preexisting organizations and networks for protest mobilization, its prevalence indicates that such movements without a figurehead leader or a coordinating center have emerged as an important player in contentious politics across the globe.

After Hong Kong's Be Water Revolution ground to a halt, the world continued to witness the eruption of these decentralized and history-making movements, including the American BLM movement after the murder of George Floyd (May 2020), Thai student protests against the military government (August 2020), the anticoup protests in Myanmar (February 2021), the "Women, Life, and Freedom" movement in Iran (September 2022), and the "A4 Revolution" in China (November 2022). All five of these incidents have a common characteristic: they appear to have arisen spontaneously and unexpectedly, without any individual or organization orchestrating them. The following are similarities they share with the Hong Kong case:

1. **Morally shocking events:** the video recorded murder of George Floyd under the brutality of Minneapolis police officers, the death of hijab-free Mahsa Amini in Iranian police detention, and the ten deaths in an Urumqi (Xinjiang's capital) fire due to draconian COVID-19 lockdown measures triggered protest waves in the United States, Iran, and China, respectively. In the case of Myanmar, the army's forcible seizure of power and the arrest of popularly elected politicians led to an uprising, and the Thai government's disbandment of a popular political party triggered the student protest.

2. **Widespread participation:** the BLM movement was estimated to have amassed fifteen million to twenty-six million people in demonstrations in the first few weeks. On June 6 alone, there were 550 cities that witnessed protest action. As such, the BLM amounted to the largest-scale social protest in American history (Buchanan, Bui, and Patel 2020). In the first three months after Mahsa Amini's death, two million Iranians took to the streets and their actions spread across 160 cities and towns, easily surpassing anti-government protests in 2009, 2017, and 2019 (Bayat 2023: 23–24). The anticoup protests in Myanmar evolved into a popular insurgency against the power-grabbing generals, involving active participation from different demographics, for instance, Buddhists, Christians, and Muslims (Frydenlund et al. 2021) and music communities (Aung 2021).
3. **Radicalized claims:** the pre–George Floyd BLM movement was divided over various ways to end racism among law enforcement, and the shock resulted in the ascendency of radical police abolitionism over other milder reform proposals (Phelps, Ward, and Frazier 2021). Breaking the taboo that few opposition politicians dared to touch, Thai student protesters used anti-monarchy slogans and directly denounced the erratic behavior of their king (M. Thompson and Cheng 2022). China's A4 Revolution opposed the continuation of heavy-handed anti-COVID-19 measures, and, although it lasted only ten days, it resulted in drastic policy changes. More importantly, it was the only post-Tiananmen protest "that successfully traced the political root for a policy problem" (Kin-man Chan 2023: 60).
4. **Cross-border activism:** Overseas activities were also an essential part of the contestations on the home front. Iranian diaspora communities have long been involved in the country's opposition movement (Cohen and Yefet 2021). China's A4 Revolution spread to overseas students whose actions shattered the myth of Little Pink, implying that Chinese youths are monolithically jingoistic nationalists. In Myanmar's prodemocracy movement, artworks exhibited and sold in the Global North also contributed to the campaign on the domestic front (Banki 2023).
5. **Social media:** the present age is saturated with social media, and it is difficult to imagine a great social movement that does not go viral in cyberspace at the same time. Iranians used digital platforms like Twitter, Instagram, and Clubhouse to circumvent the theocratic control over information flow (Yee 2022). The #Milk-

TeaAlliance has connected the prodemocracy campaigners in Thailand and Myanmar and envisioned a cross-border community "digitally dismantling Asian authoritarianism" (Dedman and Lai 2021). Even in China, where the state has mastered the art of digital Leninism, the A4 Revolution indicated there remained cracks in the Great Firewall that dissident netizens could utilize skillfully (Kin-man Chan 2023: 63–64).

The aforementioned traits demonstrate that there exist unmistakable resemblances among major decentralized movements in the contemporary era. But how does the lack of nominal leadership make possible widespread participation, claim radicalization, and cross-border activism? This book proffers that collective improvisation offers a conceptual solution. The moral shock of a pivotal event has the power to galvanize a large number of people into action, and their collaboration spans across online and offline networks. As more and more people are united by the same goal, their diversity constitutes a creative source for novel ideas, tactics, and artistic expressions that are indispensable when mounting an effective challenge to the authorities.

While more instantiations of collective improvisation elsewhere remain to be closely examined, there are tendencies that encourage contemporary social movements to follow the course of decentralization. All over the world, political organizations with mass followers are on the decline, be they political parties, labor unions, or advocacy groups. As fewer people possess membership, the mobilization decisions of organizational leaders become less effective, as they can only address a shrinking population. Concomitantly, as people are withdrawing from their organizational identities and loyalties, they are demanding more from their protest participation. It is increasingly unlikely that people will choose to join a protest exclusively because of their allegiance to a leader or an organization; instead, more participants intend to draw subjective and psychological gratification out of their protest action. There is a growing quest for authenticity when it comes to the politics of protest, as more participants are motivated by their individual convictions, rather than their group membership. Finally, as scholars of the information society have long stressed, digital media encourage the growth of horizontal networks that begin to replace hierarchical organizations with top-down command chains and rigid membership boundaries (Castells 2012; Juris 2008). As such, people are now allowed to solve their personal needs without bothering to apply for membership. All these tendencies result in a significant reconfiguration of contemporary contentious politics as it is becoming less likely that a major social movement will take place in the old-school fashion with organizational leadership.

While the earlier analysis mostly addresses the situation in democratic countries, in authoritarian societies that do not respect citizens' political liberties and curtail their freedom of association, expression, and press, protests can happen only if participants successfully manage to anonymize and disguise their connection (Fu 2017) or use their everyday relationship intensively (Pearlman 2021). Consequently, when major anti-government protests take place in China, Iran, and Hong Kong in the future, decentralization is the only way they can surface.

In short, in liberal democracies, which have largely incorporated social protests as an everyday and normal feature, decentralized movements have become occasional outlets for transformative protest activism. By contrast, in authoritarian countries, social movements must be decentralized, or they are not allowed to exist. When such protests happen in such a context, it often signals a major crisis for authoritarian rulers.

Quo Vadis Hong Kong?

When the Be Water Revolution was still in full swing, it was undoubtedly the most-attended protest in the world, and, arguably, that won overwhelming sympathy and support from Western media. In the same time frame of 2019–2020, major protests in Belorussia (against the reelection of Alexander Lukashenko), Catalonia (against the sentencing of proindependence leaders), Chile (over a metro fare hike), Iraq (against corruption and misrule), Venezuela (against the reelection of Nicolás Maduro), and elsewhere took place, and many of them resulted in much higher casualties without receiving the global spotlight that Hongkongers enjoyed.

How can we explain such an anomaly? A structuralist account would likely emphasize the distinctive geopolitical positioning of the city within the escalating rivalry between the United States and China, its historical connection to Britain, and its role in showcasing China's intentions to annex Taiwan. Furthermore, Hong Kong's role as a premier global financial center and a hub for international correspondents contributed to its heightened prominence. However, from the actionist perspective, these endowments were but latent possibilities that required human agents' intervention to be actualized. The city's geopolitical, financial, and journalistic significance does not automatically guarantee a favorable and sympathetic response from the international audience.

Facing the ELAB threat, Hongkongers intensively mobilized their assets, skills, and connections to launch a spectacular campaign for the world to see. Through countless acts of in-kind or cash donations, political consumerism, and crowdfunding, Hong Kong's affluent middle class provided ample resources for street mobilization as well as for remedial aftercare when the protests wound down. The deployment of their professional skills in filmmaking, graphic design, music composition, and dramaturgic choreography resulted in a host of creative endeavors to keep the spirit of the protest alive. Hong Kong's far-flung communities were also galvanized into action and their linguistic fluency and embedded knowledge helped gain more local sympathy. From the G20 Osaka Summit to Russia's War in Ukraine, Hongkongers have seized almost every international event to champion their cause for homeland democracy. In short, Hongkongers have earned their rightful attention through their commitment, effort, and ingenuity.

Whither goest Hong Kong? Just like the years immediately following the Umbrella Movement, the city's prodemocracy campaign was again exhausted and defeated. The repression this time was notably more severe and widespread, extending beyond just the leadership. The NSL has completely revamped the city's institutions; opposition parties, civil society organizations, free press, liberal education, and independent judiciary have all ceased to exist. Opposition leaders are either languishing in jail or taking shelter in exile. Understandably, it is much more difficult for the city's prodemocracy movement to rebound from the devastating aftermath of the Be Water Revolution than that of the Umbrella Movement. However, the city-based postmobilization activism, which continues to exploit the remnant free space, helps slow down the process of full assimilation into the mainland system. They also help document every step in the direction of autocratization, which is always a source of global embarrassment for Beijing and its underlings in the SAR government. These tenacious forms of activism under duress preserve the shared identity, connections among like-minded citizens, and their collective memory, all necessary building blocks for the next round of engagement.

Fueled by the recent wave of emigration, Hong Kong's expatriate community is expanding across various regions of the world. The baptism of the Be Water Revolution bequeathed a combative Hong Kong identity, which is sure to stay among the overseas compatriots. Although the NSL brought about the global targeting of overseas activists and their families back in Hong Kong, campaigners abroad still enjoyed more freedom of action and expression. With the decline of home front protests, the overseas Hongkongers joined hands with Tibetans, Uighurs, Taiwanese, and Falun Gong members in a broader campaign to resist the PRC's authoritarian expansion. With their established presence in Washington, DC, London, and Taipei, Hongkongers were able to ensure their concerns were heard by elected officials and policymakers in their host countries.

Engaging in campaigns abroad poses significant risks in the long run, and often it evolves into a marathon race with the homeland dictatorship in a contest to see who can eventually outlast the other. Political enthusiasm is likely to wane as time passes and more and more erstwhile activists choose to return to their own quotidian matters. Therefore, it is not surprising to see many overseas Hongkonger associations shrink in size or even cease to be active in the years to come, and it is also likely that annual commemorative events will draw fewer and fewer participants. Surviving organizations will probably take the route of professionalization and formalization, especially when it comes to policy advocacy. Migrant associations need to devise new ways to embed their Hong Kong identity in everyday and communal activities.

The politics of diaspora is also the politics of exile. From Karl Marx's time onward, the world of exiles has been driven by rumors, cliques, and strife. The correspondences between London-based Marx and his pal Friedrich Engels in Manchester were replete with gossip about other revolutionary exiles, occasionally interspersed with the former's pleas for cash assistance. Exiles are forced to live in a small world where petty interests and personal animosity often take precedence over principles. They are always closely monitored by homeland dictators, who also frequently dispatch infiltrators to sow the seeds of discord.

For Hong Kong's nascent diaspora activism, the worst-case scenario would probably resemble the post-Tiananmen exiles in the West, whose disunity and internecine denunciation despite the initial global sympathy for their plight significantly diluted their strength and potential impacts. There are several reasons for their diminishing visibility. Externally, China's overseas dissidents were fighting a geopolitically uphill battle as the PRC grew richer and more powerful and, thus, was more capable of securing the loyalty of the overseas Chinese communities and students (J. Chen 2018). The commercial interests in trade with China led the Western nations to discard their human rights concerns, thus marginalizing dissidents' voices (Hung 2022b: 8). Internally, dissidents were deeply mired in factionalism and mutual accusations, which resulted in disenchantment among their erstwhile supporters (Junker 2019: 112–17). As such, the divisive politics of Chinese prodemocracy exiles is a negative lesson for Hong Kong's diaspora movement.

By contrast, Taiwanese overseas exiles provide a more comparable and presumably more hopeful reference case. One year after the February 28 Incident of 1947, in which the Kuomintang government brutally suppressed an island-wide uprising and systemically eliminated political leaders, the first overseas proindependence organization, the Formosan League for Reemancipation led by Thomas Liao, was established in Hong Kong. The diaspora opposition began to draw more participants in the 1960s when overseas students from Taiwan grew, especially significantly in the United States. Freshly arriving on the free soil, many of them learned the first lesson of democracy via the 1960s campus radicalism and became critical of the one-party authoritarianism at home (W. Cheng 2023; Lynch 2003). Because of their involvement in dissident activities, the Kuomintang government "blacklisted" or deprived their home-returning rights. These overseas students managed to integrate into their host nations while staying concerned about their homeland. Simultaneously, they nurtured a second generation of locally born activists capable of continuing the unfinished cause for Taiwan's freedom. Making use of political space in the host countries, these diaspora activists made efforts to expose human rights abuse at home, rescue political prisoners, and pressure the governments for more proactive actions, when such campaigns were not tolerated in Taiwan. As the democratic transition in Taiwan began in the mid-1980s, overseas dissidents launched several protests against the home-returning ban, leading to the lifting of the government's blacklist in 1992. Taking Taiwan's experience as a benchmark, there was a gap of forty-four years between the emergence of the overseas opposition movement and tolerance by the home country government. The temporality of diaspora activism must be measured in decades, rather than in months or years, perhaps a novel lesson for fast-paced Hongkongers.

The history of Taiwan's overseas opposition movement also shows what kinds of transnational repression are in stock for Hong Kong's dissidents abroad. The Hong Kong SAR government already effectively imposed a home-returning ban with the announcement of a wanted list of six diaspora activists including Nathan Law in August 2020, and the dragnet was further expanded with follow-up manhunt announcements. In the past, the Kuomintang government planted a wide network of informants for surveillance, fostered parallel immigrant associations to marginalize the dissidents, and even resorted to political assassinations. There is no reason why Hong Kong's national security apparatus would not apply these old playbooks to contain the challenge from abroad, in particular, since such repression is in sync with the worldwide PRC's sharp power campaigns.

With the understanding of these formidable challenges ahead, the Be Water Revolution has bequeathed several positive legacies that were denied to overseas Taiwanese activists in their formative era of the 1960s. First, a battle-hardened and tenacious Hong Kong identity emerged and became the unifying thread among the city's overseas communities. By contrast, early postwar Taiwan was an ethnically divided society, and the cleavage between mainlanders and native Taiwanese persisted after they left Taiwan (Lien 2010). Second, while the Cold War geopolitics led Western countries to look away from human rights violations and political repression in Taiwan for the purpose of anti-communism, the more recent international configuration turned out to be more favorable to Hong Kong's overseas advocates, as their host country governments were already alerted to the threat of China's expanding authoritarianism. To be blunt, Taiwan's democratization used to stand in the way of the U.S. strategic interests, but Hongkongers' agenda is more aligned with them. Last, because of the city's post-Tiananmen migration wave in the 1990s, overseas Hong Kong communities were more established, widespread, and numerous, which easily translates into a stronger activism, whereas Taiwan's diaspora communities had to literally be built from scratch. Again, in light of the actionist sociology perspective of this book, these resources and opportunities remain only in latency at best, and they can never be activated without the determined intervention of overseas Hongkongers.

Are home-based and overseas prodemocracy Hongkongers able to wait for such a long period before realizing their cherished goal of self-determination? Or, alternatively, will they eventually give up the solemn hope that "may people reign, proud and free, now and evermore," as the underground anthem has vividly adumbrated? Perhaps the finale will arrive faster than everyone has expected since the U.S.-China rivalry has entered a crescendo phase beyond the point of no return. There is no telling how the burgeoning New Cold War will impact Hong Kong; there are too many unknown variables at present, and no self-respecting social scientist would venture into the danger zone of fortune-telling.

Although Hong Kong is geographically tiny, its population exceeds the combination of three Baltic states, from which they drew inspiration for a huge human chain rally. As the Baltic people launched a historic protest that led to the demise of the Soviet Union, there is no reason why Hongkongers cannot reapply the lesson. Sitting on the doorstep of a giant neighbor, Hong Kong is not immune to the vicissitudes of politics in the PRC. The Chinese Communist Party chairman Xi Jinping's relentless concentration of power is expected to continue unstopped, and his Hong Kong underlings have to toe the line decreed by Beijing in order to demonstrate their allegiance. Hong Kong cannot escape from China's post-COVID-19 economic downturn, as the city has been thoroughly integrated with the mainland economy. Understanding that Hong Kong's future will not be entirely decided by what will happen in the city and its overseas communities, the actionist perspective stresses that subjective preparedness and the availability of agentic power remains the key process for realizing the city's democratization in the future. In plain language, if Hongkongers decide to give up the will to fight for their freedom, their city is never going to be democratic; however, should they retain a combative spirit and remain what is called *keingaang* (adamant, or unbending) in Cantonese, they could potentially seize a future geopolitical crisis as an opportunity to renew their activism. In other words, while structural tendencies are easier to imagine and forecast, the agency factor continues to be indeterminate and always elusive to prediction, a wild card, so to speak. With this understanding, the final chapter of the Be Water Revolution—and the city's political future—remains to be written.

Appendix

Research Methods and Data

Hong Kong's Be Water Revolution was a prolonged, massive, multidimensional, and spatially dispersed movement against autocratization, which calls for the use of many research methods to understand its complexity. This book applies a mixed methods approach to examine the evolution of that eventual protest from many angles. The four main data sources are (1) journalistic sources, (2) in-depth interviews, (3) field observations, and (4) published materials.

(1) JOURNALISTIC SOURCES

The journalistic sources are based on the online archives of Hong Kong's *Apple Daily* (a newspaper) and Standnews (a news website). Both are avowedly prodemocracy and provide rich details of the city's political struggles. In 2021, both news agencies abruptly ceased operation due to a government crackdown, and this research benefited from the crowd-funded digital activism of civic-tech communities to restore their content elsewhere. Now *Apple Daily* has a permanent online archive (available at https://collection.news/appledaily) for public viewing. As for Standnews, I contracted a software engineer to write computer code to store its content in our digital storage.

Journalistic sources make up a database for protest event analysis. Following Tilly's definition (1981: 76), a protest event is an incidence of contentious gathering, in which participants assemble in a public space and raise certain collective demands. This definition excludes acts that are not sufficiently antagonistic (distributing flyers), indoor (press conference), online (crowdfunding), static (putting up a poster), and individually based (suicide). A protest event minimally requires physical presence in public space (anonymously or not) and demonstrates collective defiance. This classical definition primarily understands social movements as a public, physical, and collective phenomenon, thus understandably neglecting many online activities that are at the forefront of movement innovation. This book retains this conventional perspective because it remains a more useful measurement for understanding the rise and fall of a protest movement.

Utilizing protest events as a basic unit, we make the following decision rules: (1) Spatial contiguity: protests in adjacent places are seen as an event, and those simultaneously occurring in different places are not the same one. As a rule of thumb, the distance between Hong Kong's metro stations is used to define spatial contiguity. If participants finish their first protest and proceed to stage another in a different location, these are defined as two separate events. (2) Temporal continuity: an event can last more than one day as long as protest actions continue uninterrupted. (3) Initiatives and spin-offs: protests beget their own protests; but if they spin off new actions by different participants, they should be counted as different events. A protest event comes from the initiative of participants. If a protest changes its course after encountering police or opponents, it remains one singular event. For instance, after the largely peaceful demonstration from To Kwa Wan to Hung Hom on August 17, 2019, protesters split their ways, with some circling back to To Kwa Wan, besieging Mong Kok Police Station, blocking the road in Jordan, and destroying an office of the pro-Beijing Hong Kong Federation of Trade Unions. The latter four ensuing episodes are counted as independent ones since they were not included in the original plan.

The observation period starts in February 2019, when the Hong Kong government proposed the ELAB, and ends in June 2020, when the NSL was decreed. In total, I observed the continuous occurrence of protest events over seventy-one weeks. Each protest event is coded with the following information: date, location, demands, initiators, activities, participant numbers, police actions, and arrest numbers.

In the previous parlance of Hong Kong's activists, protests can roughly be divided into two categories: "peaceful, rational, and nonviolent" and "militant." Yet, the 2014 Umbrella Movement popularized an intermediate option—"civil disobedience"—which is more proactive than the former but stops short of using force (K. Chan 2022). This book uses "disruptive" as a label for acts associated with civil disobedience. In addition, I follow the trichotomy convention used by Tarrow (1989: 69) in his classification of Italian protest events (conventional/confrontational/violent). The three-part classification is as follows: (1) Peaceful protests are those conventional assemblies and demonstrations that do not aim to create major disruptions or cause harm or damage; (2) disruptive protests are initiatives intending to cause disruption without using force, such as strikes, blocking traffic, paralyzing a governmental agency with crowds, and so on; and (3) violent protests involve the use of physical force to cause personal harm or property damage. In my dataset, there are 1,770 protest events in total, including 1,158 peaceful (65%), 501 disruptive (28%), and 111 violent ones (6%).

Each protest event contains many different activities, or those specific actions that participants adopt when gathering together. In a peaceful rally, it is common that people collect signatures, read statements, distribute materials, or encamp themselves, and these specific forms of action are duly coded as long as they are reported. In some cases, more militant activities might take place in a largely peaceful event. A largely peaceful demonstration might experience intense standoff moments, whereby some participants decide to forestall police action or throw projectiles in anger. These unexpected activities are likely to escalate a peaceful event into a disruptive or a violent one. In this potentially mixed situation, I evaluate these on a case-by-case basis, and, if these aggressive activities remain sporadic, isolated, or inconsequential, the event is still coded as peaceful.

The activity coding method is based on Stanford University's Dynamics of Collective Action project (available at https://stanford.io/3gXKYJ8), which contains sixty-seven activities. For Hong Kong's situation, major modifications are made. First, I remove routinized and conventional activities such as leafleting and slogan chanting (because they are too frequent) as well as those that are absent (kidnapping/hostage taking). Then, I add nuances to some classifications. For instance, "blockade/blocking by protesters" is further divided into the following types: blocking the road, toll stations, railroads, airport, or building entrances; besieging; queuing to obstruct an agency or store; creating difficulties for ground movement; and traffic slowdowns (fake incidents). In addition, I add some activities that are uniquely embedded in Hong Kong's context. For example, placing one's right hand over the right eye (31) is a symbolic gesture to protest a police shooting that blinded a young female first-aider. In the end, this book's analysis ends up with 133 activities. The dataset indicates that the top five activities in terms of frequency were blocking the road (287), singing songs (284), marching (213), forming a human chain (137), and starting a fire (122).

In addition to protest event analysis, journalistic sources provide clues to 899 group statements that were made to support the movement. Among them, 285 were from alumni groups, 283 by professionals, 68 by students, 51 by civil servants, and 47 by religious organizations. The dynamics of group statements is examined in Chapter 4.

(2) IN-DEPTH INTERVIEWS

Another set of data comes from in-depth interviews. From 2019 to 2024, our research team interviewed 189 persons, Hongkongers or not, who were involved in the prodemocracy movement in various capacities. Among them, I personally conducted 147 interviews, while the other 42 were done by my research associates. In terms of nationality, 164 are Hongkongers, who might possess foreign passports, including British Overseas (National), have acquired other nationalities, or recently obtained political asylum status. Among twenty-five non-Hongkongers, twenty are Taiwanese and two Macanese, and the rest (a Malaysian, a Polish, and a Swiss) are not connected to Hong Kong either biologically or culturally.

In terms of social status at the time of interview, seventy-three were students or graduate students, thirty-seven were full-time workers or retirees, and twenty-four were staff of NGOs or labor unions. I also interviewed ten professors, ten elected district councillors, seven artistic workers (writers, photographers, and curators), six prodemocracy business owners, five journalists, and three lawyers. Ten of my interviewees did not want to reveal their personal identity. My interviewees were involved in the Be Water Revolution in different capacities. Aside from fifteen non-Hongkonger supporters and fifteen Hongkongers whose movement involvement is not obvious, forty-five interviewees were primarily engaged in diaspora activism, twenty-two in frontline street protests, twenty-two in student organizations, ten in peaceful protests and donation drives, nine in overseas assistance, eight in local community organizing, seven in communication and Lennon Walls, six in NGO/labor union organizing and yellow economic circle, five in "parenting" and driving service, three in electioneering, two in legal assistance and prisoner help each, and finally one in social work. In some cases, I interviewed these individuals more than once.

These interviewees were recruited in multiple channels. With my previous research on the 2014 Umbrella Movement, I was able to reconnect with the previous interviewees and asked them to introduce me to additional involved persons. My research team also helped reach out for more interviewees on the strength of their personal connections. Aside from snowballing, when it comes to Hong Kong's diaspora activists, I sent uninvited interview requests to their Facebook, Twitter, and Instagram accounts, and, luckily,

I received several positive responses from their admins. Some of my Hong Kong interviewees eagerly helped my research efforts, knowing that their stories need to be carefully recorded, especially when the city's academic freedom was swiftly eroded. Since June 2020, the NSL made my interview data collection more difficult, as their storytelling could easily land them in legal troubles. However, I also have benefited from the growing acceptance of online chat over secure platforms with end-to-end encryption (E2EE) features that helped to preserve the anonymity of my interlocutors. My online interviewees knew that their personal stories would not be known by PRC security operatives. In many cases, I also refrained from obtaining their personal identity (real names, locations, etc.), and the lack of personally identifiable information is not a major worry since it is not directly relevant to my research questions. There are five interviews that proceeded entirely in text chat so that we have no knowledge of their gender.

I use several set questionnaires for diverse movement involvements, including street protest, logistic support, overseas assistance, electioneering, and so on. All the interviews are transcribed into text, English or Mandarin, and these files constitute 13 MB in memory storage. Interview data are a precious source because they reveal what participants actually did during the protest wave. As a note to the severity of repression, at least six interviewees had been arrested and six had their identities obtained by the police. Four of them were listed as overseas fugitives, and two were sentenced to jail. Since I could not update all my interviewee profiles, these numbers likely only represent a fraction of the consequences of legal repression.

I did not interview people who were pro-government. My positionality as a Taiwan-based academic with a pronounced prodemocracy stance helped recruit participant interviewees as they could check out my academic publications or online op-ed pieces or review my social media page before consenting to my requests.

(3) FIELD OBSERVATIONS

Finally, some of my research data is based on my own participation observation. I was based in Boston when the Be Water Revolution erupted, and, during its course, I moved back to Taipei. I was able to make three short research trips (August and October 2019, January 2020) to Hong Kong for firsthand observation. Demonstrations, rallies, forums, film screenings, fairs, and other related events in Taiwan also presented rich opportunities to collect data. In addition, I attended some forums or met activists in Frankfurt, Ithaca, Kuala Lumpur, London, New York, Tokyo, Warsaw, and Woking. In the field, I usually had to jot down observations in my paper notebooks and expanded later when having access to a computer. As of October 11, 2024, my field note file is 196 pages and 141,000 words in Microsoft Word format.

(4) PUBLISHED MATERIALS

Like its 2014 predecessor Umbrella Movement, Hong Kong's Be Water Revolution spawned a cottage industry of book publications devoted to this topic. While the proregime camp also managed to come up with their publications to promote their version of history, this study consults mainly only those by participants and sympathetic writers and editors. Together these publications represent a rich archive into the intimate experiences among movement participants. Throughout the text, I have cited valuable materials from these publications.

Among the forty-eight nonacademic publications I reference, there are eleven report collections, eleven commentary collections, eight public history writings, seven interview collections, three photography albums, two autobiographies, comics, and novels, and one film script, visual material collection, and zine. Their publication dates run from September 2019 to May 2023. Five were published in English, and forty-three were in Chinese. In terms of publication locations, twenty-five were in Taiwan, eighteen in Hong Kong, four in New York, and one in Singapore and an unknown place.

A Glossary of Protest Phrases

Social movements are signifying agents because when they attempt to change the world, they also create new lexicons, phrases, and idioms at the same time. These emerging linguistic constructs are not merely words that describe the existing reality but words that are performative in the sense that they help bring about changes to reality. The Be Water Revolution is also a rare occasion when many Hongkongers gathered together emotionally for the same purpose—a Durkheimian moment of collective effervescence—that led to a creative outburst in language. Hong Kong's participants invented many new vocabularies whose origin and authorship were unknown and probably ultimately untraceable—an unmistakable characteristic of collective improvisation. These new expressions swiftly gained currency, and the shared linguistic practice reinforced the bond among movement participants and supporters. In terms of function, they help delineate the movement community boundary, identify the foes, inspire protest actions, and envision the future goal. Typically, these newly minted terms are spoken in Cantonese, the native tongue of the majority of Hongkongers, and their translation into Mandarin risks the loss of rich local connotations. The glossary that follows provides Cantonese romanization, Mandarin Pinyin, Chinese characters, and a brief explanation. In cases of idiosyncratic expressions that do not have Mandarin equivalents, Pinyin is not provided.

Cantonese romanization	Mandarin Pinyin	Chinese characters	Brief explanation
bat dukfui bat gotzek	*bu duhui bu gexi*	不篤灰、不割席	"Do not snitch and do not split," which is a demand for movement unity that urges participants not to report on illegal actions and not to denounce them.
boulik binjyun	*baoli bianyuan*	暴力邊緣	"The edge of violence" is a movement strategy advocated by Edward Leung to entice the government to make mistakes with provocative actions.
caang siudim	*cheng xiaodian*	撐小店	"Supporting small stores" emerged as a tactic to alleviate the economic impacts of the 2014 Umbrella Movement, and it evolved into a more ambitious project of "yellow economic circle" in 2019.
caangsaan lokkeoi	*chengsan luoqu*	撐傘落區	"Support the Umbrella Movement by going to communities" emerged as a follow-up effort by encouraging the prodemocracy movement participants to build neighborhood ties after the conclusion of the 2014 Umbrella Movement.
cai soeng cai lok	—	齊上齊落	"Entering together and leaving together" is an expression of movement solidarity by leaving no protester behind.
coihung zinji	*caihong zhanyi*	彩虹戰衣	"Rainbow warrior robe" means the casual clothing worn by protesters when coming to the rally site.
faailok kongzang	*kuaile kangzheng*	快樂抗爭	"Joyous resistance" was a tactical proposal by Hong Kong's localists who contended there was a need for more assertive actions.
faatmung	—	發夢	"Dreaming" refers to one's participation in protest actions.
fo mo	*huo mo*	火魔	"Fire magic" is a protester lingo for petrol bombs.
gaazoeng	*jiazhang*	家長	"Parents" are those movement supporters who provide resources to and take care of protesters in need.
gamsang zigaa cinsinbaa, gamsai ziceoi haukansi	—	今生只嫁前線巴，今世只娶後勤絲	"Girls will only marry frontline brothers and boys will only marry logistics sisters" is a widely circulated description about how romantic intimacy developed among young frontline protesters.

gau	*gou*	狗	"Dog" is the pejorative term used by protesters for the police. The canine appellation also applies to "dog's cars" (police vehicles) and "dog's houses" (police residence).
gongzyu	*gangzhu*	港豬	"Hong Kong pigs" is a pejorative term for apolitical and materialistic Hongkongers.
gwai	*gui*	鬼	"Ghosts" are spies, infiltrators, agents, and agents provocateurs dispatched by the government to undermine the protest movement.
gwaigei	*guiji*	鬼機	"Ghost phones" are the cell phones with a single-use sim card and only installed with necessary applications for security reasons.
gwokzaisin	*guojixian*	國際線	"International front" refers to the global campaign to enlist movement support from abroad.
gwongfuk hoenggong sidoi gaakming	*guangfu xianggang shidai geming*	光復香港、時代革命	"Liberate Hong Kong, Revolution of Our Time" is the most popular slogan from during the Be Water Revolution. Originally, it was a campaign slogan by the localist candidate Edward Leung in 2016.
hak zongsau, hung zongsik, laam baamaai, wong bongcan	—	黑裝修、紅裝飾、藍罷買、黃幫襯	"'Renovate' (read: destroy) black stores (gangster-operated stores), 'decorate' (vandalize) red stores (Chinese-owned stores), boycott blue stores (whose owners are pro-government), and support yellow stores (whose owners are pro-movement)" emerged as a rule of engagement for frontline protesters vis-à-vis the business establishment.
hingdai paasaan gokzi noulik	*xiongdi pashan gezi nuli*	兄弟爬山、各自努力	"Brothers climb the mountain and each has to contribute his effort." This slogan means that movement participants are all aiming for the same goal, and they are doing it in their own ways. The phrase has many interpretations, including the tolerance of different tactics and the freedom to take the initiative.
jungmoupaai	*yongwupai*	勇武派	"Militants" are the protesters who are willing to use disruptive or violent measures. The term first came into being during the 2014 Umbrella Movement out of dissatisfaction with the student leadership who upheld the principle of nonviolent civil disobedience.

(*continued*)

Cantonese romanization	Mandarin Pinyin	Chinese characters	Brief explanation
kongzang jungjap sangwut	*kangzheng rongru shenghuo*	抗爭融入生活	"Blending protest into life" refers to a series of experimental attempts to embed the movement in everyday practices. The idea was first proposed after the arrest spike in the wake of the two University Battles in November 2019, but it was forcibly abandoned with the onset of the COVID-19 pandemic and the NSL.
laam caau	—	攬炒	"Mutual destruction" means the campaign to leverage international sanctions against the Hong Kong government and politicians.
mangeoi	*wenju*	文具	"Stationery" refers to the standard equipment of frontline protesters, including helmets, goggles, masks, and others.
mansyun	*wenxuan*	文宣	"Communicative materials" created to convey the movement messages.
mou daaitoi	*wu datai*	無大台	Its literal meaning is "no main stage," which is to say that the movement can proceed without a command center.
pindei hoifaa	*biandi kaihua*	遍地開花	"Flowers blossoming everywhere" means the geographic proliferation of protest actions and the adaptation of novel tactics.
pongtingsi	*pangtingshi*	旁聽師	"Court observers" are those who attend the court proceedings in order to express their support for the defendants.
saanbing	*sanbing*	傘兵	"Umbrella soldiers" or "paratroopers" refer to the first-time district council candidates inspired by the Umbrella Movement.
saanhau zouzik	*sanhou zuzhi*	傘後組織	"Post-Umbrella organizations" are the community, professional, and political organizations that emerged in the wake of the Umbrella Movement.
saaubing	*shaobing*	哨兵	"Scouts" are those movement participants on the streets who provide the latest information on police deployment.
sapbaatkeoi hoifaa	*shibaqu kaihua*	十八區開花	"Flowers blossoming in 18 districts" means to spread protests across all of Hong Kong's administrative regions.

sauzuk	*shouzu*	手足	“Brothers and sisters” are the terms used to describe protesters in the Be Water Revolution.
si nei gaau ngomun woping jauhang si mutjung dik	*shi ni jiao women heping youxing shi meiyong de*	是你教我們和平遊行是沒用的	“It is you who taught us that peaceful demonstration was useless” is an often used saying to justify disruptive actions.
siliu or *siniu*	—	獅鳥	“A half-lion and half-bird creature” is a euphemism for vigilante violence against proregime mobsters.
siudeoi	*xiaodui*	小隊	“Teams” are the groups that frontline protesters form for the purpose of the division of labor.
taajat boudai ceoizaau soenggin or sometimes shortened as *boudai zijoek*	—	他日煲底除罩相見 煲底之約	“A reunion without masks under the rice cooker the other day,” “the promise under the rice cooker,” envisioned the future success of the movement when protesters can gather together without using face masks to conceal their identities. Hong Kong’s Legislative Council Complex appears like a giant electronic rice cooker, and its main entrance area is endearingly referred to as the space under the home appliance.
toulung siudeoi	*tulong xiaodui*	屠龍小隊	“The Dragon Slaying Brigade” was one of the best-known teams of militants who granted interviews to media reporters.
tungloujan	*tongluren*	同路人	“Fellow travelers” are those who share the same prodemocracy commitment. It emerged as a common identity and appellation during the Be Water Revolution.
waaminleng	—	畫面靚	“Nice looking” is often used to criticize those who insist that rallies and demonstrations have to be orderly in order to look good on camera.
wo nei fannhok, wo nei faangung, wo nei sak	—	和你返學, 和你返工, 和你塞	“Going to school with you,” “going to work with you,” and “congesting with you,” respectively, all meaning the intentional creation of traffic jams during rush hours.

(*continued*)

Cantonese romanization	Mandarin Pinyin	Chinese characters	Brief explanation
wo nei fei	*he ni fei*	和你飛	"Flying with you" means protest gatherings in the airport.
wo nei lunch	—	和你 lunch	"Lunch with you" means holding protest rallies during the lunch break.
wo nei se	*he ni xie*	和你寫	"Write with you" is the activity of writing letters collectively to imprisoned protesters.
wo nei shop	—	和你 shop	"Shopping with you" means protest gatherings in shopping malls.
wo nei sing	—	和你 sing	"Singing with you" means protest by sing-alongs.
wo nei zip zi hok	*he ni zhe zhi he*	和你摺紙鶴	"Folding origami cranes with you" means collectively folding papers to express the concern for others.
woleifei	*helifei*	和理非	"Peaceful, rational, and nonviolent" is the action guideline upheld by Hong Kong's moderate prodemocracy movement.
wongsik gingzaihyun	*huangse jingjiquan*	黃色經濟圈	"Yellow economic circle" is a proposed project of a citywide solidarity economy envisioned that could sustain the protest activism over the long haul.
zeoicesi	*zhuicheshi*	追車師	"Vehicle chasers" refer to those supporters who surround and chase after the prison bus to express their solidarity.
zipfonghok	*jiefangxue*	接放學	"School pickup" refers to the efforts among private vehicle owners to transport protesters away from the conflict zone.
ziutouleon	*jiaotulun*	焦土論	"Scorched earth policy" refers to the strategy for more disruptive protest actions in Hong Kong with the expectation that China will suffer more as a consequence.

Notes

INTRODUCTION

1. Unknown author, "Trump Says Tiananmen Square–Style Crackdown in Hong Kong Would Harm China Trade Deal," *Straits Times*, August 19, 2019, available at https://bit.ly/3MESD00, accessed on April 13, 2023.

2. Kaixin Peng et al., "Lida ju yi san qi qi ren" [1377 were arrested in the Polytech], HK01, November 29, 2019, available at https://bit.ly/3UzjEUp, accessed on April 13, 2023.

3. Fanxu Kong, "Xiuli fengbo yizhounian" [One year of the extradition controversy], HK01, June 9, 2020, available at https://bit.ly/3RppI0N, accessed on November 21, 2023.

4. Unknown author, "Da jiankong" [The great prosecution], The Initium, July 24, 2020, available at https://bit.ly/3MBuEi3, accessed on April 13, 2023.

5. Hong Kong Democracy Council, "Hong Kong Reaches a Grim Milestone," available at https://bit.ly/3mvhrwJ, accessed on October 8, 2024.

6. Austin Ramzy and Tiffany May, "'Our Hands and Feet Are Tied': Hong Kong's Opposition Quits in Droves," *New York Times*, August 16, 2021, available at http://bit.ly/46RmybK, accessed on May 30, 2023.

7. Clement So, "Xianggang renkou liandie sannian" [Three consecutive years of population decline in Hong Kong], Radio France Internationale, December 8, 2022, available at https://bit.ly/3KWu8Kt, accessed on April 13, 2023.

8. Zixu Wang and John Yoon, "In Mourning the Queen, Some in Hong Kong Mourn the Past," *New York Times*, October 29, 2022, available at https://nyti.ms/400Aa0Z, accessed on April 13, 2023.

9. Fan Wang, "Hong Kong Anthem: Google Won't Alter Search Results amid Protest Song Row," BBC, December 12, 2022, available at https://bit.ly/3RFATne, accessed on May 30, 2023.

10. Kate Conger, "YouTube Disables 210 Channels That Spread Disinformation about Hong Kong Protests," *New York Times*, August 22, 2019, available at https://nyti.ms/40dR780, accessed on April 16, 2023.

CHAPTER 1

1. Unless indicated otherwise, all interviewee names are pseudonyms.

2. The following two sections reuse some materials published in M. 2020.

3. See the interview with Alex Chow, the student leader of the Umbrella Movement, in Shirley Leung, "Wuye menghui tongku, zouchu shanghen queli mubiao" [Amid midnight crying and dreaming, the attempt to bury trauma and seek new goals], Protonmedia, April 28, 2023, available at https://bit.ly/40MyaJW, accessed on April 29, 2023.

CHAPTER 2

1. Hong Kong Public Opinion Research Institute, *Xiuding taofan tiaoli minyi diaocha* [A report on public opinion regarding the revision of fugitive amendment], July 31, 2019, available at https://bit.ly/429rVRE, accessed on May 3, 2023.

2. Adolfo Arranz, "Arrested Hong Kong Protesters: How the Numbers Look One Year On," *South China Morning Post*, June 11, 2020, available at https://bit.ly/3LP37Jd, accessed on May 3, 2023.

3. Xian Zhou, "Shui shi shehui de chifenzhe" [Who are the stakeholders in the society?] *Am 730*, August 19, 2019, available at https://bit.ly/3HF3dRa, accessed on May 5, 2023. Another progovernment lawmaker was startlingly honest, as he vehemently denounced young protesters whose actions disrupted the "harvest period" for the middle-aged middle class like him, unknown author, "Chen jianbo cheng shouchengqi you gongming" [Chan Kin-por's "Harvest Period" gains resonance], Indiemedia, June 14, 2019, available at https://bit.ly/3v07eMH, accessed on August 16, 2023. Common to these rather frank pronouncements is the view that radical protesters were socially and economically unestablished.

4. Unknown author, "Cockroaches That Would Slay Dragons: Hong Kong Apostasy," China Heritage, available at https://bit.ly/3HIaArj, accessed on May 5, 2023.

5. For a dramatic story of how a couple of protesters both fell in love and then later broke up with each other during the movement, see Yeung 2022: 35–77.

6. The 612 Humanitarian Relief Fund Annual Report of 2021, June 2021, available at https://t.ly/LfIK2, accessed on October 10, 2024.

7. Jiayu Lu, "Jing zhi xinghuotongmeng she xiheiqian" [Police claimed spark alliance laundered black money], HK01, December 19, 2019, available at https://bit.ly/3Cy4STJ, accessed on March 28, 2022.

8. According to a journalist witness, there was also a female volunteer in Nam Cheong station (another transfer station to Yuen Long), encouraging T-shirt wearing protesters to change for her free clothes. However, compared to Mei Foo's case, the effort here appeared to be an unorganized intervention by an individual (A Hoi 2021: 92).

CHAPTER 4

1. Jiyao Wang and Zhenhai Guan, "Zhanling lifahui san xiaoshi quanjilu" [A full recorder of occupying the legislative council for three hours], Hong Kong Feature, July 3, 2019, available at https://bit.ly/3NlgOzR, accessed on August 7, 2023.

2. See unknown author, "Liang jiping: Xiangxiang taren tongku" [Brian Leung: Imaging others' suffering], Standnews, available at https://bit.ly/41oSXW6, accessed on August 8, 2023.

3. See the full text, "Jinzhong xuanyan quanwen" [The full text of Admiralty Declaration], available at https://bit.ly/41jL3Nw, accessed on August 8, 2023. My English translation departs from the official version.

4. Unknown author, "Zhonglianban guohui zao danxi tuhei" [The state emblems of central liaison office was egged and painted black], *Liberty Times*, July 21, 2019, available at https://bit.ly/47V0zBQ, accessed on December 13, 2023.

5. Unknown author, "Xianggang dazhuan xuejie fabiao kengqiang bake xuanyan" [Hong Kong's university students publicized a powerful class boycott declaration], YouTube, September 3, 2019, available at http://y2u.be/jQRr713_kGo, accessed on August 8, 2023.

6. Unknown author, "Xianggangren, fankang" [Hongkongers, Resist!], *Liberty Times*, October 5, 2019, available at https://bit.ly/3NqVJnE, accessed on December 13, 2023.

7. Cited from an anonymous post on LIHKG, July 24, 2019, available at https://bit.ly/3Rn6MPV, accessed on August 9, 2023.

8. See unknown author, "Linchuang xinlixue boshi xiehui yu zhengfu ji butong zhengjianzhe baorong chuli liannongqiang" [The association of doctors in clinical psychology urged the government and people with different political opinions to tolerate Lennon Walls], Radio Television Hong Kong, available at https://bit.ly/3NssBwt, accessed on August 9, 2023.

9. Unknown author, "Xianggang yiqun huaxue gongchengshi shengming" [A statement from a group of Hong Kong's chemical engineers], from an anonymous post on LIHKG, August 14, 2019, available at https://bit.ly/48cIwXI, accessed on August 9, 2023.

10. Shuji Zhen, "Xianggang jingcha zhiqin fangbao jing zhiyi mangrenyong guaizhang xijing" [Hong Kong's riot police on duty suspected blind peoples' canes as assault weapons], Radio France Internationale, June 15, 2019, available at https://bit.ly/3GI016A, accessed on December 14, 2023.

11. Qiaoxin Hu, "Jingquan zai shang qianxian yingshi cuileiyan" [Police dogs on the front line were forced to breathe tear gas], HK01, October 23, 2019, available at https://bit.ly/3ThC8dA, accessed on August 9, 2023.

12. Unknown author, "Xianggang jingsao fa qi jingcha qinshu lianxian" [Hong Kong's police wives formed a coalition of police family members], NTDTV, August 2, 2019, available at https://bit.ly/3GKkB6l, accessed on December 14, 2023.

13. Unknown author, "Xianggang xinyimin ye fansongzhong" [Hong Kong's new migrants also opposed extradition to China], *Liberty Times*, June 2, 2019, available at https://bit.ly/3tngwBN, accessed on December 14, 2023.

14. A post on Facebook, May 28, 2019, available at https://bit.ly/3v55txz, accessed on August 9, 2023.

15. The full text is available at https://bit.ly/472KlWa, accessed on August 9, 2023.

16. More available at https://bit.ly/3TkVBdd, accessed on August 9, 2023.

17. Jieling Zhu, "Shinai falianshu fanxiuli" [Housewives collected signatures to oppose amendment], HK01, May 31, 2019, available at http://y2u.be/zGadfiEIPIg, accessed on August 10, 2023.

18. See the video clip on YouTube, August 31, 2019, available at http://y2u.be/y7yRDOLCy4Y, accessed on December 14, 2023. As of this day, there have been 38.8 million views.

19. Jean Chen, "Fan songzhong biandi kaihua de shijiao jinhua" [The visual evolution of the well-spread anti-extradition movement], Reporter, October 31, 2019, available at https://bit.ly/41lTOqo, accessed on August 12, 2023.

20. James Pomfret and Sara Cheng, "Hong Kong Man Jailed for Nine Years in First National Security Case," Reuters, July 30, 2020, available at https://bit.ly/3v23U3O, accessed on December 14, 2023.

CHAPTER 5

1. Shirley Leung, "Cong liandeng jialeba dao HKDC zhi xing zongjian" [From Campbell Macaroni on LIHKG to the chief executive in HKDC], Protonmedia, April 28, 2023, available at https://bit.ly/41Cg9hR, accessed on May 15, 2023.

2. As of May 15, 2023, the "We HK No China Extradition" YouTube channel has 21,300 subscribers and hosts thirty-two video clips, available at https://bit.ly/3BJRWfj.

3. See the Facebook post available at https://bit.ly/3o11f7h, for Joshua Wong's Facebook page, which existed after Wong's imprisonment. The cited post was dated November 22, 2020. A later visit on October 11, 2024 has found that specific post has been taken down.

4. Unknown author, "Zhouting huoxuan BBC jinguo baiming" [Agnes Chow was selected in BBC's one hundred heroines], BBC, November 25, 2020, available at https://bit.ly/3GIUVa2, accessed December 3, 2023.

5. The following four sections reuse some material published in M. Ho 2023a.

6. The DNLM Directory is available at https://bit.ly/43cD7xl, accessed on May 21, 2023.

7. The subsequent discovery of China's global secret police stations confirmed my interviewees' suspicion. In April 2023, the Federal Bureau of Investigation arrested two Chinese Americans who were involved in the PRC's covert policing in New York City. They were accused of intimidating overseas political dissidents, including human rights activists for Hong Kong. *New York Times*, April 17, 2023, available at https://nyti.ms/3WpBmL5, accessed on May 21, 2023.

8. A personal anecdote is of relevance here. In November 2019, I was "uninvited" by a Malaysian Chinese Association for a previously agreed upon lecture on the then ongoing protests in Hong Kong in Kuala Lumpur due to the direct intervention from the Chinese embassy. Despite the rude cancellation, other prodemocracy Malaysian Chinese organizations stepped in and, with their facilitation, I had the opportunity to share my observation and met those pro-Hong Kong voices that were suppressed by the conservative senior leaders.

9. According to a preelection survey, 36% of respondents in Hong Kong favored Trump, and 42% were pro-Biden, which made the city the second-highest territory/county in the Asia Pacific in terms of its rate of support for Trump, trailing only behind Taiwan (42%). Unknown author, "Who Do People in Asia-Pacific Want to Win the US Presidential Election?" YouGov, October 15, 2020, available at https://bit.ly/41kz6am, accessed on June 23, 2023.

10. Kai Chi Leung, "Liangnianban nei yu sishiwan ming xianggang jumin jing jichang ligang" [Within two and a half years, more than four hundred thousand Hong Kong residents exited from the airport], The Initium, December 23, 2023, available at https://bit.ly/41n3q4f, accessed on May 25, 2023.

11. Cora Engelbrecht, "'We Are Fleeing the Law': Hong Kong Protesters Escape to Taiwan," *New York Times*, December 8, 2019, available at http://bit.ly/3RINeHr, accessed on May 26, 2023.

12. A collection of short stories published in Taiwan best depicted the mood of aimlessly drifting among these youngsters, see Mu 2022.

13. James Griffiths, "Hong Kong Set the Bar for Charter Cities. But It's Not a Blueprint That Can Be Transported," CNN, September 14, 2020, available at https://cnn.it/39y5tIF, accessed on September 23, 2021.

CHAPTER 6

1. Unknown author, "Timeline: 59 Hong Kong Civil Society Groups Disband following the Onset of the Security Law," Hong Kong Free Press, June 30, 2022, available at https://bit.ly/41jLVlm, accessed on December 14, 2023.

2. The International Federation of Journalists (2022: 15) put the number at five hundred thousand. However, I chose a higher figure, which is based on an interview with a former officer of *Apple Daily*.

3. See the statement of Green Bean Media, available at https://bit.ly/46W3wkr, accessed on June 4, 2023.

4. Unknown author, "Xianggang wangmei chuangbanren mei canyu chuxuanan que bei dianming" [One Hong Kong's online media founder wasn't involved in the primary, but criticized], VOA, August 24, 2022, available at https://bit.ly/3GJhQlQ, accessed on June 5, 2023.

5. Fengjing Chen, "Zai laji niandai zhongxin zoujin yijia shudian" [In the age of garbage, walking again into a bookstore], The Initium, October 12, 2021, available at https://bit.ly/48ezgm2, accessed on June 11, 2023.

6. Ziliu Ling, "Liu zai xianggang de ren" [Those who stayed in Hong Kong], The Initium, November 10, 2022, available at https://bit.ly/3Nq5mTI, accessed on June 14, 2023.

7. Unknown author, "Yiquan shuguan qunian ban qingjiu gongyin taizaizhi gongdu huodong pang yiming beikong wei fangyitiaoli ji wupai shoujiu" [Punch book held an event drinking sake and reading Dazai Osamu together, but was accused of violating antipandemic regulations and selling alcohol without a permit], Inmediahk, March 1, 2023, available at https://bit.ly/3RiZ35D, accessed on December 14, 2023.

8. Among them, a Telegram channel (@youarenotalonehk) has 72,939 followers, as of June 26, 2023.

9. The Witness (available at https://www.facebook.com/thewitnesshk) and the Court News (available at https://www.facebook.com/hkcourtnews) have on Facebook 69,000 and 27,000 followers, respectively, assessed on December 14, 2023.

10. Chuyan Yu, "Jianzhengzhe yu pangtingshi" [Witness and those who participated in the courtroom]. The Initium, January 5, 2021, available at https://bit.ly/4ave7WG, accessed on June 26, 2023.

11. Wen Cheng, "Shouzong pangtingshi shandongan liang beigao zuicheng qiu shier ji san ge yue" [The first case of courtroom hearers sentencing of two for incitement, for twelve and three months, respectively], Radio Free Asia, October 27, 2022, available at https://bit.ly/3NthgMF, accessed on June 26, 2023.

References

A Hoi. 2021. "Qieryi shijian: Wujing shifen" [The July 21 incident: Moments without police]. In *Fan xiuli fengbao: Caifang zhanchang* [The anti-ELAB storm: The battlefield of journal reporting], edited by Chris Yeung, 92–97. Hong Kong: Hong Kong Journalists Association.

Almeida, Paul D. 2003. "Opportunity Organizations and Threat-Induced Contention." *American Journal of Sociology* 109 (2): 345–400.

Aminzade, Ron, and Doug McAdam. 2001. "Emotion and Contentious Politics." In *Silence and Voice in the Study of Contentious Politics*, by Ronald R. Aminzade, Jack A. Goldstone, Doug McAdam, Elizabeth J. Perry, William H. Sewell, Sidney Tarrow, and Charles Tilly, 14–51. Cambridge: Cambridge University Press.

Anderson, Benedict. 1983. *Imagined Communities: Reflections on the Origin and Spread of Nationalism*. London: Verso.

Andrews, Kenneth T., and Michael Biggs. 2006. "The Dynamics of Protest Diffusion: Movement Organizations, Social Networks, and News Media in the 1960 Sit-Ins." *American Sociological Review* 71 (5): 752–77.

Au, Loong-yu. 2020. *Hong Kong in Revolt: The Protest Movement and the Future of China*. London: Pluto.

Aung, Pinky Htut. 2021. "Sonic Resistance in Myanmar: Anthems of Social Change." Nusasonic, available at https://bit.ly/3thK43S, accessed on August 19, 2023.

Austin, J. L. 1955. *How to Do Things with Words*. Oxford: Clarendon.

Banki, Susan. 2023. "Art Is Happening in Myanmar, and Outside of It: Transnational Solidarity Art." *Globalizations* 20 (7): 1048–64.

Bauhinia Project. 2021. *Hong Kong without Us: A People's Poetry*. Atlanta: University of Georgia Press.

Bayat, Asef. 2017. *Revolution without Revolutionaries: Making Sense of the Arab Spring*. Stanford, CA: Stanford University Press.

———. 2023. "Is Iran on the Verge of Another Revolution?" *Journal of Democracy* 34 (2): 19–31.

Bennett, W. Lance, and Alexandra Segerberg. 2013. *The Logic of Connective Action: Digital Media and the Personalization of Contentious Politics*. Cambridge: Cambridge University Press.

Biggs, Michael. 2005. "Strikes as Forest Fires: Chicago and Paris in the Late 19th Century." *American Journal of Sociology* 110 (6): 1684–714.

Bob, Clifford. 2010. *The Marketing of Rebellion: Insurgents, Media, and International Activism*. Cambridge: Cambridge University Press.

———. 2015. "The United Nations: Gay versus Anti-Gay Players in Transnational Contention." In *Breaking Down the State: Protestors Engaged*, edited by Jan Willem Duyvendak and James M. Jasper, 205–24. Amsterdam: Amsterdam University Press.

Bourdieu, Pierre. 1977. *Outline of a Theory of Practice*. Translated by R. Nice. Cambridge: Cambridge University Press.

Britt, Lory, and David Heise. 2000. "From Shame to Pride in Identity Politics." In *Self, Identity, and Social Movements*, edited by Sheldon Stryker, Timothy J. Owens, and Robert W. White, 239–51. Minneapolis: University of Minnesota Press.

Buchanan, Larry, Quochtrung Bui, and Jugal K. Patel. 2020. "Black Lives Matter May Be the Largest Movement in U.S. History." *New York Times*, July 3, 2020. Available at https://bit.ly/3RkZn3U, accessed on August 19, 2023.

Bunce, Valerie, and Sharon Wolchik. 2011. *Defeating Authoritarian Leaders in Post-Communist Countries*. Cambridge: Cambridge University Press.

Carothers, Thomas, and Richard Youngs. 2015. *The Complexities of Global Protests*. Washington, DC: Carnegie Endowment for International Peace.

Carrico, Kevin. 2022. *Two Systems Two Countries: A Nationalist Guide to Hong Kong*. Berkeley: University of California Press.

Carroll, John M. 2022. *The Hong Kong-China Nexus*. Cambridge: Cambridge University Press.

Castells, Manuel. 2012. *Network of Outrage and Hope: Social Movements in the Internet Age*. Oxford: Polity.

Chan, Anita. 2020. "The Emergence of Labor Unions from within Hong Kong's Protest Movement." *Asia-Pacific Journal* 18 (24): 1–8.

Chan, Debby Sze Wan. 2022. "The Consumption Power of the Politically Powerless: The Yellow Economy in Hong Kong." *Journal of Civil Society* 18 (1): 69–86.

———. 2023. "Political Resistance in the Marketplace: Consumer Activism in the Milk Tea Alliance." *Journal of Contemporary Asia* 54 (4): 643–66.

Chan, Debby Sze Wan, and Ngai Pun. 2020. "Economic Power of the Politically Powerless in the 2019 Hong Kong Pro-Democracy Movement." *Critical Asian Studies* 52 (1): 33–43.

Chan, Hoi Hing. 2019. "Jiefang yinfa zhongchan: Juda de waiwei liliang" [Neighbors, gray-haired, and middle class: The mighty external forces]. In *Xianggangren 2.0* [Hongkongers 2.0], edited by Reng Fu Wang, 60–66. Taipei: Zhennada.

Chan, Jenny, Mark Selden, and Ngai Pun. 2020. *Dying for an iPhone: Apple, Foxconn, and the Lives of China's Workers*. Chicago: Haymarket Books.

Chan, Katy Pui Man. 2021. "Behind the 'Racism' of the 2019 Hong Kong Protests." *HAU: Journal of Ethnographic Theory* 11 (2): 863–68.

Chan, Kin-man. 2020. *Chen jianmin yuzhong shujian* [Chen Kin-man's letters from prison]. Hong Kong: Step Forward.

———. 2022. "Democracy Movement and Alternative Knowledge in Hong Kong." In *Knowledge and Civil Society*, edited by Johannes Glückler, Heinz-Dieter Meyer, and Laura Suarsana, 235–51. Berlin: Springer.

———. 2023. "Unwritten Endings: Revolutionary Potential of China's A4 Protest." *Sociologica* 17 (1): 57–66.

Chang, Chu-chin, and Thung-hong Lin. 2020. "Autocracy Login: Internet Censorship and Civil Society in the Digital Age." *Democratization* 27 (5): 874–95.

Chang, Min-Chi. 2023. "Cong xianggang fansongzhong tuxiang kan shehui yundong zhong de dongneng" [An observation on agency in social movements via 2019–2020 ongoing Hong Kong protests' graphics]. *Yishu pinglun* [Arts review] 45:155–94.

Chang, Paul Y. 2015. *Protest Dialectics: State Repression and South Korea's Democracy Movement, 1970–1979*. Stanford, CA: Stanford University Press.

Chang, Paul Y., and Kangsan Lee. 2021. "The Structure of Protest Cycles: Inspiration and Bridging in South Korea's Democracy Movement." *Social Forces* 100 (2): 879–904.

Chen, Chih-Jou Jay, and Victor Zheng. 2022. "Changing Attitudes toward China in Taiwan and Hong Kong in the Xi Jinping Era." *Journal of Contemporary China* 31 (134): 250–66.

Chen, Jie. 2018. "The Chinese Political Opposition in Exile: A Chequered Development." *Europe-Asia Studies* 70 (1): 108–29.

Chen, Yun-chung, and Mirana M. Szeto. 2015. "The Forgotten Road of Progressive Localism: New Preservation Movement in Hong Kong." *Inter-Asia Cultural Studies* 16 (3): 436–53.

Cheng, Edmund W. 2020. "United Front Work and Mechanisms of Countermobilization in Hong Kong." *China Journal* 83:1–33.

Cheng, Edmund W., and Wai-Yin Chan. 2017. "Explaining Spontaneous Occupation: Antecedents, Contingencies and Spaces in the Umbrella Movement." *Social Movement Studies* 16 (2): 222–39.

Cheng, Edmund W., Francis L. F. Lee, Samson Yuen, and Gary Tang. 2022. "Total Mobilization from Below: Hong Kong's Freedom Summer." *China Quarterly* 251:629–59.

Cheng, Joseph Yu-shek, ed. 2005. *The July 1 Protest Rally: Interpreting a Historic Event*. Hong Kong: City University of Hong Kong Press.

Cheng, Wendy. 2023. *Island X: Taiwanese Student Migrants, Campus Spies, and Cold War Activism*. Seattle: University of Washington Press.

Chenoweth, Erica. 2020. "The Future of Nonviolent Resistance." *Journal of Democracy* 31 (3): 69–84.

Chenoweth, Erica, and Maria J. Stephan. 2011. *Why Civil Resistance Works: The Strategic Logic of Nonviolent Conflict*. New York: Columbia University Press.

Cheung, Jacky. 2022. *Shangcheng houyi* [Legacies of a harmed city]. Taichung: White Elephant.

Chinese University of Hong Kong Centre for Communication and Public Opinion Survey. 2020. *Xianggang fan xiuli yundong zhong de minyi zhuangkuang yanjiu baogao* [A research report on public opinion in Hong Kong's anti-extradition law amendment bill movement]. Available at https://bit.ly/418zPtS, accessed on April 6, 2023.

Chong, Ja Ian. 2020. "Support for Trump in Hong Kong and Taiwan Is Unsurprising (But Misguided)." *The Diplomat*. Available at https://bit.ly/3RmvXlZ, accessed on December 3, 2023.

Chong, Ja Ian, and Hsin-Hsin Pan. 2022. "Evolution of Our Times: Developing Democratic Identities in Hong Kong and Taiwan." *Pacific Affairs* 95 (3): 441–73.

Chow, Rey. 1995. *Xie zaiguo zhi wai* [Writing the diaspora]. Hong Kong: Oxford University Press.

Choy, Jeffrey, ed. 2020. *Sanxia cunzhi: Xianggang fansongchong shehuiyundong wenxuan zuopin ji* [The will under the umbrella: A collection of artistic communication materials of Hong Kong's anti-ELAB movement]. Hong Kong: Backdrop Studio.

Chung, Hiu-Fung. 2020. "Changing Repertoires of Contention in Hong Kong: A Case Study on the Anti-Extradition Bill Movement." *China Perspectives* 2020 (3): 57–63.

Chung, Sanho. 2023. "'Because Hongkongers Should Support Hong Kong': Entanglement of National Identity, Political Ideology, and Football Fandom in Hong Kong." *Journal of Sport and Social Issues* 47(3): 203–27.

Chung, Sze-yuen. 2001. *Xianggang huigui lichen: Zhong shiyuan huiyilu* [The retrocession of Hong Kong: Sze-yuen Chung's memoir]. Hong Kong: Chinese University of Hong Kong Press.

Chung, Yiu Wa. 2021. *Shijian yexu bu zhanzai women zhebian* [Time maybe is not on our side]. Taipei: Spring Hill.

Citic Besiegement Team. 2020. *Zhongxin wekun riji* [Dailies of Citic Tower besiegement]. Hong Kong: Glastree.

Clarke, Killian. 2014. "Unexpected Brokers of Mobilization: Contingency and Networks in the 2011 Egyptian Uprising." *Comparative Politics* 46 (4): 379–94.

Cohen, Ronen A., and Bosmat Yefet. 2021. "The Iranian Diaspora and the Homeland: Redefining the Role of a Centre." *Journal of Ethnic and Migration Studies* 47 (3): 686–702.

Cress, Daniel M., and David A. Snow. 1996. "Mobilization at the Margins: Resources, Benefactors, and the Viability of Homeless Social Movement Organizations." *American Sociological Review* 61 (6): 1089–1109.

Daddy, Tian, ed. 2019. *Fan songzhong sheying ji: Wo yuan rongguang gui xianggang* [A photography albumen of the anti-extradition movement: Glory to Hong Kong]. Taipei: Kiwi Fruit Studio.

Dapiran, Antony. 2020. *City on Fire: The Fight for Hong Kong.* London: Scribe.

Davies, Michael C. 2024. *Freedom Undone: The Assault on Liberal Values and Institutions in Hong Kong.* New York: Columbia University Press.

DB Channel, ed. 2022. *Xianggang shenhao de pianke* [Great moments of Hong Kong]. Taipei: 1841 Press.

Dedman, Adam K., and Autumn Lai. 2021. "Digitally Dismantling Asian Authoritarianism: Activist Reflections from the #MilkTeaAlliance." *Contention: The Multidisciplinary Journal of Social Protest* 9 (1): 1–36.

della Porta, Donatella. 1988. "Recruitment Process in Clandestine Political Organization: Italian Left-Wing Terrorism." In *From Structure to Action: Comparing Social Movement Research across Cultures*, edited by Bert Klandermans, Hanspeter Kriesi, and Sidney Tarrow, 155–69. Greenwich, CT: JAI.

———. 1995. *Social Movements, Political Violence, and the State.* Cambridge: Cambridge University Press.

———. 2013. *Clandestine Political Violence.* Cambridge: Cambridge University Press.

———. 2015. *Social Movements in Times of Austerity: Bringing Capitalism Back into Protest Analysis.* Oxford: Wiley.

———. 2018. "Radicalization: A Relational Perspective." *Annual Review of Political Science* 21:461–74.

———. 2020. *How Social Movements Can Save Democracy: Democratic Innovations from Below.* Cambridge: Polity.

della Porta, Donatella, and Herbert Reiter, eds. 1998. *Policing the Protest: The Control of Mass Demonstrations in Western Democracies*. Minneapolis: University of Minnesota Press.

Diani, Macro. 2001. "Social Capital as Social Movement Outcome." In *Beyond Tocqueville: Civil Society and the Social Capital Debate in Comparative Perspective*, edited by Bob Edwards, Michel W. Foley, and Macro Diani, 207–18. Hanover, NH: Tufts University Press.

———. 2015. *The Cement of Civil Society: Studying Networks in Localities*. Cambridge: Cambridge University Press.

Diani, Mario, and Doug McAdam, eds. 2003. *Social Movements and Networks: Relational Approaches to Collective Action*. Oxford: Oxford University Press.

Duara, Prasenjit. 2016. "Hong Kong as a Global Frontier: Interface of China, Asia, and the World." In *Hong Kong in the Cold War*, edited by Priscilla Roberts and John M. Carroll, 211–30. Hong Kong: Hong Kong University Press.

Durkheim, Emile. 1915. *The Elementary Forms of the Religious Life*. Translated by Joseph Ward Swain. New York: Free Press.

Edwards, Bob, and John D. McCarthy. 2004. "Resources and Social Movement Mobilization." In *Blackwell Companion to Social Movements*, edited by David A. Snow, Sarah A. Soule, and Hanspeter Kriesi, 116–52. Oxford: Blackwell.

Edwards, Bob, John D. McCarthy, and Dane R. Mataic. 2019. "The Resource Context of Social Movements." In *Wiley Blackwell Companion to Social Movements*, edited by David A. Snow, Sarah A. Soule, Hanspeter Kriesi, and Holly J. McCammon, 79–97. Oxford: Wiley-Blackwell.

Einwohner, Rachel L. 2003. "Opportunity, Honor and Action in the Warsaw Ghetto Uprising of 1943." *American Journal of Sociology* 109 (3): 650–75.

———. 2006. "Identity Work and Collective Action in a Repressive Context: Jewish Resistance on the 'Aryan Side' of the Warsaw Ghetto." *Social Problems* 53 (1): 38–56.

Fantasia, Rick. 1989. *Cultures of Solidarity: Consciousness, Action, and Contemporary American Workers*. Berkeley: University of California Press.

Fleischauer, Stefan. 2016. "Taiwan's Independence Movement." In *Routledge Handbook of Contemporary Taiwan*, edited by Gunter Schubert, 68–84. London: Routledge.

Fominaya, Christina Flesher. 2014a. *Social Movements and Globalization: How Protests, Occupations and Uprisings Are Changing the World*. New York: Palgrave Macmillan.

———. 2014b. "Debunking Spontaneity: Spain's 15-M/Indignados as Autonomous Movement." *Social Movement Studies* 14 (2): 142–63.

———. 2020. *Democracy Reloaded: Inside Spain's Political Laboratory from 15-M to Podemos*. Oxford: Oxford University Press.

Fong, Brian C. H. 2014. "The Partnership between the Chinese Government and Hong Kong's Capitalist Class: Implications for HKSAR Governance, 1997–2012." *China Quarterly* 217:165–220.

———. 2017. "One Country, Two Nationalisms: Center-Periphery Relations between Mainland China and Hong Kong, 1997–2016." *Modern China* 43 (5): 523–56.

———. 2021a. "Diaspora Formation and Mobilisation: The Emerging Hong Kong Diaspora in the Anti-Extradition Bill Movement." *Nations and Nationalism* 28 (3): 1061–79.

———. 2021b. "Exporting Autocracy: How China's Extra-jurisdictional Autocratic Influence Caused Democratic Backsliding in Hong Kong." *Democratization* 28 (1): 185–202.

Frenzel, Fabian, Anna Feigenbaum, and Patrick McCurdy. 2014. "Protest Camps: An Emerging Field of Social Movement Research." *Sociological Review* 62 (3): 457–74.

Frydenlund, Iselin, Pum Za Mang, Phyo Wai, and Susan Hayward. 2021. "Religious Responses to the Military Coup in Myanmar." *Review of Faith and International Affairs* 19 (3): 77–88.

Fu, Diana. 2017. *Mobilizing without the Masses: Control and Contention in China*. Cambridge: Cambridge University Press.

Gamson, William A. 1975. *The Strategy of Social Protest*. Homewood, IL: Dorsey.

Gan, Wendy. 2017. "Puckish Protesting in the Umbrella Movement." *International Journal of Cultural Studies* 20 (2): 162–76.

Gerbaudo, Paolo. 2012. *Tweets and the Streets: Social Media and Contemporary Activism*. New York: Pluto.

———. 2017. *The Mask and the Flag: Populism, Citizenism, and Global Protest*. Oxford: Oxford University Press.

Giddens, Antony. 1984. *The Constitution of Society: Outline of the Theory of Structuration*. Berkeley: University of California Press.

Gitlin, Todd. 2012. *Occupy Nation: The Roots, the Spirit, and the Promise of Occupy Wall Street*. New York: Harper Collins.

Glasius, Marlies, and Armine Ishkanian. 2018. "The Square and Beyond: Trajectories and Implications of the Square Occupations." In *Global Cultures of Contestation: Mobility, Sustainability, Aesthetics and Connectivity*, edited by Esther Peeren, Robin Celikates, Jeroen de Kloet, and Thomas Poell, 27–48. London: Palgrave Macmillan.

Goldstone, Jack A. 2004. "More Social Movements or Fewer? Beyond Political Opportunity Structures to Relational Fields." *Theory and Society* 33 (3): 333–65.

Goldstone, Jack A., and Charles Tilly. 2001. "Threat (and Opportunity): Popular Action and State Response in the Dynamics of Contentious Action." In *Silence and Voice in the Study of Contentious Politics*, 179–94. Cambridge: Cambridge University Press.

Goodwin, Jeff, James M. Jasper, and Francesca Polletta, eds. 2001. *Passionate Politics: Emotion and Social Movements*. Chicago: University of Chicago Press.

Gould, Deborah. 2002. "Life during Wartime: Emotion and the Development of ACT UP." *Mobilization: An International Quarterly* 7 (2): 177–200.

Graeber, David. 2013. *The Democracy Project: A History, a Crisis, a Movement*. New York: Allen Lane.

Granovetter, Mark. 1978. "Threshold Models of Collective Behavior." *American Journal of Sociology* 83 (6): 1420–43.

Gundelach, Peter, and Jonas Toubøl. 2019. "High-and Low-Risk Activism: Differential Participation in a Refugee Solidarity Movement." *Mobilization: An International Quarterly* 24 (2): 199–220.

Gunning, Jeroen, and Ilan Zyi Baron. 2014. *Why Occupy a Square: People, Protests and Movements in the Egyptian Revolution*. Oxford: Oxford University Press.

Hardt, Michael, and Antonio Negri. 2017. *Assembly*. Oxford: Oxford University Press.

He, Rowena Xiaoqing. 2014. *Tiananmen Exiles: Voices of the Struggle for Democracy in China*. London: Palgrave Macmillan.

———. 2020. "To Lead or Not to Lead: Campus Standoff in Hong Kong's Water Movement." *Journal of International Affairs* 73 (2): 119–34.

Hirschman, Albert O. 1970. *Exit, Voice, and Loyalty: Responses to Decline in Firms, Organizations, and States*. Cambridge, MA: Harvard University Press.

Ho, Lawrence Ka-Ki. 2020. "Rethinking Police Legitimacy in Postcolonial Hong Kong: Paramilitary Policing in Protest Management." *Policing: A Journal of Policy and Practice* 14 (4): 1015–33.

Ho, Ming-sho. 2018. "From Mobilization to Improvisation: The Lessons from Taiwan's 2014 Sunflower Movement." *Social Movement Studies* 17 (2): 189–202.

———. 2019. *Challenging Beijing's Mandate of Heaven: Taiwan's Sunflower Movement and Hong Kong's Umbrella Movement*. Philadelphia: Temple University Press.

———. 2020. "How Protesters Evolve: Hong Kong's Anti-Extradition Movement and the Lessons Learned from the Umbrella Movement." *Mobilization: An International Journal* 25 (5): 711–28.

———. 2021. "'Dried Mango': Taiwan's Fiercely Democratic Young Voters." *Journal of the European Association for Chinese Studies* 2:197–203.

———. 2023a. "Hongkongers' International Front: The Diaspora Activism during and after the 2019 Anti-Extradition Protest." *Journal of Contemporary Asia* 54 (2): 238–59.

———. 2023b. "Relational Tactics and Trust in High-Risk Activism: Anonymity, Preexisting Ties, and Bonding in Hong Kong's 2019–20 Protest." *International Journal of Comparative Sociology* 65 (4): 499–516.

———. 2024. "Movement Meaning of Money: Monetary Mobilization in Hong Kong's Prodemocracy Movement." *Sociological Review* 72 (2): 432–50.

Ho, Ming-sho, and Wei An Chen, 2021, "Peddling the Revolution? How Hong Kong's Protesters Became Online Vendors in Taiwan." *Made in China Journal* 6 (3): 94–99.

Ho, Ming-sho, and Chun-hao Huang, 2017. "Movement Parties in Taiwan (1987–2016): A Political Opportunity Explanation." *Asian Survey* 57 (2): 343–67.

Ho, Ming-sho, Chun-hao Huang, and Liang-ying Lin. 2020. "The Sunflower Imagination: The Movement Perception and Evaluation from the Grassroots." In *Sunflowers and Umbrellas Social Movements, Expressive Practices, and Political Culture in Taiwan and Hong Kong*, edited by Thomas Gold and Sebastian Veg, 42–67. Berkeley: University of California Berkeley Institute of East Asian Studies.

Ho, Ming-sho, and Wai Ki Wan. 2023. "Universities as an Arena of Contentious Politics: Mobilization and Control in Hong Kong's Anti-Extradition Movement of 2019." *International Studies in Sociology of Education* 32 (2): 313–36.

Ho, Ming-sho, and Yun-Chung Ting. 2023. "Contentious Institutionalization of Protests under Democracy: The Evidence from Taiwan, 1986–2016." *Government and Opposition*. Available at https://doi.org/10.1017/gov.2023.25.

Holbig, Heike. 2020. "Be Water, My Friend: Hong Kong's 2019 Anti-Extradition Protests." *International Journal of Sociology* 50 (4): 325–37.

Holland, Laurel L., and Sherry Cable. 2002. "Reconceptualizing Social Movement Abeyance: The Role of Internal Processes and Culture in Cycles of Movement Abeyance and Resurgence." *Sociological Focus* 35 (3): 297–314.

Hon, Lai Chu. 2022. *Heiri* [Darkness under the Sun]. Taipei: Acropolis.

Hong Kong Cherishers, eds. 2020. *Xiaoshile de liannongqiang* [Lennon Walls that have disappeared]. Hong Kong: Isaiah.

Hong Kong Public Opinion Research Institute. 2019. *Women xianggangren gundong diaocha yanjiu baogao 8* [We the Hongkonger's rolling surveys: The eighth report]. Available at https://bit.ly/3KXu8JW, accessed on April 13, 2023.

Huang, Shu-Mei. 2018. "Liminoid Space and Place-Fixing in Urban Activism." *Inter-Asia Cultural Studies* 19 (3): 359–71.

Hui, Po-keung. 1999. "Comprador Politics and Middleman Capitalism." In *Hong Kong's History: State and Society under Colonial Rule*, edited by Tak-wing Ngo, 30–45. London: Routledge.

Hui, Victoria Tin-bor. 2020. "Crackdown: Hong Kong Faces Tiananmen 2.0." *Journal of Democracy* 31 (4): 122–37.

———. 2021. "Hong Kong's New Police State." *The Diplomat*, Available at http://bit.ly/3RGceyM, accessed on December 13, 2023.

Hung, Ho-fung. 2022a. *City on the Edge: Hong Kong under Chinese Rule*. Cambridge: Cambridge University Press.

———. 2022b. *Clash of Empires*. Cambridge: Cambridge University Press.

Ibrahim, Zuraidah, and Jeffie Lam, eds. 2020. *Rebel City: Hong Kong's Year of Water and Fire*. Singapore: World Scientific.

International Federation of Journalists. 2022. *The Story That Won't Be Silenced: Hong Kong Freedom of Expression Report 2021/22*. Available at https://bit.ly/3RFPsap, accessed on May 30, 2023.

———. 2023. *Journalists in Exile: A Survey of Media Workers in the Hong Kong Diaspora*. Available at https://bit.ly/3tdlfpR, accessed on June 3, 2023.

Invisible Committee. 2009. *The Coming Insurrection*. Los Angeles: Semiotext(e).

Ip, Iam-chong. 2020. *Hong Kong's New Identity Politics: Longing for the Local in the Shadow of China*. London: Routledge.

Jasper, James M. 1997. *The Art of Moral Protest: Culture, Biography, and Creativity in Social Movements*. Chicago: University of Chicago Press.

———. 1999. "Recruiting Intimates, Recruiting Strangers: Building the Contemporary Animal Rights Movement." In *Waves of Protest: Social Movements since the Sixties*, edited by Jo Freeman and Victoria Johnson, 65–82. New York: Rowman and Littlefield.

———. 2004. "A Strategic Approach to Collective Action: Looking for Agency in Social-Movement Choices." *Mobilization: An International Quarterly* 9 (1): 1–16.

———. 2006. *Getting Your Way: Strategic Dilemmas in the Real World*. Chicago: University of Chicago Press.

———. 2012. "Introduction: From Political Opportunity Structures to Strategic Interaction." In *Contention in Context: Political Opportunities and the Emergence of Protest*, edited by Jeff Goodwin and James M. Jasper, 1–33. Stanford, CA: Stanford University Press.

———. 2014. *Protest: A Cultural Introduction to Social Movements*. Oxford: Wiley.

———. 2015. "Playing the Game." In *Players and Arenas: The Interactive Dynamics of Protest*, edited by James M. Jasper and Jan Willem Duyvendak, 9–32. Amsterdam: Amsterdam University Press.

———. 2018. *The Emotions of Protests*. Chicago: University of Chicago Press.

Junker, Andrew. 2019. *Becoming Activists in Global China: Social Movements in the Chinese Diaspora*. Cambridge: Cambridge University Press.

Juris, Jeffrey S. 2008. *Networking Futures: The Movements against Corporate Globalization*. Durham, NC: Duke University Press.

Kaeding, Malte Philipp. 2017. "The Rise of 'Localism' in Hong Kong." *Journal of Democracy* 28 (1): 157–71.

Kang, Jiyeon. 2018. *Igniting the Internet: Youth and Activism in Postauthoritarian South Korea*. Honolulu: University of Hawai'i Press.

Keck, Margaret E., and Kathryn Sikkink. 1998. *Activists beyond Borders: Advocacy Networks in International Politics*. Ithaca, NY: Cornell University Press.

Ketchley, Neil. 2017. *Egypt in a Time of Revolution: Contentious Politics and the Arab Spring*. Cambridge: Cambridge University Press.

King, Brayden G., and Nicholas A. Pearce. 2010. "The Contentiousness of Markets: Politics, Social Movements, and Institutional Change in Markets." *Annual Review of Sociology* 36:249–67.

Kitschelt, Herbert. 1986. "Political Opportunity Structures and Political Protest: Anti-Nuclear Movements in Four Democracies." *British Journal of Political Science* 16 (1): 57–85.

Koinova, Maria, and Dženeta Karabegović, eds. 2020. *Diaspora Mobilizations for Transitional Justice*. London: Routledge.

Koopmans, Ruud. 1993. "The Dynamics of Protest Waves: West Germany, 1965 to 1989." *American Sociological Review* 58 (5): 637–58.

Krastev, Ivan. 2014. *Democracy Disrupted: The Politics of Global Protest*. Philadelphia: University of Pennsylvania Press.

Krasynska, Svitlana, and Eric Martin. 2017. "Formality of Informal Civil Society: Ukraine's EuroMaidan." *Voluntas: International Journal of Voluntary and Nonprofit Organization* 28 (1): 420–49.

Kriesi, Hanspeter, Ruud Koopmans, Jan Willem Duyvendak, and Marco G. Giugni. 1995. *New Social Movements in Western Europe*. Minneapolis: University of Minnesota Press.

Ku, Agnes Shuk-mei. 2012. "Remaking Places and Fashioning an Opposition Discourse: Struggle over the Star Ferry Pier and the Queen's Pier in Hong Kong." *Environment and Planning D* 30 (1): 5–22.

Kurzman, Charles. 2004. *The Unthinkable Revolution in Iran*. Cambridge, MA: Harvard University Press.

Kwan, Chun Hoi. 2020. *Xianggang dadao* [Hong Kong Boulevard]. Hong Kong: HK Feature.

Lai, Ruby Y. S. 2023. "Home as a Site of Resistance/Repression? The Intersection of Family, Politics and the Hong Kong 2019 Protest Movement." *Sociological Review* 72 (2): 412–31.

Lai, Yan-ho. 2022. "A 'Leader-Full' Movement under Authoritarianism: Mobilization Networks in Hong Kong's Anti-Extradition Movement." In *Authoritarianism and Civil Society in Asia*, edited by Anthony J. Spires and Akihiro Ogawa, 3–23. London: Routledge.

Lai, Yan-ho, and Ming Sing. 2020. "Solidarity and Implications of a Leaderless Movement in Hong Kong: Its Strengths and Limitations." *Communist and Post-Communist Studies* 53 (4): 41–67.

Larana, Enrique, Hank Johnston, and Joseph R. Gusfield, eds. 1994. *New Social Movements: From Ideology to Identity*. Philadelphia. Temple University Press.

Lary, Diana, and Bernard Luk. 1994. "Hong Kong Immigrants in Toronto." In *Reluctant Exiles: Migration from Hong Kong and New Overseas Chinese*, edited by R. Skeldon, 139–62. New York: M. E. Sharpe.

Lau, Chun Kong. 2020. *Yuanlang heiye* [A dark night in Yuen Long]. Hong Kong: Lauyeah.

Lau, Kwong Shing. 2020. *Bei xiaoshi de xianggang* [Hong Kong that was forced to disappear]. Taipei: Gaea Books.

Law, Nathan. 2016. "After the Mong Kong conflict: The Collective Aphasia among Progressive Democrats" [Wangjiao chongtu hou: Jinbu minzhupai de jiti shiyu]. *The Reporter*, February 16, 2016. Available at https://bit.ly/47SkW2T, accessed on December 3, 2023.

———. 2021. *Freedom: How We Lost It and How We Fight Back*. New York: Experiment.

Lee, Ching Kwan. 2022. *Hong Kong: Global China's Restive Frontier*. Cambridge: Cambridge University Press.

Lee, Ching Kwan, and Ming Sing, eds. 2019. *Take Back Our Future: An Eventful Sociology of the Hong Kong Umbrella Movement Paperback*. Ithaca, NY: Cornell University Press.

Lee, Francis L. F. 2018. "Changing Political Economy of the Hong Kong Media." *China Perspectives* 2018 (3): 9–18.

———. 2019. "Solidarity in the Anti-Extradition Bill Movement in Hong Kong." *Critical Asian Studies* 52 (1): 18–32.

———. 2023. "Proactive Internationalization and Diaspora Mobilization in a Networked Movement: The Case of Hong Kong's Anti-Extradition Bill Protests." *Social Movement Studies* 22 (2): 232–49.

Lee, Francis L. F., and Joseph M. Chan. 2018. *Media and Protest Logics in the Digital Era: The Umbrella Movement in Hong Kong.* Oxford: Oxford University Press.

Lee, Francis L. F., Michael Chan, and Hsuan-Ting Chen. 2020. "Social Media and Protest Attitudes during Movement Abeyance: A Study of Hong Kong University Students." *International Journal of Communication* 14 (2020): 4932–51.

Lee, Francis L. F., Edmund W. Cheng, Hai Liang, Gary K. Y. Tang, and Samson Yuen. 2022. "Dynamics of Tactical Radicalisation and Public Receptiveness in Hong Kong's Anti-Extradition Bill Movement." *Journal of Contemporary Asia* 52 (3): 429–51.

Lee, Francis L. F., Gary Tang, Samson Yuen, and Edmund W. Cheng. 2020. "Five Demands and (Not Quite) Beyond: Claim Making and Ideology in Hong Kong's Anti-Extradition Bill Movement." *Communist and Post-Communist Studies* 53 (4): 22–40.

Lee, Francis L. F., Samson Yuen, Gary Tang, and Edmund W. Cheng. 2019. "Hong Kong's Summer of Uprising: From Anti-Extradition to Anti-Authoritarian Protests." *China Review* 19 (4): 1–32.

Lei, Ya-Wen. 2018. *The Contentious Public Sphere: Law, Media, and Authoritarian Rule in China*. Princeton, NJ: Princeton University Press.

Lemonik, Mikaila Mariel. 2013. "Moral Shocks/Outrage." In *Wiley-Blackwell Encyclopedia of Social and Political Movements*, edited by David A. Snow, Donatella della Porta, Bert Klandermans, and Doug McAdam. Oxford: Wiley Blackwell. DOI:10.1002/9780470674871.wbespm436.pub2.

Leung, M. K. 2019. "Technology Aids Unity of Hong Kong Movement." *Financial Times*, June 27, 2019. Available at https://bit.ly/473rbzj, accessed on November 12, 2023.

Li, Yao-Tai, and Ka Yi Fung. 2022. "Donating to the Fight for Democracy: The Connective Activism of Overseas Hong Kongers and Taiwanese in the 2019 Anti-extradition Bill Movement." *Global Networks* 22 (2): 292–307.

Li, Yao-Tai, and Bin-Jou Liao. 2023. "An 'Unsettling' Journey? Hong Kong's Exodus to Taiwan and Australia after the 2019 Protest." *American Behavioral Scientists*. DOI:10.1177/00027642231192025.

Li, Yao-Tai, and Jenna Ng. 2021. "Moral Dilemma of Striking: A Medical Worker's Response to Job Duty, Public Health Protection and the Politicization of Strikes." *Work, Employment and Society* 36 (5): 967–76.

Li, Yao-Tai, and Katherine Whitworth. 2022. "Contentious Repertoires: Examining Lennon Walls in Hong Kong's Social Unrest of 2019." *Journal of Contemporary Asia* 53 (1): 124–45.

———. 2023. "Redefining Consumer Nationalism: The Ambiguities of Shopping Yellow during the 2019 Hong Kong Anti-ELAB Movement." *Journal of Consumer Culture* 23 (3): 517–35.

———. 2024. "Coordinating and Doxing Data: Hong Kong Protesters' and Government Supporters' Data: Strategies in the Age of Datafication." *Social Movement Studies* 23 (3): 355–72.

Lian, Joseph. 2022. *Jingxin ji: Hou yusan yundong xianggang zhengzhi pinglun* [A collection of shocks: Political commentaries after the Umbrella Movement]. Taipei: 1841 Press.

Liang, Hai, and Francis L. F. Lee. 2021. "Opinion Leadership in a Leaderless Movement: Discussion of the Anti-extradition Bill Movement in the LIHKG Web Forum." *Social Movement Studies* 22 (5): 670–88.

Lien, Pei-te. 2010. "Pre-emigration Socialization, Transnational Ties, and Political Participation across the Pacific: A Comparison among Immigrants from China, Taiwan, and Hong Kong." *Journal of East Asian Studies* 10 (3): 453–82.

Lin, Kevin. 2021. "A New Chapter for Hong Kong's Labour Movement?" *Made in China Journal* 6 (3): 80–85.

Ling, Minhua. 2020. "Living between Incongruous Worlds in Hong Kong." *HAU: Journal of Ethnographic Theory* 10 (2): 308–12.

Liu, Wen, JN Chien, Christina Chung, and Ellie Tse, eds. 2022. *Reorienting Hong Kong's Resistance: Leftism, Decoloniality, and Internationalism*. London: Palgrave Macmillan.

Loveman, Mara. 1998. "High-Risk Collective Action: Defending Human Rights in Chile, Uruguay, and Argentina." *American Journal of Sociology* 104 (2): 477–525.

Luders, Joseph. 2006. "The Economics of Movement Success: Business Responses to Civil Rights Mobilization." *American Journal of Sociology* 111 (4): 963–98.

Lui, Lake. 2023a. "National Security Education and the Infrapolitical Resistance of Parent-Stayers in Hong Kong." *Journal of Asian and African Studies* 58 (1): 86–100.

———. 2023b. "Winning Quietly: Hong Kong Educators' Resistance to National Security Education." *Sociological Review* 72 (2): 451–70.

Lui, Lake, Ken Chih-Yan Sun, and Yuan Hsiao. 2021. "How Families Affect Aspirational Migration amidst Political Insecurity: The Case of Hong Kong." *Population, Space, and Place* 28 (4): e2528.

Lynch, Daniel. 2003. "Taiwan's Democratization and the Rise of Taiwanese Nationalism as Socialization to Global Culture." *Pacific Affairs* 75 (4): 557–74.

Ma, Ngok. 2011. "Hong Kong's Democrats Divide." *Journal of Democracy* 22 (1): 54–67.

———. 2012. "Political Parties and Elections." In *Contemporary Hong Kong Government and Politics*, edited by Wai-man Lam, Percy Luen-tim Lui, and Wilson Wong, 159–78. Hong Kong: Hong Kong University Press.

———. 2020. *Fankang de gongtongti: 2019 xianggang fansongzhong yundong* [A community in resistance: Hong Kong's anti-extradition movement of 2019]. Taipei: Rive Gauche.

Ma, Ngok, and Edmund W. Cheng. 2021. "Professionals in Revolt: Specialized Networks and Sectoral Mobilization in Hong Kong." *Social Movement Studies* 22 (5): 648–69.

Maeckelbergh, Marianne. 2011. "Doing Is Believing: Prefiguration as Strategic Practice in the Alterglobalization Movement." *Social Movement Studies* 10 (1): 1–20.

Maher, Thomas V. 2010. "Threat, Resistance, and Collective Action: The Cases of Sobibór, Treblinka and Auschwitz." *American Sociological Review* 75 (2): 252–72.

Mahtani, Shibani, and Timothy McLaughlin. 2023. *Among the Braves: Hope, Struggle, and Exile in the Battle for Hong Kong and the Future of Global Democracy*. New York: Hachette Books.

Marks, Gary, and Doug McAdam. 1999. "On the Relationship of Political Opportunities to the Form of Collective Action: The Case of the European Union." In *Social Movements in a Globalizing World*, edited by Donatella della Porta, Hanspeter Kriesi, and Dieter Rucht, 97–111. London: Palgrave Macmillan.

Matthews, Gordon. 2020. "The Hong Kong Protests in Anthropological Perspective: National Identity and What It Means." *Critique of Anthropology* 4 (2): 264–69.

Matthews, Gordon, Eric Kit-wai Ma, and Tai-lok Lui. 2008. *Hong Kong, China: Learning to Belong to a Nation*. London: Routledge.

McAdam, Doug. 1982. *Political Process and the Development of Black Insurgency, 1930–1970*. Chicago: University of Chicago Press.

———. 1983. "Tactical Innovation and the Pace of Insurgency." *American Sociological Review* 48 (6): 735–54.

———. 1986. "Recruitment to High-Risk Activism: The Case of Freedom Summer." *American Journal of Sociology* 92 (1): 64–90.

———. 2003. "Beyond Structural Analysis: Toward a More Dynamic Understanding of Social Movements." In *Social Movements and Networks: Relational Approaches to Collective Action*, edited by Mario Diani and Doug McAdam, 281–98. Oxford: Oxford University Press.

McAdam, Doug, and Hilary Schaffer Boudet. 2012. *Putting Social Movements in Their Place: Explaining Opposition to Energy Projects in the United States, 2000–2005*. Cambridge: Cambridge University Press.

McAdam, Doug, and W. Richard Scott. 2005. "Organizations and Movements." In *Social Movement and Organizational Theory*, edited by Gerald F. Davis, Doug McAdam, W. Richard Scott, and Mayer N. Zald, 4–40. Cambridge: Cambridge University Press.

McCarthy, John D., and Mayer N. Zald. 1987. "Resource Mobilization Theory and Social Movements." In *Social Movements in an Organizational Society*, edited by Mayer N. Zald and John D. McCarthy, 15–42. New Brunswick, NJ: Transaction Books.

Meek, Laura A., and Bai Hua. 2023. "Fugitive Hong Kong." *Current Anthropology* 64 (4): 436–48.

Melucci, Alberto. 1996. *Challenging Codes: Collective Action in the Information Age*. Cambridge: Cambridge University Press.

Meyer, David S. 1990. *A Winter of Discontent: The Nuclear Freeze and American Politics*. New York: Praeger.

Meyer, David S., and Sidney Tarrow, eds. 1998. *The Social Movement Society*. Lanham, MD: Rowman and Littlefield.

Mitchell, Katharyne. 1999. "Hong Kong Immigration and the Question of Democracy: Contemporary Struggles over Urban Politics in Vancouver B.C." In *Cosmopolitan Capitalists: Hong Kong and the Chinese Diaspora at the End of the Twentieth Century*, edited by G. Hamilton, 152–66. Seattle: University of Washington Press.

Mok, Chit Wai John. 2022. "Violent Repression, Relational Positions, and Emotional Mechanisms in Hong Kong's Anti-Extradition Movement." *Mobilization: An International Quarterly* 7 (3): 297–317.

Moore, Barrington, Jr. 1978. *Injustice: The Social Bases of Obedience and Revolt*. London: Routledge.

Moss, Dana. 2022. *The Arab Spring Abroad: Diaspora Activism against Authoritarian Regimes*. Cambridge: Cambridge University Press.

Mu, Yu. 2022. *Yanjie* [Streets filled with smoke]. Taipei: ECUS Publishing House.

Nachman, Lev. 2018. "Misalignment between Social Movements and Political Parties in Taiwan's 2016 Election: Not All Grass Roots Are Green." *Asian Survey* 58 (5): 874–97.

Nachman, Lev, Shelley Rigger, Chit Wai John Mok, and Nathan Kar Ming Chan. 2021. "Taiwanese Are Sympathetic but Uncertain about Hong Kong Refugees." *Foreign Policy*. Available at https://bit.ly/3J669GF, accessed on March 9, 2023.

Näre, Lena, and Maija Jokela. 2022. "The Affective Infrastructure of a Protest Camp: Asylum Seekers' 'Right to Live' Movement." *Sociological Review* 71 (1): 165–82.

Nepstad, Sharon Erickson. 2004. "Persistent Resistance: Commitment and Community in the Plowshares Movement." *Social Problems* 51 (1): 43–60.

———. 2015. *Nonviolent Struggle: Theories, Strategies, and Dynamics*. Oxford: Oxford University Press.

Nepstad, Sharon Erickson, and Christian Smith. 1999. "Rethinking Recruitment to High-Risk/Cost Activism: The Case of Nicaragua Exchange." *Mobilization: An International Quarterly* 4 (1): 25–40.

Ng, Vitrierat, and Kin-man Chan. 2017. "Emotion Politics: Joyous Resistance in Hong Kong." *China Review* 17 (1): 83–115.

Oberschall, Anthony. 1993. *Social Movements: Ideologies, Interests, and Identities*. New Brunswick, NJ: Transaction Books.

O'Donnell, Guillermo, and Philippe C. Schmitter. 1986. *Transitions from Authoritarian Rule: Tentative Conclusions about Uncertain Democracies*. Baltimore: John Hopkins University Press.

Parkinson, Sarah Elizabeth. 2013. "Organizing Rebellion: Rethinking High-Risk Mobilization and Social Networks in War." *American Political Science Review* 107 (3): 418–32.

Pearlman, Wendy. 2021. "Mobilizing from Scratch: Large-Scale Collective Action without Preexisting Organization in the Syrian Uprising." *Comparative Political Studies* 54 (10): 1786–817.

Peña, Alejandro M., Larissa Meier, and Alice M. Nah. 2021. "Exhaustion, Adversity, and Repression: Emotional Attrition in High-Risk Activism." *Perspectives on Politics* 21 (1): 27–42.

Pepper, Suzanne. 2008. *Keeping Democracy at Bay: Hong Kong and the Challenge of Chinese Political Reform*. Lanham, MD: Rowman and Littlefield.

Phattharathanasut, Tuwanont. 2024. "From Bad Student to Transnational Activist: Netiwit Chotiphatphaisal and Transnational Activism in Northeast and Southeast Asia." *TRaNS*, DOI:10.1017/trn.2023.15.

Phelps, Michelle S., Anneliese Ward, and Dwjuan Frazier. 2021. "From Police Reform to Police Abolition? How Minneapolis Activists Fought to Make Black Lives Matter." *Mobilization: An International Quarterly* 26 (4): 421–41.

Pickerill, Jenny, and John Krinsky. 2012. "Why Does Occupy Matter?" *Social Movement Studies* 11 (3–4): 279–87.

Piven, Frances Fox, and Richard A. Cloward. 1977. *Poor People's Movements: Why They Succeed, How They Failed*. New York: Vintage Books.

Pleyers, Geoffrey. 2010. *Alter-globalization: Becoming Actors in the Global Age*. Cambridge: Polity.

Polletta, Francesca. 1999. "'Free Spaces' in Collective Action." *Theory and Society* 28 (1): 1–38.

Przeworski, Adam. 1986. "Some Problems in the Study of the Transition to Democracy." In *Transitions from Authoritarian Rule: Comparative Perspectives*, edited by Guillermo A. O'Donnell, Philippe C. Schmitter, and Lawrence Whitehead, 47–64. Baltimore: John Hopkins University Press.

Pu, Sang. 2020. "Xianggang fansongzhong yundong: Fansi yu celue" [Hong Kong's anti-extradition movement: Reflections and tactics]. *Taiwan minzhu jikan* [Taiwan Democracy Quarterly] 17 (4): 167–75.

Putnam, Robert D. 2001. *Bowling Alone: The Collapse and Revival of American Community*. New York: Simon and Schuster.

Ren, Rex, and Daniel Chan. 2022. *Shaonian* [May you stay forever young]. Taipei: 1841 Press.

Revolution of Our Times Team, The. 2022. *Shidai geming dianying fangtanlu* [People in "Revolution of Our Times"]. Taipei: Spring Hill.

Roberts, Priscilla, and John M. Carroll, eds. 2016. *Hong Kong in the Cold War*. Hong Kong: Hong Kong University Press.

Rowen, Ian. 2015. "Inside Taiwan's Sunflower Movement: Twenty-Four Days in a Student-Occupied Parliament, and the Future of the Region." *Journal of Asian Studies* 74 (1): 5–21.

Rucht, Dieter, and Friedhelm Neidhardt. 2002. "Towards a 'Movement Society'? On the Possibilities of Institutionalizing Social Movements." *Social Movement Studies* 1 (1): 7–30.

Sawyers, Traci M., and David S. Meyer. 1999. "Missed Opportunities: Social Movement Abeyance and Public Policy." *Social Problem* 46 (2): 187–206.

Schock, Kurt. 2005. *Unarmed Insurrections: People Power Movements in Nondemocracies*. Minneapolis: University of Minnesota Press.

Schradie, Jen. 2019. *The Revolution That Wasn't: How Digital Activism Favors Conservatism*. Cambridge, MA: Harvard University Press.

Scott, James C. 1985. *Weapons of the Weak: Everyday Form of Peasant Resistance*. New Haven, CT: Yale University Press.

———. 1990. *Domination and the Arts of Resistance: Hidden Transcripts*. New Haven, CT: Yale University Press.

———. 1998. *Seeing Like a State: How Certain Schemes to Improve the Human Condition Have Failed*. New Haven, CT: Yale University Press.

Sewell, William H. Jr. 2005. *Logics of History: Social Theory and Social Transformation*. Chicago: Chicago University Press

Shirky, Clay. 2008. *Here Comes Everybody: The Power of Organizing without Organizations*. New York: Penguin.

———. 2010. *Cognitive Surplus: Creativity and Generosity in a Connected Age*. New York: Penguin.

Shiu, Ka-chun. 2022. *Shiqiang sheng hua: Zuojianji ji qita* [Flowers on the stone wall: Prison notes and others], rev. ed. Hong Kong: Hillway.

Shum, Maggie. 2021. "When Voting Turnout Becomes Contentious Repertoire: How Anti-ELAB Protest Overtook the District Council Election in Hong Kong 2019." *Japanese Journal of Political Science* 22 (4): 248–67.

———. 2023. "Transnational Activism during Movement Abeyance: Examining the International Frontline of Hong Kong's 2019 Anti-Extradition Bill Movement." *Journal of Asian and African Studies* 58 (1): 143–66.

Sinn, Elizabeth. 2014. *Pacific Crossing: California Gold, Chinese Migration, and the Making of Hong Kong*. Hong Kong: Hong Kong University Press.

Skocpol, Theda. 1979. *States and Social Revolutions: A Comparative Analysis of France, Russia and China*. Cambridge: Cambridge University Press.

———. 2002. *Diminished Democracy: From Membership to Management in American Civic Life*. Norman: University of Oklahoma Press.

Smith, Anthony D. 1991. *National Identity*. London: Penguin.

Smith, Jackie. 2008. *Social Movements for Global Democracy*. Baltimore: Johns Hopkins University Press.

Snow, David A., and Robert D. Benford. 1988. "Ideology, Frame Resonance and Participant Mobilization." In *From Structure to Action: Comparing Social Movement Research Across Cultures*, edited by Bert Klandermans, Hanspeter Kriesi, and Sidney Tarrow, 197–218. Greenwich, CT: JAI.

Snow, David A., and Dana M. Moss. 2014. "Protest on the Fly: Toward a Theory of Spontaneity in the Dynamics of Protest and Social Movements." *American Sociological Review* 79 (6): 1122–43.

Snow, David A., E. Burke Rochford Jr., Steven K. Worden, and Robert D. Benford. 1986. "Frame Alignment Processes, Micromobilization, and Movement Participation." *American Sociological Review* 51 (4): 464–81.

So, Alvin Y. 1999. *Hong Kong's Embattled Democracy: A Societal Analysis.* Baltimore: Johns Hopkins University Press.

Soule, Sarah A. 2009. *Contention and Corporate Social Responsibility.* Cambridge: Cambridge University Press.

Soule, Sarah, and Jennifer Earl. 2006. "A Movement Society Evaluated: Collective Protest in the United States, 1960–1986." *Mobilization: An International Quarterly* 10 (3): 345–64.

Staggenborg, Suzanne. 2020. *Grassroots Environmentalism.* Cambridge: Cambridge University Press.

Standnews. 2020. *Lizhi* [The records of Standnews]. Unknown publisher.

Stryker, Sheldon, Timothy J. Owens, and Robert W. White, eds. 2000. *Self, Identity, and Social Movements.* Minneapolis: University of Minnesota Press.

Su, Chris Chao, Michael Chan, and Sejin Paik. 2022. "Telegram and the Anti-ELAB Movement in Hong Kong: Reshaping Networked Social Movements through Symbolic Participation and Spontaneous Interaction." *Chinese Journal of Communication* 15 (3): 431–48.

Sussman, Nan M. 2010. *Return Migration and Identity: A Global Phenomenon, a Hong Kong Case.* Hong Kong: Hong Kong University Press.

Tam, Vivian. 2020. *Tian yu hei xing yu liang: Fanxiuli yundong de ren he shi* [Stars are brighter in dark nights: People and things in anti-ELAB movement]. Hong Kong: Breakthrough.

Tang, Aubrey. 2022. "The Parasites of Language: 'President Trump, Please Liberate Hong Kong.'" *Language and Dialogue* 12 (1): 35–53.

Tang, Gary. 2023. "The Intervention of the Anti-Extradition Bill Movement in the Norms of Citizenship in Hong Kong." *Journal of Asian and African Studies* 58 (1): 26–45.

Tang, Gary, and Edward W. Cheng. 2021. "Affective Solidarity: How Guilt Enables Cross-generational Support for Political Radicalization in Hong Kong." *Japanese Journal of Political Science* 22 (4): 198–214.

Tang, Thomas Yun-tong, and Michelle W. T. Cheng. 2022. "The Politicization of Everyday Life: Understanding the Impact of the 2019 Anti-Extradition Law Amendment Bill Protests on Pro-Democracy Protesters' Political Participation in Hong Kong." *Critical Asian Studies* 54 (1): 128–48.

Tarrow, Sidney. 1989. *Democracy and Disorder: Protest and Politics in Italy 1965–75.* Oxford: Clarendon.

———. 1993. "Cycles of Collective Action: Between Moments of Madness and the Repertoire of Contention." *Social Science History* 17 (2): 281–307.

———. 1994. *Power in Movement: Social Movements, Collective Action and Politics.* Cambridge: Cambridge University Press.

———. 2011. *Power in Movement: Social Movements and Contentious Politics*, 3rd ed. Cambridge: Cambridge University Press.

Taylor, Verta. 1989. "Social Movement Continuity: The Women's Movement in Abeyance." *American Sociological Review* 54 (5): 761–75.

Thompson, E. P. 1980. *The Making of the English Working Class.* London: Penguin Books.

Thompson, Mark R., and Edmund W. Cheng. 2022. "Transgressing Taboos: The Relational Dynamics of Claim Radicalization in Hong Kong and Thailand." *Social Movement Studies* 22 (5): 802–21.

Tilly, Charles. 1978. *From Mobilization to Revolution*. Reading, MA: Addison-Wesley.
———. 1981. *As Sociology Meets History*. New York: Academic Press.
———. 1998. "Political Identities." In *Challenging Authority: Historical Study of Contentious Politics*, edited by Michael Hanagan, Leslie Page Moch, and Wayne Te Brake, 3–16. Minneapolis: University of Minnesota Press.
———. 2002. *Stories, Identities, and Political Change*. Lanham, MD. Rowman & Littlefield.
———. 2004. *Social Movements, 1786–2004*. Boulder, CO: Paradigm.
———. 2008. *Contentious Performances*. Cambridge: Cambridge University Press.
Tilly, Charles, and Sidney Tarrow. 2007. *Contentious Politics*. Oxford: Oxford University Press.
Ting, Tin-yuet. 2020. "From 'Be Water' to 'Be Fire': Nascent Smart Mob and Networked Protests in Hong Kong." *Social Movement Studies* 19 (3): 362–68.
To Freedom Committee, eds. 2020. *Zhi ziyou: Xianggang kangzheng yinian jishi* [To freedom: A chronicle of Hong Kong's one-year struggles]. Hong Kong: Times Creative Culture.
Tong, Kin-long, and Samson Yuen. 2021. "Disciplining Student Activism: Secondary Schools as Sites of Resistance and Control in Hong Kong." *Sociological Forum* 36 (4): 984–1004.
Touraine, Alain. 1988. *The Return of the Actor: Social Theory in Postindustrial Society*. Translated by Myrna Godzich. Minneapolis: University of Minnesota Press.
Traugott, Mark. 2010. *The Insurgent Barricade*. Berkeley: University of California Press.
Tsang, Eileen Y. H., and Jeffrey S. Wilkinson. 2022. "The Home as a Barometer of Society: 'Practices of Intimacy' to Moderate Family Intergenerational Conflict in the 2019 Summer of Dissent." *China Review* 22 (1): 307–34.
Tsang, Steve. 1997. "Strategy for Survival: The Cold War and Hong Kong's Policy Towards Kuomintang and Chinese Communist Activities in the 1950." *Journal of Imperial and Commonwealth History* 25 (2): 294–317.
Tsui, Anna, and Chris Chan. 2021. "Hong Kong's New Union Movement Faces Big Challenges from Covid, National Security Law." *Labor Note*, March 2, 2021. Available at https://bit.ly/3GFoqtx, accessed on May 30, 2023.
Tufekci, Zeynep. 2017. *Twitter and Tear Gas: The Power and Fragility of Networked Protest*. New Haven, CT: Yale University Press.
22 Hongkongers. 2019. *Ziyou liuyue* [The free June]. Taipei: Showwe.
Urman Aleksandra, Justin Chun-ting Ho, and Stefan Katz. 2021. "Analyzing Protest Mobilization on Telegram: The Case of 2019 Anti-Extradition Bill Movement in Hong Kong." *PLoS ONE* 16 (10): e0256675.
Useem, Bert. 1980. "Solidarity Model, Breakdown Model, and the Boston Anti-Busing Movement." *American Sociological Review* 45 (3): 357–69.
Veg, Sebastian. 2016. "Creating a Textual Public Space: Slogans and Texts from Hong Kong's Umbrella Movement." *Journal of Asian Studies* 75 (3): 673–702.
———. 2017. "The Rise of 'Localism' and Civic Identity in Post-handover Hong Kong: Questioning the Chinese Nation-State." *China Quarterly* 230:232–47.
Walder, Andrew G. 2009. "Political Sociology and Social Movements." *Annual Review of Sociology* 35:393–412.
Wang, Dan J., and Sarah A. Soule. 2016. "Tactical Innovation in Social Movements: The Effects of Peripheral and Multi-Issue Protest." *American Sociological Review* 81 (3): 517–48.
Wang, Klavier Jieying, Hope Reidun St. John, and Eliz Miu Yin Wong. 2017. "Touching a Nerve: A Discussion on Hong Kong's Umbrella Movement." In *Protest Camps in In-*

ternational Context: Spaces, Infrastructures and Media of Resistance, edited by Gavin Brown, Anna Feigenbaum, Fabian Frenzel, and Patrick McCurdy, 109–33. Oxford: Policy.

Wasserstrom, Jeffrey. 2023. "Protesters of the World, Unite." Public Books. Available at https://bit.ly/3GJYDAJ, accessed April 14, 2023.

Whitworth, Katherine, and Yao-Tai Li. 2023. "Visual Framing: The Use of COVID-19 in the Mobilization of Hong Kong Protest." *China Quarterly* 253:19–34.

Wilson, Andrew. 2006. *Ukraine's Orange Revolution*. New Haven, CT: Yale University Press.

Wiltfang, Gregory L., and Doug McAdam. 1991. "The Costs and Risks of Social Activism: A Study of Sanctuary Movement Activism." *Social Forces* 69 (4): 987–1010.

Wong, Bernard P. 1994. "Hong Kong Immigrants in San Francisco." In *Reluctant Exiles: Migration from Hong Kong and New Overseas Chinese*, edited by R. Skeldon, 235–55. New York: M. E. Sharpe.

Wong, Kevin Tze-wai, Victor Zheng, and Shirley Po-san Wan. 2022a. "Minyi yu shehui yundong zhouqi: Xianggang fanxiuli yundong de gean fenxi" [Public opinion and social movement cycle: An analysis of Hong Kong's anti-ELAB movement]. In *2020 zhongguo xiaoying: Taigang minzhong de taidu bianqian* [2020 China impact: Attitude changes in Taiwan and Hong Kong], edited by Michael Hsin-huang Hsiao, Chih-Jou Jay Chen, and Victor Zheng, 123–58. Hong Kong: Hong Kong Institute of Asia-Pacific Studies Chinese University of Hong Kong.

———. 2022b. "2019 xianggang shehui kangzheng: Shimin zhichi yinyou chutan" [The 2019 social protest in Hong Kong: A preliminary investigation of citizen support]. In *2020 zhongguo xiaoying: Taigang minzhong de taidu bianqian* [2020 China impact: Attitude changes in Taiwan and Hong Kong], edited by Michael Hsin-huang Hsiao, Chih-Jou Jay Chen, and Victor Zheng, 159–94. Hong Kong: Hong Kong Institute of Asia-Pacific Studies Chinese University of Hong Kong.

Wong, Stan Hok-Wui, Karl Ho, Harold D. Clarke, and Kelvin Chun-man Chan. 2023. "Does Loyalty Discourage Exit? Evidence from Post-2020 Hong Kong." *Journal of Asian and African Studies* 58 (1): 101–19.

Wu, Rwei-ren. 2021. "Peripheral Nationalisms of Taiwan and Hong Kong under China's Influence: A Comparative-Nationalism Perspective." In *China's Influence and the Center-Periphery Tug of War in Hong Kong, Taiwan and Indo-Pacific*, edited by Brian C. H. Fong, Wu Jieh-min, and Andrew J. Nathan, 59–73. London: Routledge.

Yang, Shen. 2019. "Enclave Deliberation and Social Movement Mobilization: The DDays in Occupy Central." *Social Movement Studies* 19 (2): 144–59.

Yee, Vivian. 2022. "Despite Iran's Efforts to Block Internet, Technology Has Helped Fuel Outrage." *New York Times*, September 29, 2022. Available at https://bit.ly/41nVEqO, accessed on August 19, 2023.

Yeung, Willie Sau. 2022. *Xianggang bimi xingdong* [Clandestine actions in Hong Kong]. Taoyuan: Duyanlong.

Youngs, Richard, ed. 2022. *Global Civil Society in a Geopolitical Age: How Civic Activism Is Being Reshaped by Great Power Competition*. Washington, DC: Carnegie Foundation for International Peace.

Yuen, Samson. 2018. "Contesting Middle-Class Civility: Place-Based Collective Identity in Hong Kong's Occupy Mongkok." *Social Movement Studies* 17 (4): 393–407.

———. 2021. "The Institutional Foundation of Countermobilization: Elites and Pro-Regime Grassroots Organizations in Post-Handover Hong Kong." *Government and Opposition* 58 (2): 316–37.

———. 2023. "Tolerant Solidarity with Violent Protesters: Evidence from a Survey Experiment." *Journal of Conflict Resolution* 67 (9): 1731–56.

Yuen, Samson, and Edmund W. Cheng. 2017. "Neither Repression nor Concession? A Regime's Attrition against Mass Protests." *Political Studies* 65 (3): 611–30.

Yuen, Samson, and Kin-long Tong. 2021. "Solidarity in Diversity: Online Petitions and Collective Identity in Hong Kong's Anti-Extradition Bill Movement." *Japanese Journal of Political Science* 22 (4): 215–32.

Zald, Mayer N., and John D. McCarthy, eds. 1987. *Social Movements in an Organizational Society.* New Brunswick, NJ: Transaction Books.

Index

Ming-sho Ho is Distinguished Professor of Sociology and Researcher at the Taiwan Social Resilience Center at National Taiwan University. He is the author of *Challenging Beijing's Mandate of Heaven: Taiwan's Sunflower Movement and Hong Kong's Umbrella Movement* (Temple) and *Working Class Formation in Taiwan: Fractured Solidarity in State-Owned Enterprises, 1945–2012*.

www.ingramcontent.com/pod-product-compliance
Lightning Source LLC
Chambersburg PA
CBHW020344270326
41926CB00007B/313

* 9 7 8 1 4 3 9 9 2 4 8 5 3 *